The Trials of Jimmy Hoffa

THE TRIALS
OF
JIMMY HOFFA

An Autobiography

JAMES R. HOFFA

as told to DONALD I. ROGERS

HENRY REGNERY COMPANY · CHICAGO

Contents

1	A Valentine for Mom	1
2	A Boy with a Job	8
3	Viola Hoffa, Breadwinner	17
4	The Ninth Grade Graduate	22
5	Toward Sweet Independence	31
6	Greener and Thornier Pastures	38
7	The Other End of the Trucks	55
8	Depression City, 1935	68
9	Brooding Days and Gathering Storms	83
10	Josephine	93
11	The Midwestern Council	105
12	The Dedicated Few	112
13	Growth: How High Is Up?	119
14	Brother Against Brother	128
15	Ohio, the South, and the CSDC	140
16	The Presidency	146
17	Only the Beginning	156
18	Trial by Headline	171
19	*Life* Magazine's Role	177
20	The Relentless Adversary	185
21	Drums Along the Potomac	190
22	If at First You Don't Succeed	200
23	No Ethics, No Honor, No Law	228

24 The Spy Who Came to Dinner   238
25 The Sergeant-at-Arms   244
26 The Frame-Up and the Voodoo Man   250
27 Tippens and Partin   261
28 When You Peel an Onion, You Cry   273
29 Reimbursement Without Pay   285
    Appendix: The Cast   303

The Trials of Jimmy Hoffa

1

A Valentine for Mom

For the first few days of my life, Mom told me, I was referred to as "The Tumor," because the doctor had insisted, initially, that my mother was afflicted by some kind of growth, and that the swelling was certainly not another child. The science of obstetrics hadn't advanced too far in the autumn of 1912 when Mom consulted the town's general practitioner about her condition.

Early on the cold morning of February 14, 1913, I presented irrefutable evidence that the lump was not a tumor at all but me, the third child of John and Viola Hoffa, U.S. citizens living in Brazil, Indiana.

They named me for Uncle Jim, my father's brother, and gave me my mother's family name, Riddle, for a middle name. Hoffa. James Riddle Hoffa. Hoffa is a fairly well-known name around southwest Indiana and parts of Pennsylvania.

My father, John Cleveland Hoffa, was the third generation of his family to live in the southwestern part of that state. Before that my forebears lived in Pennsylvania and, according to family lore, were among the earliest of the Pennsylvania Dutch settlers. So I guess I'm of Pennsylvania Dutch descent. German, Dutch, and Irish.

By tradition the Pennsylvania Dutch, or Germans, are

farmers, settled people, land people, comfortable. I don't know what motivation ran through the Hoffa line, but, as near as I can learn, no Hoffa in the five generations that I can trace ever farmed the land unless forced to by hard times, though now and again a Hoffa became a "gentleman farmer," farming as a hobby. I've got a severe case of green thumb and love to work in my yard and garden, and I've often wondered if it's an accumulation of family frustrations after so lengthy a denial of the land.

My great grandparents, John Hoffa and Mary Cook Hoffa, were honest-to-goodness pioneers in Owen County, Indiana. They had migrated from Pittsburgh and the coal-mining regions of Pennsylvania. They lived in a one-room, mud-chinked log cabin built on rented farm land in the north part of the county near the village of Cunot. They spent most of their lives in and around Cunot, moving to better living quarters as time went on.

Great-grandfather John Hoffa was a blacksmith who worked in the coal mines. So was my grandfather, Jacob Hoffa. So was my father, John Cleveland Hoffa. My father plied his skill as a metalsmith to the repair of drills and other mine implements rather than to the shoes of mules. He was more of a specialist, I guess.

Grandfather Jacob Henry Hoffa was born on January 25, 1848, near Cunot. He died when I was about eight and a half, but I remember him well, an old man who looked tough and rugged. He talked much of the outdoors, which he loved, as I do.

He spoke often, too, of the many chores he had to do at home when he was a boy. He hinted that it was the dreariness of his chores that caused him to take an early interest in his father's craft and to accompany him whenever he could. He served as apprentice to his own Dad, then became a smith on his own before his twentieth birthday.

Grandpa married Nancy Jane Asher, daughter of a pros-

perous farm family. The Ashers, also pioneer settlers in
Owen County, hailed originally from Kentucky, Tennessee,
and North Carolina.

My own father, the youngest of Jake Hoffa's children, died
a year before grandfather. Dad had two older brothers:
James, for whom I am named, and Charles. All were big
men, bigger than I.

I remember my father well, though I was only seven when
he died. As an adult, I have been back to the place where he
was born and the home he lived in near Cunot. It was a sort
of farm that wasn't really worked as a farm, though they
kept pigs, chickens, a cow, and a mule. But I understand
from what people tell me that nearly everyone had that
much livestock in those days. Chickens and pigs didn't
count, and one cow and one mule didn't make a farm. The
stock was, in fact, with the exception of the mule, just "meat
and milk" for the table. The mule paid his keep by doing
the plowing, haying, and harvesting.

The home of my father's childhood had four big rooms
and an outside summer kitchen. There was a medium-sized
barn to house the cow and mule and store the hay, and then
there were numerous outbuildings, including pens, chicken
coops, toolsheds, and, naturally, the privy. All were of un-
painted pine or oak and were bleached silvery white by the
elements, a hue I've seen duplicated by the application of
very expensive pigments to extremely costly homes.

Uncle Jim has told me that the three boys toiled long and
hard on that homesite, cultivating and husbanding the vegetables, meat, and milk for the table while grandfather was
touring the coal mines of the region, plying his trade as a
blacksmith.

My father went through nine grades of school and was
therefore considered a high school graduate. The one-room
elementary school in Cunot had one teacher who taught six
grades. When she finished with them, students were expected

to go to Cloverdale to attend classes for the seventh, eighth, and ninth grades. When you "graduated" from the ninth grade, with ceremonies at which you received a diploma, you were as well educated as you could be in the public school system of southwestern Indiana in those days.

There is no indication that Dad ever thought about going on to college. Not many people did in those days. Besides, he liked the work of his father and grandfather and apparently was eager to serve his brief apprenticeship and strike out on his own.

Father's first job was his only job. He held it all of his life and, according to his boss, served well and faithfully. He worked for a man named Ben Merchon, a coal prospector who used a steam-powered drilling rig to locate the veins of coal that underlie that part of Indiana like black, meandering underground streams.

Ben and Dad worked together on the rig and traveled throughout their part of the country on contract, taking core samples from deep in the earth. It was on such an assignment that he met my mother, Viola Riddle, daughter of Stephen and Jennetta Riddle, fairly prosperous farmers of Jessup, in Parke County, Indiana.

Mother recalls that in the late summer of 1908 Ben Merchon and John Hoffa had a considerable amount of drilling work in the Parke County area, and they moved their equipment to Jessup and looked for a place where they could find room and board.

They found rooms at the house of a family named West on a farm just outside Jessup. The farm adjoined the Riddle farm, and Elizabeth "Lizzie" West and my mother were "best friends." I guess it wasn't long before the young boarder, John Hoffa, age twenty-eight, took notice of the young and pretty neighbor, Viola "Ola" Riddle, age eighteen, who came to call on Lizzie West.

There are snapshots of my father to confirm mother's

claim that he was a most handsome man. He stood six feet tall, weighed 190 pounds, and had powerful shoulders and a muscular frame with the narrow waist and hips of an athlete. He had thick, black hair and dark, level eyes set off by a high forehead. A striking man, strong yet graceful.

I point this out because it's obvious I didn't inherit my father's looks. His muscles, perhaps, but not his handsomeness. I favor my mother and the Riddles. My features look pretty on my mother, but on a man—well, if my Jo loves me, it's probably not because she finds me a Rock Hudson.

As fall came to Jessup, Indiana, in 1908, it became clear to the townspeople that John Hoffa, the coal driller, was courting Viola Riddle. When the news seeped back to Cunot, it surprised Father's brothers and his friends, for it had been assumed he was a confirmed, if not militant, bachelor.

Throughout that winter, Father called on the Riddles whenever his working schedule permitted, and the couple was invited to church affairs and other sociables—which in those days constituted public confirmation of betrothal. On May 15, 1909, they were married. Their first home was with Grandma and Grandpa Hoffa back in Cunot, and they lived there about a year until near the time my sister Jennetta was born, when they moved to a house about two miles distant from my grandparents' home.

Then, for reasons that have never been clear to me, the entire branch of the Hoffa family moved to Brazil, Indiana, breaking a family association with Cunot that had lasted seventy-five years. My father had a reason, for the head-quarters of the Ben Merchon drilling company was located in Brazil, but I've always wondered about the others—somehow I never asked.

Grandfather apparently grew tired of the nomadic life of a mine blacksmith and seized an opportunity to take over the blacksmith shop on Brazil's main street. So within a short time there were four new Hoffa households in Brazil:

Grandpa and Grandma, Father and Mother, Uncle Jim and Aunt Ella, and Uncle Charlie and Aunt Ruth. All lived in a part of the community called Stringtown, an area occupied mostly by miners and blue-collar laborers.

Mother and Dad rented a home on North Vandalia Street in Stringtown, an A-frame house of three rooms: living room in front, bedroom in the middle, kitchen in the rear.

There, in the middle room, my brother Billy was born, and there, on St. Valentine's Day, 1913, my life began.

My first recollection of home, however, is not the Vandalia Street house but our second Brazil home: the much larger house on Church Street, outside the designated area of Stringtown. I remember it as square and white with four large rooms and a nice back yard. It was only a short distance from the Lambert Street School, where Jennetta, Billy, and I began our education. Nancy, my younger sister, was sent to a private kindergarten, an arrangement that indicated, I assume, that our family fortunes were much improved.

Part of the improvement, I suspect, came from the fact that Mom was taking in laundry. Billy and I had regular chores assigned to us for picking up and delivering the laundry. Jennetta helped Mom with the washing and ironing. And there was a standing order that, at the first sign of rain, no matter where we were, we had to make a beeline for the back yard and snatch clothing from the lines and get it inside.

It was fun. We worked together. It was a good family life. We were all happy.

My father's work took him away a great deal of the time, but when he was home, it was like Fourth of July every day. When he took a breather from work, he cast it aside entirely. My sisters and brother and I recall that he seemed to get a lot of enjoyment out of us kids. He actually played with us —played our games: hide 'n' seek, and tag, and marbles. And he'd take us fishing out near Harmony, in Fish Creek. We'd stop at Grandpa Hoffa's blacksmith shop and watch the work and drop in at the drugstore for a phosphate drink. Whenever a circus or a carnival or a medicine show came to town, he'd be sure to take us if he was home.

He had big, hard, comfortable hands that made you feel secure when you crossed the street, and he had a deep, resonant voice that, though seldom raised, commanded attention. He neither drank nor smoked, and he seemed always to smell of shaving soap.

When he died in 1920, I was seven years old. With his death the lives of his family changed drastically.

2

A Boy with a Job

I never thought of us as being poor. I didn't think we were especially unfortunate. I knew that money was hard to get and that it had to be worked for. I realized that it took a great deal of money to pay for essential things—the rent and food and clothing—and that not much was left over for other things. But as a boy I never gave much thought to the circumstances of others. If some families seemed to have more money and fewer pressures and more perceptible pleasures, I took it as a natural phenomenon.

We remained a happy family. Hardworking, sometimes even experiencing borderline hunger, but happy. We enjoyed our work, our home, our family and friends. If things seemed different from life in other families, it was because our father had died, and we were without a father to earn money. We had to do it ourselves. It was a harsh but simple fact of life.

It is probable that my father died of a massive stroke. No one diagnosed his fatal attack then, so we'll never know.

He left us to go on a drilling trip with Ben Merchon. A robust, smiling giant, he kissed us all good-bye as we stood in a line on the front stoop. He returned a week later, wasted and confused, unable to keep his balance.

Mother put him to bed and sent for the doctor. That

doctor called in another physician for consultation. They were unable to diagnose Dad's illness and recommended that he be sent to the hospital.

He never returned.

When mother visited him at the hospital—a day-long trip by train—he made a request that may seem to some to be strange. He asked that, if he died, he be brought home first, before being sent to the undertaker's. Mother kept her promise.

The day that Dad died, we four kids were at Uncle Jim's farm. We had been sent there the day before. At the time he died, Billy and I must have been playing out in the fields. As I think of it, though, that's probably the way he would have wanted it to be.

I dimly remember the funeral. There was a big clan of us Hoffas when you counted in all of the cousins, and there were many Riddles and a great many friends of the family. To a boy, it was an impressive event.

That same day mother called us children to stand in front of her in the kitchen. She was never one to mince words. She would now have to be both mother and father to us, she said. She would have to work, she said. And we, she declared, would all have to help.

That was all she said about it. Then—or ever.

Long after I became an adult, I discussed this incident with her. Mom admitted that she was in desperate financial straits when my father died. He had been ill for four months, and enormous medical bills had accumulated. The rent was overdue, and groceries had to be bought on a strictly cash basis because the bills were so long unpaid. No one in the family was in a position to help, but only if her children were actually starving would Viola Hoffa have accepted handouts.

In 1920 there was no such thing as welfare or relief or aid to dependent children. The burden of feeding five mouths

was hers alone. If she couldn't do it, her children would
have to go to an orphanage. Period.

The first thing she did was move out of the house on
Church Street, the home where she had spent her happiest
years, and into a small apartment above Grandpa Hoffa's
blacksmith shop. That might have worked out all right, but
Grandpa, too, took sick. So she moved us back to Vandalia
Street, into the A-frame three-room house that had been our
first home in Brazil and was to be our last in that town.

Grandpa moved in with us, an invalid, and there he died
a little less than a year after Dad had passed on.

I'm glad we lived in a small town in the rural Midwest. I
would not have had such a happy childhood, otherwise. As
it was, my life was confined not to the A-frame house, nor to
the precincts of Stringtown. Our "home" was the whole
township of Brazil and all of its sprawling peripheral
countryside.

Billy and I had the appetites of plow horses, and though I
cannot ever remember a serious scarcity of food at home,
three or four meals a day were simply never enough, so we
learned to forage the town and countryside. There's an unwritten law in the Midwest that cultivated fruit that hangs
over fences is in the public domain. Billy and I knew where
it all was to be found. We knew its ripening schedule, from
peaches and cherries in the early summer, to plums, apples,
and grapes. We knew the cultivated nut trees that spread
beyond fence limits, and we knew where the wild nut trees
grew in the nearby woods. We knew the streams to fish with
each changing season, and we knew where to snare rabbits,
woodcock, and even pheasant.

I didn't like to kill wild things. I didn't like to trap, for it
seemed cruel. I didn't want to shoot them. Yet we knew,
because Mother was so pleased when we brought game
home, that the food was very useful to our family budget.
So, in time, Billy and I became very adroit in the use of the

humane and painless snare. Billy, being older, dealt the coup de grace to the animals and birds.

We had our chores. Mother was a frontier-type woman, being economical with the use of words, downright parsimonious in the bestowal of praise, and unwavering in the matter of discipline, particularly where it concerned fatherless children. The chores and studies came first, and even when these tasks had been completed, she did not see the need for any nonsense or silliness. I don't mean that she was gloomy or didn't like a joke. She was warm and loving and fun to be with. Her credo was simply that Duty and Discipline were spelled with capital D's. Her viewpoint was not an uncommon one among women of her day in her part of the world, and especially not uncommon among women in her circumstances. She took her responsibilities seriously and expected her offspring to regard their responsibilities in the same light.

She was reasonable and just and never shrewish—which, I realize now, she might well have been with adequate justification.

Although there was no one who shaved in our A-frame home, there was a razor strap displayed prominently in the kitchen. It wasn't for strapping razors. Mom didn't have to use it often. It was sufficient that we knew she knew how to use it. Likewise, she had a large bottle of castor oil, which I scarcely believe was maintained there on the shelf for its normal purpose. It was as potent a discipline-enforcer as was the guillotine to a French criminal.

Mother's policy was to tell us what she expected us to do. After that she assumed it would be done, without reminder. In school she expected us to get good marks. We did. If we didn't, well, Report Card Day was either very gay or very scary around our house.

She expected me to hurry home from school. She expected me to change my clothes as quickly as possible. She expected me to do my allotted chores as expeditiously as possible. She expected me to remain in the yard, on the ready for errand or assignment, until she gave me permission to "go and play." This was true even if the "play" meant trying to catch a mess of fish sorely needed for supper or embarking on such a vital assignment in springtime as garnering a bucketful of cowslip greens from the swamp or dandelion greens from the pasture.

Mom ran a laundry business to the limit of her capacity. She also cooked in a restaurant on Main Street and frequently did housework in some of the big homes on "The Hill."

My chores revolved around the laundry operation. I had to split kindling for the big kitchen stove and see that the coal scuttle was kept filled and the ashes cleaned from beneath the grate. The ashes had to be sifted, too, and unburned coals salvaged in a separate pail. I also had to lug water and keep the big clothes boiler full, as well as the "well" at the end of the stove.

In addition, I had a regular route for picking up laundry and for delivery of same when it was clean. I used a wagon in summer and a sled in winter. Billy helped with the heavier loads, though he had many chores of his own, among them tending the kitchen garden. Billy and I also took turns at the washer and wringer cranks.

Jennetta had to clean up the kitchen after breakfast before she left for school. Mother prepared the breakfast, and most of the time she saw that it was served properly on the table, then left for her work, either at the restaurant or at one of the big homes on The Hill. My oldest sister also had to see to it that we were dressed properly. We had to be not only clean but suitably outfitted according to the weather. Shoes were too expensive to be worn without rubbers in slush or on a rainy day. Our schedules were too exacting to allow time for colds that were contracted unnecessarily just because some preoccupied boy forgot mittens, scarf, or hat. It was Jennetta's responsibility to see that we were respectably and properly outfitted, and Mom checked off each detail of our dress when we returned from school.

Little Nancy, too, had her chores. She helped Jennetta around the house, dusting, cleaning, putting away, and both girls, of course, helped with the laundry as much as they could, especially with hanging out the clothes. Mom alone did the ironing, though both girls served an apprenticeship at that craft under her hovering and critical supervision. She always kept an array of flatirons upended on the back of the stove, and to my recollection, the ironing board, held aloft by a trestle of crisscrossed legs, was never folded up and put away except on Sunday, the Day of the Big Dinner.

Sunday was a special day for all the Hoffas, and the routine was about the same in our house as it was in the homes of Grandpa and my uncles and aunts.

First our bodies were purified, and Mom checked all the details—fingernails, behind the ears, the crinkle at the back of the neck, the hollow in front of the Achilles tendons of boys who went barefoot from Friday afternoon to churchtime.

Next we turned our attention to the purification of our hearts. Dressed starch-white-clean, we trooped off to the Christian Church of Brazil to attend a rather formal service patterned after the eastern Congregational Church order of worship. The standard operating procedure was to begin with the singing of a hymn, followed by a prayer, with the congregation still standing, then the singing of the doxology, "Praise God from whom all blessings flow . . ." Then came the reading of the Scripture lesson, to which, ultimately, the sermon made reference. That was followed by a choral selection and the offertory, the taking of the collection. The offertory was followed by the church announcements (meetings of the various groups) and the singing of a hymn. Then there was the sermon, lasting just about half an hour, and the benediction, and an organ recessional as we filed out of church.

Mother went home after church services, but we had to remain for Sunday school, a session lasting nearly an hour in which we learned the meaning of some passage in the Bible, customarily based on a little "Reader" that was handed to us each week by our Sunday-school teacher. The Reader was a four-page pamphlet with colored pictures, and its text, printed in big block letters for young eyes, told the same story that the teacher discussed at class.

All told it made for about two and a half hours of inactivity, and I am grateful that neither Billy nor I was ever graded for our attentiveness or application to the subject matter under consideration. I'm afraid we were far too active to have been regarded, ever, as model Sunday-school students.

Long before the class ended, both Billy and I were thinking about what Mom was doing at home.

What she was doing was preparing our Sunday Dinner, beyond doubt the Biggest Event of the Week.

Perhaps there were weekdays when there were more potatoes and macaroni than there was meat. Probably Mom had to plan very carefully during the week. I was too young to notice the subtle balances between the costly and the inexpensive foods. But on Sunday we Hoffas observed a Feast Day.

Mom was a wonderful cook. She handled her stove the way a concert pianist addresses his Steinway, adjusting draft and damper, gauging the efficiency of the coal bed in the firebox, and combining her engineering skill with artistry to prepare the foods. She produced magical Sunday dinners; the memory of them will remain with me as long as I breathe.

Many times it was a roast; she must have had to plan and

scrimp to put it on the table. Frequently, it was a pot roast, so delicious and aromatic that my mouth waters at the memory. In the season that they were most available in Brazil, Indiana, and thus least expensive, we enjoyed great roasts of pork, rib roasts, hams, roast lamb, veal, and chops of varying kinds. And chicken. Chicken was Mom's specialty. With pullets, roasters, or hens her skill was unsurpassed.

On Sundays, dressed so fine we were uncomfortable, we feasted.

It was the same in every Hoffa household in the vicinity, and frequently we visited around for Sunday dinner. Relatives put out their best, with pickles and preserves and special desserts on that one day of the week when we rested, young and old, from our everyday duties.

We weren't a very religious family, though Sunday did have its share of religion. We were too busy, I guess, meeting each day's challenges, to devote much thought to whys and wherefores. We had no time available in which to break any of the Ten Commandments, hence we observed them. Besides, there was Mom, to whom life was real and very earnest. We liked our own family dinners, but we liked it also when we were invited out to Grandpa Riddle's farm or to Uncle Jim Hoffa's farm. Both were located on Shady Lane, beyond the end of the trolley line. On Sundays, when Mom was with us, someone would meet us with car or carriage at the end of the line. On other holidays, sometimes Billy and I would ride to the end of the car tracks, then hike to Jim's farm, about three-quarters of a mile beyond. Grandpa Riddle's farm was about three-quarters of a mile beyond that.

It was at Uncle Jim's one Sunday afternoon that I cut my hand. Billy and I had been assigned the chore of catching a plump pullet and fulfilling its destiny at the chopping block. I held the bird by feet and neck, and Billy swung the ax. It was a heavy implement for Billy, and when the handle caught in a patch on the knee of his pants, the blade missed its mark and cut deeply into the back of my hand, severing tendons.

Billy and I both began to yowl, and Mom ran out of the house. She hollered for Uncle Jim to get the Model T going and for Aunt Ella to bring some clean strips of bed sheet for bandages. They hustled me off to the doctor, where I was told that I would probably never have the full use of my right hand again.

What the doctor said was true—for a while. For several weeks the hand was numb and stiff. I learned, though, that with great effort and enormous pain, I could move the fingers and manipulate the hand. I decided it would be my secret to exercise the hand in private until one day I could show my mother that I had full use of it. They say that you forget pain. Perhaps in most cases you do, but I was not quite eight years old when that happened, and I can still remember vividly the excruciating pain of exercising those fingers.

It was worth it. I regained full use of the hand six to eight months after the accident.

The pullet, having escaped the roasting pan, lived to be an old hen and was a consistently good egg-layer, undoubtedly determined to produce to the utmost to forestall a repeat trip to the block. She laid eggs as though she was scared not to.

3

Viola Hoffa, Breadwinner

If I seem to be dwelling at length on my childhood, my purpose is twofold. First, I would like to dispel the notion that mine was an unhappy childhood, or that I was unduly deprived, or that I was reared in abject poverty. My detractors have tried, at times, to imply that I carry a grudge against big business or rich people because of an unfortunate background. I don't think my background was very unfortunate or very unusual. I wish my father had lived. I wish I had been able to complete my education. Other than that, I look back on a rich and rewarding life as child, adolescent, and young man.

My second reason is to show, without emotional demonstration, the remarkable independence, responsibility, resourcefulness, and steadfastness of my widowed mother, Viola Riddle Hoffa. Sometimes I worry over my fear that her kind of person is disappearing from the world, at least in our so-called civilized society.

I don't believe that hardship is a virtue or that it is essential in tempering strong and noble character. Steadfastness and dedication are not confined to the poor. Sometimes they are qualities that are harder to maintain over the long stretch when you are poor, and thus seem of greater value when observed in the less elegant areas of our society.

To Viola Hoffa there were no alternatives. There was no one to whom we could turn for help. There was no welfare program, no help for herself or for her dependent children. Either she must work, or she must starve. Or, worse, lose her children to the state.

My record shows that I have been in the forefront in the creation of welfare programs. It is a sin against our nation when anyone is allowed to be hungry or cold or inadequately clothed or improperly treated for illness or disability. Thus I am glad that we have created or are in the process of creating fine and far-reaching welfare programs in most parts of this country.

It is therefore with reluctance that I have come to the realization that now we must address ourselves to the other side of the coin and try to determine where, and to what extent, we are destroying that basic quality of self-reliance and proud independence that has distinguished the American middle class throughout this nation's history.

Having studied the effect of the programs on the few who are adversely affected by them, we must then seek solutions. At this point in history it might prove unwise to soften, by any degree, America's sturdy backbone. We must find alternatives that will permit us to buttress the lower economic levels of our society with readily accessible welfare programs without destroying the individual desire for self-reliance and self-betterment.

The raw courage of my mother, exemplified day in and day out while her children were growing to adulthood, has influenced my thinking, and that of my brother and sisters, perhaps more than anything else in life. Viola Riddle Hoffa's life as a mother has been the personification of the class struggle born of the Industrial Revolution. As a member of the labor movement, I am an extension of that struggle.

As an activist in the labor movement, I have dedicated

myself to the creation of jobs for all who wish them and to ensuring the payment of proper compensation so that the worker can live in dignity and self-provided security. And, if there is anything about the background of the boy that influenced the life of the man, it was this.

After Grandpa Hoffa died we moved to Clinton, into a two-room house that stood behind a larger house on Third Avenue, a neighborhood of coal miners and other laboring people. It was not at all a grand neighborhood, but it was not shabby. It was inelegant, and there was sometimes coal dust from the mines and soot from the trains, but it was a settled, sturdy neighborhood.

We had been there only a short time when Billy and I, exploring, found the frame of an old bicycle on the town dump. We salvaged it and then instituted a vigil over the junk pile until we had collected the basic necessities to re-build a bicycle that would actually work. It was our proudest possession and remained such until we were both grown men, doing serious work.

The "Hoffa Home Laundry" grew out of our move to Clinton. Its equipment consisted of a large hand-cranked washing machine, a hand-operated wringer, two big laundry tubs for the boiling of clothes, and a network of clothes lines in the back yard. In the summer the whole operation was conducted from the back porch and in the back yard.

Depending on the size of the family, the cost was one to two dollars per week for the complete family wash. As I re-call, the rent for our house was six dollars a month. Yet the Hoffa Home Laundry had one serious drawback: it simply didn't make enough money to sustain the family. When there were long stretches of bad weather, there was no in-come from the laundry. The automatic dryer had yet to be invented.

To fill in, Mom worked as a waitress and also as a cook in some of the restaurants. Another time she was an ironer at the Vermillion County hospital. The job was ironing sheets and pillow cases, by hand.

Mom liked it in Clinton because it was not far from several of her relatives and also near her girlhood friend, Lizzie West, now Lizzie Guinn. But she soon came to the conclusion that Clinton contained too few opportunities for the employment of a young widow whose income requirements were not any less than those of a family with a working father. Something steady, she decided, would be better than the unpredictable livelihood to be earned in Clinton.

She never explained why she chose Detroit. It was a big city, of course, beginning to boom with the automobile business, so I suppose she thought her chances best there. Anyway, we moved to an apartment on Merritt Street, on the west side of Detroit. The house, once a stately dwelling, now housed four families. Our home was three rooms on the ground floor rear.

In 1924, when we moved there, we were among the first of the migrants. Because we came from the rural areas of the Midwest, we were immediately identified as hillbillies. Billy and I took exception to this appellation, and on several occasions we had to register our displeasure with our fists.

Our section of Detroit was occupied predominately by Poles, Slavs, and other people with Middle-European backgrounds. They were thrifty, hardworking, and exceptionally clean people, and the parents were strict disciplinarians. But they were also clannish, especially the kids, and there was an unwritten law, not revealed to parents, that new kids in the neighborhood had to establish themselves with their knuckles. Billy and I did so. It was not easy. It was not done overnight. We learned never to look for a fight and never to run from one. We learned that unless you were willing to fall into line and accept the pecking order of an existing clan, you had to establish your right to maintain your own private domain. This was accomplished by bloody noses and

shiners, but finally we won acceptance into the neighborhood youth's social order. And, eventually, there came a day
when we could walk home from school without encountering
a couple of toughs who wanted to kick the hillbillies around.

Mom may have moved to Detroit to find a steady pay envelope, but she couldn't leave behind the drudgery of her
work in Clinton. Her first job in Detroit was for five and a
half days a week in—you've guessed it—a laundry, as a
presser and ironer.

4

The Ninth Grade Graduate

Two brand new experiences awaited Mom soon after she moved to Detroit: she went into debt, and she told her first and, to my knowledge, only lie. To get the money to move to Detroit and set up there she sold whatever furniture was salable from the Clinton home. The rest she gave away, thus cutting down what would have been an unmanageable moving bill.

When we moved into the house on Merritt Street, she needed furniture right away, so she bought all of the basic necessities for a four-room apartment on "time." Her brother had to co-sign for it. Not once did Mom miss a payment on the furniture. Finally, the bill was paid in full, right on schedule. The accomplishment pleased her enormously.

Then one day one of the ladies in the laundry told her about Turnstead's, an automobile parts factory. They were hiring there for the production line, her informant said, at considerably more money than they were paying at the laundry.

Mom hustled out to Turnstead's and applied for a job. The hiring boss cautioned her that they wanted only people with previous production-line experience. She looked him straight in the eye and assured him she was thoroughly experienced and seasoned. In truth, she had never been in a factory and had seen the outside of only a few of them. She was as green as anyone could possibly be.

Thus began the years during which the "experienced" worker screwed a tap onto a threaded piece of stock as it moved past her on a conveyor line. For eight hours a day, five days—and sometimes six—a week she tightened taps onto their threads. She did it day in and day out for four years, without vacation, until one day she doubled over in pain and learned that she had a seriously infected appendix. At least the enforced stay in the hospital provided an opportunity for a good, relaxing time.

During her convalescence mother looked over the job market and decided to expand her career as well as her experience-rating by hiring out as a polisher of radiator caps at Fisher Body's Fleetwood plant. That was a pretty good job, and she stayed with it, off and on, for years, and for a long time whenever we kids saw an especially glittery radiator cap gleaming in the sun, we'd think, gee, probably Mom polished that one.

The Depression ended the concept of the "regular job," even at such a solid and stable plant as Fisher Body, and during periods of layoff Mom worked around in various manufacturing plants, whenever she could. When she couldn't find factory work, she took employment in one of the laundries, or in the laundry room of one of the hospitals. Once she worked in a bakery, "polishing up an old skill," as she put it, and another time she had a one-day-a-week job as a cleaning woman on the passenger boats running between Detroit and Cleveland. The cleaning was done when the boats were tied up at dockside, so she didn't get the benefit of a voyage across the lake.

For the record, Mom worked until 1948. She had started

keeping house at age nineteen, had to go to work as a widow at age twenty-six, and worked for thirty-two years, quitting when she was fifty-eight.

Her children think that Viola Riddle Hoffa is a titan among human beings, one whose patience, steadfastness, determination, and sheer courage mark her as an exceptional person. The children of Johnny Hoffa may have been deprived of a father, but heaven blessed them twice over when it gave them Viola Riddle for a mother.

Her parents called her "Viola." Dad called her "Buddy." Her closest friends call her "Ola." We who can call her "Mom" are uniquely privileged.

My mother has always been a doer. She does it; she doesn't talk about it. She tried to instill the same characteristic in us. I began working at various chores for pay when I was about eleven years of age. I turned over every penny I earned to my mother. The feeling of pride that it gave me surpassed any value the money might have had for me, yet she never said anything more than "Thank you, Jimmy," and "Thank you, Billy." There was never any praise to turn our heads or make us think we were doing something special; for, in fact, we were doing nothing special. We were doing what most kids were doing in those days.

Though none of the adults seemed to have much money in the Detroit neighborhood where I grew up, jobs for a kid weren't hard to find. I cleaned basements and garages, raked leaves from small yards, trimmed scraggly hedges, carried in coal and wood, sifted ashes and retrieved unburned coals, split kindling on a half-dozen different chopping-blocks, ran errands for over-scheduled housewives, and for a brief period enjoyed a reputation as a competent painter, having earned the right to paint our neighbor's fence and another's front stoop.

On weekends I sacked potatoes at C. L. Smith's grocery. There was no hourly rate, nor even a piece rate. I got fifty cents for the job, and I sacked as many potatoes as Mr. Smith thought needed to be sacked. Mr. Smith had an uncanny knack of predicting most accurately the number of bags of potatoes he would sell in the coming week. When I arrived on Saturday morning at eight o'clock, there were usually no more than one or two sacks left in stock. Conversely, I never knew him to run out of sacked potatoes.

After a few weeks, when Mr. Smith observed that I was an earnest worker and not likely to goof off when unwatched, he entrusted me with the glamour job of running deliveries in response to telephone orders.

Tips of pennies and nickels—and occasionally even a dime or two—swelled my earnings. More importantly, my activities as a delivery boy attracted the attention of other merchants, and before long I was acknowledged as *the* delivery boy in our neighborhood. Storekeepers would hail me on the street and make dates with me to work for them.

My delivery work led to other jobs, too: sweeping out stores and storage rooms and loading platforms, helping to unload trucks, assisting in such varied assignments as uncrating vegetables or eggs, removing canned goods from their cartons and stacking them on shelves, ultimately even assisting in arranging canned food displays in the windows or near the counters.

It was good work. I enjoyed doing it and was satisfied when I did it well. It taught me much, if not about the retail business, certainly about life. I wasn't aware of it, but it also taught me quite a bit about myself. That had value transcending all other rewards from those early labors.

We went to school, too, and our marks, as I've said, were required to meet with Mom's satisfaction or we heard about it. I'm afraid that on some occasions Billy got more than a tongue lashing: that large disciplinary bottle of castor oil came with us from Clinton to Detroit, a firm and fast member of the Hoffa family as long as one child remained in school. However, it was to Billy's ultimate benefit that he never grew fond of that dual-purposed nostrum: he couldn't even read those marvelous magazines, *War Birds, Spads,* and *War Aces,* and such like, because invariably they described the use of castor oil in the engines of those "aeroplanes," and without fail Richtofen's bullets smashed the engine of the hero's plane and sent the juice of the castor bean cascading down his face.

We went to the school at the corner of Calvary and McMillan Streets, the Neinas School, though to me it was always just "The School." We all entered nervously. A city school, we were sure, would hold many mysteries, and surely we would embarrass ourselves.

We were surprised, then, when the lady with whom we registered told us we were to move ahead one grade because the Indiana schools were more advanced than the city schools. There were occasions during the next year or two when we reflected that this was not as much of a favor as it seemed at the time.

Each night Mom checked us. She asked us what our assignments were. We told her. Then she asked us if we had done them. We responded. She didn't read over our homework. What she read was our report cards, glancing occasionally at the bottle of castor oil.

Jennetta and Nancy were straight-'A' students. I passed everything, gaining an occasional A and averaging out with B's. Billy wasn't really a bad student, but he liked to think about other things than homework. He drank quite a bit of castor oil.

With my B's and B-minuses I escaped the Great American Bottled Cure, but I won no prizes from the school authorities—except in gym. Gym was a different thing. It's funny about gymnastics and exercise in general. My muscles have always made themselves known to me, a sort of itching or pressuring telling me they have to be exercised. I have

always exercised regularly, and do so to this day, sometimes
to the extent that Jo thinks I'm some kind of a nut. But it
makes me feel good. Clean. Refreshed.

In gym I won medals—bronze, silver, and even gold—and
for the decathlon, and I got to represent our school in
meets throughout the city. I'm still rather proud of my
achievement, for I worked hard.

The most enduring memory I have of life at Neinas School
was my bashfulness in the classroom and around the
teachers. When I was with the boys, I wasn't at all bashful
or timid. I wasn't exactly gregarious when the fellows were
together, but I certainly wasn't what you'd call retiring. But
in the classroom it was an entirely different matter.

The presence of girls, for one thing, probably inhibited
me. But the teachers, also, seemed so crisp and antiseptic,
standing aloof with all the embodiment of authority and
discipline, that I seemed to freeze up. They weren't at all
like Mom, and the girls seemed nothing like Jennetta or
Nancy.

Looking back, I realize, of course, that some of those
teachers were warm and charming and gentle. My feelings
simply prove, I guess, that the highly valued instincts of
children can go awry. As for the girls, well, I can say in all
honesty that they didn't interest me too much, aside from
arousing occasional curiosity, until I was well launched into
manhood.

I'm glad that the thrill of discovery and the magic of falling in love for the very first time were saved for Jo. I've
lived half a hundred years, and no greater blessing has ever
been bestowed on me than the great fortune of loving and
marrying Josephine. But that all came later—much later.

There was a wonderful surprise waiting for Billy and me
when we graduated from the ninth grade of Neinas. For
months Mom had harbored a secret. The silver coins that
Billy and I earned and turned over to her had been kept

aside and hidden away, and for our commencement ceremonies she bought us beautiful blue suits—really good
quality blue cheviot worsted—and new shoes to go with
them. The suits had double-breasted coats and flared
knickers. They were just superb.

I still have my diploma. It's the only one I ever earned.

Neither my mother nor the rest of the family intended
that I would quit school after graduating from Neinas. I was
automatically enrolled in high school, and Mom filled out
some forms and sent them to the proper authorities.

Just as soon as summer vacation started, however, I got a
good job in a grocery store at regular wages. I handled most
of the stock, did the unpacking, and made the displays,
handled the cleaning, ran the errands, and made some of
the deliveries.

Billy and Jennetta were working, too, and when all of us
kids turned our earnings over to Mom, the family was in
better financial shape than it had been since my father died.

It was a situation that we found very pleasant.

Billy and I discussed the idea of working instead of studying. Both of us partially favored it, though Mom had impressed us again and again with the need for an education.
We both knew how hard she had worked, how great had
been her struggle, to get us through the ninth grade. Perhaps we owed it to her to go ahead and finish high school.
Three years to a kid is a mighty long time, though, and we
thought also of the time she would have to spend pinching
pennies if we were to return to classes.

Finally, I got up courage to broach the subject to her after
supper one night. She folded her hands and sat and thought
about it for several minutes without saying a word.

"I don't think I have to tell you how important an education is, Jimmy," she said at last. "You know what it can
mean to your life. I don't want you thinking that you have
to work, just because you're big enough and strong enough.

We're getting along fine and we will be able to manage if you keep at school."

She paused and thought some more, then added, "But I don't want you to go to school because *I* want you to; I want you to go because *you* want to."

Well, what could anyone do? I looked at Billy, and he shrugged. I guess that I had to *want* to go back to school whether I *liked* the idea or not. Next day I returned to work at the grocery store realizing that the summer was waning and that my days for earning were numbered.

The fact that I was only fourteen galled me. It didn't seem right to have to spend so much time at inconsequential pursuits before being able to get down to man's business. And it was man's business that interested me, not kid's.

Our enrollment at Western High School was automatic, but it was necessary for incoming new students to go to school shortly before the fall term began to sign in. I received a notice in the mail assigning me a specific hour.

I have often wondered, since, if my life would have turned out differently had there been fewer new kids lined up that day, or more people to handle the administrative work. As it turned out, I had to wait a considerable length of time for my interview.

I didn't know any of the kids sitting near me, so I sat there thinking. I thought about the long, lean, hard years Mom had put in, and how difficult it still was for her to keep steadily employed, though by now she was a skilled craftsman.

Real poverty is one thing I hope I never have to experience. Nothing is more wearing, more debilitating, more enervating, it seems to me, than the perpetual struggle to make ends meet and never quite being able to do it. The blinding, frustrating despair of "almost poverty" was a strong and bitter memory to me that day as I thought of giving up my job in the grocery store.

They were calling out the kids' names alphabetically. Just about the time they got to the G's I stood up and walked out of that classroom. Mom had said one thing that I kept remembering. She had said, "Jim, you'll have to make up your own mind."

I had made it up. I walked down the long, carbolic-scented corridor and out through the massive front doors of Western High School. They closed behind me with a pneumatic hiss, irrevocably sealing off whatever childhood or adolescence there was remaining for me.

It was my own secret Confirmation or Bar Mitzvah, for on that day I decided I was a man. I was ready for man's responsibilities and for man's estate.

At the foot of Western High's stone front steps awaited Life, a man's life, in a man's world.

I descended the steps to meet it. I didn't think at the time, as I might have thought, that life never comes up to meet you halfway. You have to take the initiative. You have to go to it.

5

Toward Sweet Independence

The sign on the corner of the building said "Dry Goods."
Mr. Leonard appeared to be a product of the store itself,
arid, crackly brittle, uncommonly clean, though unaccount-
ably imparting an impression of mustiness. He seemed stern,
with the hint of dry frost in his light blue eyes.

I stood ramrod erect before his unbelievably cluttered
desk. There were certain formulas I believed should be followed on an occasion such as this. I had read and re-read
the Horatio Alger books and was a devout believer in all of
the virtues spelled out in them, essentially those that described how to get and how to hold a job. My shoes were
polished to mirror brightness; my woolen stockings were
pulled up tight and straight, and the elastic bands around
my calves held them there with such determination that my
legs ached. My knickerbockers were fresh-pressed, with the
creases on the sides, as was proper. I wore my tight-knit navy
blue sweater with the oval neck. Above it a superwhite shirt
showed, with tie knotted firmly and tucked down into the
sweater. I had completed a checklist before leaving the
house: hair combed, face and ears washed, neck scrubbed,
hands scoured, nails cleaned.

Even if I felt like one of the lilies of the field confronting
Solomon in all of his glory, I knew it was the right way—the

31

only way—to present myself to Mr. Leonard. This was emphatically clear in the gospel according to Horatio Alger.

"Hmm," said Mr. Leonard. "Hmmm. Yes." He directed this observation to Mom, who stood behind me in her very best Sunday finery. She had declined a seat offered by Mr. Leonard in order, I knew, to preserve her official starchiness.

"Um . . . yes," he said, "we do need a boy." His eyes flicked toward me.

"We need a boy who is a hard worker," he said.

"I-I-I'm a hard worker!" I blurted, and it seemed to me I had shouted deafeningly.

"We need a boy who is steady."

"I'm very steady." I modulated my voice.

"Eh? What's that? Speak up, boy."

"I-I'm very steady."

"We need a boy who can do many different kinds of jobs."

Pause. I didn't know quite how to answer that. I nodded my head in agreement.

"He's very adaptable," Mom affirmed. "He's very quick to learn."

It seemed to me either that Mr. Leonard was searching for a loophole to ease himself out of the bargain or that maybe he hoped to discover a flaw in the candidate so he could settle the issue once and for all.

"Our . . . ah . . . boy must have very . . . ah . . . good, presentable clothes," he said. "He . . . ah . . . must have a jacket." He peered over his spectacles, directing his unasked question to both of us.

"He has a very nice new navy blue jacket," Mom said, referring to the coat of my new graduation suit.

Suddenly, as if by magic, Mr. Leonard thawed as though someone had pushed a switch.

"Splendid, splendid," he said. "I think you'll be just the man, James. How soon can you get that jacket?"

"R-right away, sir."

"Splendid. Splendid. Then you can start immediately."
He held out his hand. "I hope you'll be happy here, son."

Thus my career began at Frank & Cedar's Dry Goods and
General Merchandise.

It was a full-scale department store with several specialty
shops. My job was stockboy. I had to keep the shelves filled,
and when the clerks were rushed, I was encouraged to wait
on customers. My pay was two dollars a day—twelve dollars
a week, with now and then a dollar or two extra for working
late on Saturday nights.

At age fourteen, and in those days, it was a handsome
stipend.

I found it to be exciting work. Merchandising has a fascination all of its own, and in a good store such as Frank &
Cedar's an employee had a sense of satisfaction in doing a
good job for the customer.

A stockboy got around the store a great deal more than
the average clerk, and not being a specialist in handling the
sale of one line of goods, I was sent wherever I was needed.

Christmas was an especially exciting time, with the interesting inventory beginning to arrive by the first of November. The stockboy also had one special privilege. He got
to help with the toy displays and to assist in the assembling
of many wonderful items in the toy department. I took full
advantage of that assignment.

I also took advantage of my employee's discount and,
under Mom's urging, began to build a wardrobe. It was
then, I guess, that I acquired a taste for good quality clothing, something that has remained with me all of my life. One
of the many barbs tossed at me by Robert Kennedy had to
do with my attire. It was calculated to hit a nerve in a
tender spot. It did, but not because of vanity, as Kennedy
supposed, but because it reminded me of Mom and those
good early years of my "career." As a boy of fourteen I knew
the difference between pride and vanity. It is a lesson,

learned easily by the poor, that may elude the rich. I took
pride in looking my best; I was never vain about it.

They were good to me at Frank & Cedar's. My bosses
liked me. I liked them. I enjoyed the work. I felt the same
excitement that the department heads felt when merchandise moved well, or when a special display produced good
results. I felt that I was part of a large commercial family
and that each member shared each other's fortunes.

Every now and again one of my superiors—who were
legion—would tell me that I had a great future in the store.
There was an esprit de corps there that could almost be felt
in the atmosphere, and it was especially good for a growing
boy. It gave me a sense of identity, a feeling of belonging.

I now look back on my two years at Frank & Cedar's as, I
suppose, some men recall their days at boarding school or
college, a time of work, but also a time filled with laughter
and enjoyment. There were hundreds of amusing incidents
—I can't remember many now—and in retrospect it seems
that I was laughing a great deal of the time and hurrying
home to recount for mother and the others the details of
some side-splitting event. To a teen-ager in any circumstances, the world is a gay and sometimes even a giddy place,
created for the full enjoyment of God's noblest creatures:
the upcoming generation.

Though I worked long hours, it seems to me now that I
had more leisure time then than at any other point in my
life. I'd rush home from work, get into my overalls, and,
after handling a few routine chores around the house, pursue some seasonal recreation. I played a lot of sandlot baseball and belonged to a neighborhood nine that played a
regular schedule. I also fished a great deal, and I know it's
not tricks of an angler's memory that cause me to recall
some magnificent lunkers from the lake. I was most knowl-
edgeable in the ways and manners of the bass.

I loved sports, and do to this day, and I loved the outdoors and nature. On windy days when fish wouldn't bite, I'd walk for miles along the lakeshore, "communing" with nature. Perhaps the greatest by-product of the human evolution has been the creation of centers of commerce and culture on waterways—on seaports, on rivers, and in a few choice places on freshwater lakes, sources of transportation and power. And yet despite the explosion generated by the Industrial Revolution, questing nature-lovers have still reserved areas for tranquil withdrawal from the hurried world.

It seems almost disloyal for the head of a union whose membership comprises hundreds of thousands of truck drivers to observe that it is a pity, in some respects, that the advent of the truck, the locomotive, and the airplane has made it necessary to locate our cities on waterways. Transportation is just as good and fully as inexpensive and the wheels of commerce turn just as rapidly and efficiently in metropolitan centers where there isn't a drop of water in sight as near water. Have you noticed, though, that it didn't take them long to get recreational waterways close to such once parched and sandy cities as Dallas, Phoenix, and Las Vegas?

There was a time, when I was a teen, when I knew every bird to be found at my lakeside, and where it nested. I could identify the former owner of a feather on the beach, or recognize the parentage of a bird's egg fragment. I knew also the names of the trees and wildflowers. I could identify black birch, which had edible bark, and sassafras root, and wintergreen. My healthy appetite followed me through my teens, and nature's bounty provided some relief for a boy's perpetual hunger pangs.

I didn't realize it at the time, but I was also a dedicated and insatiable reader during that period. Though I read everything that came my way, my liking for nonfiction slightly outweighed my taste for fiction. In the latter category, however, I felt at times that I had the currently popular novelists of the times working nights to keep up with me. I read all the James Oliver Curwood books, until I felt I would be as much at home in the Yukon as I was in Frank & Cedar's store.

I can't remember the sequence that my reading took, but I read and enjoyed the entire Jalna series by Mazo de la Roche. I also liked Joseph C. Lincoln's wry characters and, somewhat later, Kenneth Roberts's sturdy Americans. Who did not read Zane Grey?

Kids around my neighborhood swapped the daily papers, buying and reading one and exchanging it for another that was regularly purchased by a pal. We did the same things with the magazines, and they went the rounds until they were dog-eared—everything from Western and adventure stories to *Popular Mechanics*.

The newspapers, then, were filled with blood and thunder on the home front. Gang wars in New York and Chicago. Shoot-outs between good guys and bad guys in Kansas City. Raids by federal agents. Stories of death and blindness and paralysis caused by bootleg liquor.

There were accounts, too, of wild buying on the stock exchanges in New York and frenzied trading for millions in the grain pits of Chicago. A group of Rhode Islanders tried to corner the wool market and failed. Cotton regained its role as King of Commodities in world trade.

And in Detroit the nation's industrial sinews grew and hardened. Increasingly there were stories of labor violence, of bitter strikes and police intervention, of broken limbs and gashed heads, of traveling goon squads, of imported strikebreakers. The headlines showed that there was war all around us, as close as a block away on some occasions.

To a teen-age kid none of this mattered much. I had a job that I liked, and my life was good.

That's just about the way the adult world felt, too. A great many Americans all across the nation had made the postwar transition from the country to the city. Most had entered urban life scared and insecure but believing desperately in the promise of steady work and ready promotions to be found in the industrial centers.

A large proportion of them had been caught up in the flowing tide of productivity and were steadily employed and confident of greater rewards in the near future. They had small concern for the minority who felt they were being exploited, and even less concern for a smaller minority reaping vast fortunes in paper wealth in the securities markets.

It was such a short time ago. The public was unaware or apathetic until disaster struck. Did we learn a lesson? Did we learn that we cannot be indifferent to problems in our society just because they don't affect the majority? I wonder.

6

Greener and Thornier Pastures

After the stock market crash and the onset of the depression, even a boy could feel the difference in the atmosphere at Frank & Cedar's. Many of the sales people and department heads who used to joke with me became serious adults, withdrawn and unmindful of the backroom activities that demanded my time. It wasn't long before there were layoffs and a doubling of workloads among the survivors. The tension increased. So did the sullenness.

"The thing to do," said my friend Walt Murphy, four years my senior, "is to get into the food business. People have to eat, no matter what. I don't care how much of a depression you have, the food and grocery business won't be so hard hit."

I brought this philosophy home to Mom to discuss around the dinner table.

"Well," she said, "there is logic in what he says. The notion has merit, though heaven knows he hasn't given you the formula for escaping the depression altogether. Hard times have hit the groceries, too."

"Mom," I said, "I think we've got to face it: I'll never get a raise at Frank & Cedar's. They complain all the time about the bad business. I'll be lucky if I don't get laid off."

"Well, don't worry about it. If you do, you can return to high school."

"High school? In the middle of the depression? Oh, no, I'll get a job—or keep this one. Who knows, *you* might get laid off."

"Suppose you let me worry about that. Meantime, I don't think you ought to start jumping from job to job—not in the middle of a depression."

"Oh, I'm not worried about getting a job. I can always get a job, Mom."

"It's good to have confidence, Jimmy, but it's foolish to be overconfident and not look at things as they really are."

This theme set the stage for many discussions in our home. As a bone of contention it is smooth worn and has been gnawed at through all the centuries—the wiser, older parent attempting to teach restraint, prudence, and practicality to the impetuous young for whom the world has no fears, nor life any mysteries.

Ultimately, Mom worked out an acceptable negotiated truce.

"Jimmy," she said, "when I let you quit school and take up a man's work, you became more a man than a boy, required to make a man's decisions. I decided then that unless I absolutely had to, I wouldn't interfere in any decisions that you might make. That's what I made up my mind to do, and I still feel the same way.

"Now if you have decided that you want to move on to another job someplace else after two years at Frank & Cedar's, I have only one bit of advice to give you. Make certain you have the other job firmly in hand, and make sure it's just the job you want, before you give your notice at Frank & Cedar's."

I assured her that I would observe those simple precautions. She probably suspected that I had already started sniffing around for something with higher pay and greater opportunity. Well, I had spoken to a couple of people at Kroger's warehouse and plant.

The grocery stores I had worked in during my school years were neighborhood stores, part of the Kroger chain. They were good stores and carried an excellent line of goods with a wide range of price and quality.

The headquarters offices and the main warehouse of Kroger's were located only a few blocks away, and a great many of the men in our neighborhood worked in the plant —really a warehouse and distributing point—while many of the womenfolk were employed in the offices. All in all, I figured I had some excellent connections at Kroger's when you counted in the several store managers and assistant managers whom I knew.

And Kroger's met that depression-proof qualification: it was a part of the food industry. In fact, it was a very important food chain. From my vantage point in the retailing industry, where the money-pinch among the customers was making itself felt in department sales and fear about the prospects for continued employment was causing former good customers to hold onto their greenbacks, the food business—any part of the food business—looked mighty attractive.

I began contacting friends and acquaintances who worked at Kroger's. Within a week I had an appointment with the boss of the night shift in the warehouse. A day later I was hired, and after serving a two-week notice at Frank & Cedar's, I reported to my new job—in the warehouse, where I had many friends. My assignment was in the produce department.

A railroad siding ran along two sides of the giant warehouse, and the produce department was located near those sidings. Long lines of "reefer" cars came in every day to await the night crews who unloaded them.

To me, the cars held a special kind of romance as I

thought of the long distances some of those cars had come, carrying intact their highly perishable cargoes.

From California's Imperial Valley came lettuce, cabbage, spinach, carrots, beets, and from the surrounding hills of that Valley came, in season, rhubarb, asparagus, and avocados. Cars brought melons from Florida, cantaloupes from Arizona and south Texas, tomatoes from Florida, eggs from Delaware, Maryland, and Virginia, cherries from Michigan's upper peninsula and celery from the midlands, apples from such distantly separated places as Oregon and upstate New York, and citrus fruits from Florida, Texas, Arizona, and southern California.

I thought of the man-hours involved in getting one head of lettuce to the city dwellers of Detroit from its birth as a seed in the Imperial Valley to its ultimate repository in someone's icebox, and I was filled with a sense of insignificance—aware, more than ever before, of the fact that I was but a tiny and expendable cog in a complex machine.

It would have been all right in Kroger's warehouse if the slightly larger cogs had not been so abrasive. No one had bothered to lubricate that part of the machine, and many small and expendable cogs were crushed, cast out, and replaced with indifferent abandon as they came into malfunctioning contact with the slightly larger gears one step closer to the Big Wheels.

The part of the vast distributing machine that reposed in Kroger's warehouse in 1930 functioned poorly, protestingly, and without maintenance or concern. A depression-supplied reserve of new cogs waited outside the gates to serve as replacement parts to the grinding, destructive machine.

There was a time, after I quit Kroger's, and following that lengthy period of bitterness, mistrust, and revulsion, when I wondered if I hadn't made a terrible mistake in leaving Frank & Cedar's. Surely I was happy there, though my earnings were smaller and the potential seemed limited.

Only much later did I come to realize that if it had not been for the experience at Kroger's warehouse, I might not have come so soon in life to feel so strongly about the labor movement, or to have realized the plight of the small guy functioning at the low end of the economic totem. I might not have known at so impressionable an age the problems of the little fellow behind the scenes, the nameless, faceless guy who keeps the machine going. I might not have realized the truth about his fears, his constant insecurity, his pointless frustrations, his perpetual submersion in a pool of hopelessness. I might not have comprehended his need to have someone speak on his behalf against the injustices he faces and to represent his interests to his employer and to the public.

Had I not learned his basic needs firsthand, and been hurt and torn by the same conditions that bruised him, I might not have had so rewarding a life, one blessed by the special feeling of fulfillment that comes to those who dedicate themselves to the labor movement.

I joined the labor movement at Kroger's. I joined it out of a need for self-preservation—laced liberally with some honest anger at injustices so blatant they were obscene. "Man's inhumanity to man" was constant and gleefully adhered to in the lower reaches of the economy found amidst the sweat and smells and curses and blisters of Kroger's produce warehouse.

The cause of most of the unhappiness at Kroger's was squat and bandy-legged, a "yapper," like a militantly ill-tempered small dog. Truckers have heard me speak about the fellow as the kind of guy who causes unions. He is, but I cannot exonerate the kind of management that permitted him to function, and, we suspected, encouraged him to discharge his duties in the way that he did.

I won't name him, for he is still living. But the men who worked under him in Kroger's warehouse in 1930 never referred to him as anything but "The Little Bastard," an appellation he earned.

The Little Bastard was perverted. I use the word in its pure sense. I know nothing about his sexual aspirations of the time, but he had an unclean, unhealthy personality, which showed in the way he got his "kicks," getting as they say, "his jollies" by abusing and threatening the people who worked under his supervision and making their lives miserable. His greatest thrill, manifested by a triumphant smile, came when he was able to fire someone and make it stick with the management. The more desperately the man needed the job—perhaps he had a sick wife or many hungry children or was on the verge of losing his home to creditors —the greater the thrill to The Little Bastard when he sent the man packing to the breadlines.

Only a perverted mind could find enjoyment in such actions. He was queer, peculiar. He occupied the ramrod position immediately above the sweat labor, like a top field hand. At the time he had kindred souls in tens of thousands of commercial enterprises across the continent. His kind helped make the depression more terrifying and dreadful than it need have been. I have never forgiven or forgotten the man, and I'll carry my contempt for him as long as I live.

He never made a request. He never issued an order. Everything was in a regal, irritated *command*. He had an annoying way of urging us to greater speed in unloading the reefers. He'd holler, "MOVE! MOVE! MOVE!" But it would come out, "HOOVE! HOOVE! HOOVE!" He sounded for all the world like a little drill sergeant in a British line outfit. The difference was that we were not at war, we were not protected by any terms of enlistment, and there was no intelligent "higher command" to which we could appeal or that limited the abuses. He was supreme. He had absolute power and was an absolute dictator.

We started our shift at 5:00 P.M. During the first half of
the night we were responsible for unloading the reefers and
boxçars. During the remainder of the night we would assem-
ble individual orders for the separate retail stores in the
Kroger chain that were serviced from our warehouse, then
we would load those orders onto designated trucks according
to a specific order that permitted the driver to unload from
the very back of the truck at his first stop and, if the order
were small, proceed to additional stores. We also had to
observe strict rules in packing and stacking, else heavy merchandise on top of the load would crush the lighter or more
delicate produce beneath.

The man who didn't observe these basic but sometimes
complex rules of stacking was summarily fired. He did the
work under a constant barrage of invective and an omnipresent harangue that deprecated one's brain, judgment,
ambition, and parentage. The Little Bastard hovered over
all like an angel of death.

The oldest fellow in our crew was a man named Sam Calhoun. He was, if I recall correctly, thirty-three at the time.
Sam had belonged to a union when he worked for an express
agency, and under the abuses heaped upon us by our foreman he quietly urged us to unionize.

Sam was a calm man, a thoughtful person, and it bothered
him that the younger men lost their tempers and shouted
back at the boss—frequently, in this manner, hastening an
end to their employment. "Don't say a word," he'd caution,
then he'd tell us that officially and with legal means and in a
dignified way we could end the abuses—through union
representation.

We had, he explained, many grievances that should be
presented to the management in a formal way. And some
grievances were of much greater importance than the annoy-
ances presented by the immediate boss in the warehouse.

Our pay of thirty-two cents an hour wasn't the lowest in town, he said, but it could stand improvement. Of greater concern to us was the fact that while for a forty-eight-hour week we could earn $15.36, we had to put in sixty, seventy, sometimes eighty hours at the warehouse to get forty-eight hours of work, for we were paid only for the actual work-time spent in loading or unloading.

There were no regular work rules, I observed, and our contemptible little foreman could make them up as he went along and thus *create* grounds for firing anyone he didn't like.

In addition, hard working breadwinners were often fired without cause simply to make room for college boys and school kids, relatives of the "brass" who wanted tuition money or pocket cash to increase their vacationtime fun.

There was no job security whatsoever, and the desperate unemployed would form lines around the warehouse, waiting for the nightly firings, hoping to be chosen as replacements.

In the face of the outrageous meanness of our foreman, Sam Calhoun urged us to remain calm and to bide our time until we could form a union and affiliate with a national or international group.

There was one drawback. Unions were not at all popular in Detroit in those days. Some organizing had taken place prior to the depression, but with the sudden onslaught of unemployment, workers lucky enough to have some kind of steady job were scared to death even to be seen talking to anyone suspected of union organizing activities.

The open shop was decreed for the entire city. Those who tried to organize were locked out. Strikebreaking crews and goon squads were formed quickly and easily by managements simply by recruiting among hungry and frightened men. A chance to earn some money to buy bread and pay part of

the rent outweighed any notions of loyalty to the down-
trodden working class, and the poor creatures eagerly took
jobs to break strikes—either the easy way or the hard way.

Fate was advocating a rocky course for us at Kroger's
warehouse.

There was a near-member of my family in my work crew,
Jim Langley, an Indiana boy like myself and at the time
the unofficial fiancé of my sister Jennetta, whom he married
later. Jim was a frequent visitor at our home, as may have
been expected, and he had used what influence he had to
help me get my job at Kroger's. I liked Jim and regarded
him as kinfolk. He and I talked over Sam's proposition and
the many sides and angles of the situation.

We concluded that organization offered the only sensible
course left open to us. We might incur the wrath of the
management; we might even invite the use of strikebreakers
and some kind of violence. But if we didn't organize, we
knew, our lives would continue to be miserable; one by one
we would be fired for no reason, and ultimately someone
would beat up our sadistic foreman, resulting, perhaps, in a
more serious problem. We wanted the boss neutralized and
humanized; we didn't want him killed. We knew that only
orders from the management would force him to treat us
decently. Otherwise, left on his own, he would continue to
merit the nickname we had bestowed on him and earn the
hatred of the men who worked under him.

People hate what they fear. When someone sets himself
up as a little tin god and wields absolute power over your
children's diet, clothes, shelter, and medical attention, he is
feared. When that tin god abuses that power, uses it indis-
criminately merely for laughs, he is hated with a bitterness
and depth that can never be understood by those who have
not experienced it.

Therefore, organization of a union, it seemed to us, was

the safest and wisest course. We would gladly have quit Kroger's and gone anywhere else where working conditions were better, but the depression had settled over the city like a pall and had strangled and smothered the last spark of economic life. There was no place else for us to go. Our foreman knew that—and gloated over it.

The management's own system set the stage for us. Because of the numerous "rest periods" during each night, when we were not paid and were on our own, we had ample time to make plans.

We could not merely confront management; we would simply be fired. Strikebreakers would be moved in to take over our jobs. Goons would be recruited to beat us up, and if we left the premises and didn't hurry fast enough, Detroit city police would work us over with their nightsticks. We knew that all of us would be considered to be "lagging" sufficiently to merit a second beating at the hands of the cops. After that we could simply join the ranks of the unemployed, nursing our bruises and waiting for our wounds to heal.

Sam Calhoun, who had experience in these things, agreed to my plan for pulling it off. We would wait until a carload of expensive and perishable produce was on the siding. "If a man doesn't have a heart you can appeal to," I said, "you gotta hit him in the pocketbook."

It made sense. I cautioned that, though we would hit the management in the pocketbook, we should not ask for too much. We would make it easy on our employers, make it possible for them to comply with our demands. Thus we would firm up the union and get it established.

That was our plan. We set about recruiting the other workers in that hellhole under the big shed. We talked to each one quietly and earnestly and spelled out our plans in detail. We watched for the injustices against individuals wrought under the reign of terror at the hands of our stupid foreman. When the boss insulted someone, we got to the bitter worker at the next break. When someone was given the short end of the deal on a work schedule, we talked to him about getting a guarantee of a certain amount of work each week, to be divided evenly among all employees at our level. When someone was fired without cause, we'd talk to his best friends about the need for job security and for specific grounds on which an employee could be fired.

I'm afraid that Jim and I were ready to call a strike as soon as we got a majority of the fellows to agree to our plans, but wise old Sam Calhoun kept calming us down, cautioning us to take it easy until exactly the right time.

It came one night at midnight in the spring of 1931— April, I think, possibly May.

At midnight two men left the warehouse to go to a lunch cart for their evening meal. This was the long-standing custom. The foreman, who was being particularly bitchy that night, went out to the gate and hired two men from the line of watching unemployed. When the two lunchers returned, the lout smilingly informed them that they no longer worked for Kroger's.

This was a horrible mistake, because he did it in front of the entire work force of about 175 men.

We may not have had 100 percent support for our budding union before that incident, but by one o'clock that morning, the entire night crew at Kroger's was ready to strike— that being regarded as the next best thing to the exquisite pleasure of beating the foreman to pulp.

Had we struck at that time and had goon squads been brought in that night, I have the feeling that the goons would have been candidates for the morgue before they knew what hit them. I have rarely seen so many men so angry over one incident.

Word was passed around the warehouse that the union was ready to act, was perfecting its plans, and that every-

one would be informed at the proper time as to what was
to be done.

To a man, they supported us. We waited for that carload
of expensive perishables.

It arrived four days later.

A switcher had snaked three or four cars onto the siding.
They were reefers, closed up tight against the spring warmth,
and their drains were dripping melting ice along the right
of way.

One by one, the foreman addressed himself to the cars,
untacking the duplicate of the manifest from the side and
breaking the seal so the doors could be slid open.

As soon as we slid open the door of the second car, we
knew what we had. You didn't have to read the shipping
orders. A cloud of sweet pungency broiled out into the shed,
smelling of rich earth and hot sunshine and flowering vines.
It was strawberries—luscious, fat, red, juicy strawberries—all
crated and waiting to be transshipped to the retail counters.
Not many other varieties of produce are more perishable.

I nodded and smiled. All the men knew what I meant.
The time for action had come.

We fell to the task of unloading with unaccustomed vigor.
If our boss had been endowed with the most elementary
perception, he would have noticed that we were more cheer-
ful than we had been in a long time. He detested any sign
of happiness on the job, but he didn't seem to notice.

We worked until the trucks were about half loaded with
crates of strawberries and the heat was building up inside
the trailers. Everyone was watching me. Suddenly I set down
a crate, straightened up, sighed, and walked away from the
loading line. I sauntered to another part of the loading
platform and stood there, hands in my pockets. The entire
crew walked over and joined me.

I don't suppose that even one of the 175 men in that crew
has ever forgotten the look on the face of our foreman.

Most of them were young "sweat labor," and in all their lives they had never known anyone who was so cordially and universally disliked.

The Little Bastard had been standing on a platform, a vantage point he occupied in order to overlook the operations. He also fancied that the elevation gave his voice greater carrying power.

At the time of the incident his back was turned to the line; he was apoplectically berating one of the men he had summoned to his throne. When the boss was finished, the man turned away and headed toward a different part of the shed, toward me.

"Hey, you," shouted the boss. "You. Where the hell do you think you're goin'? Get back to that line and get to work. If you don't feel like workin' there are plenty outside that do!"

He turned to look at the loading line. It wasn't there.

He blinked. His mouth fell open. He turned ashen under the high glare of the lights. His body swung in an arc, and he saw the men streaming toward me.

"What the hell do you guys think you're doin'?" he screamed, "Get back there. Get back, goddammit, or I'll fire every one of you bastards!"

Someone shouted an invective involving a reflexive verb.

He stiffened and actually hopped up and down on his little platform. "By God," he roared, "not one of you s.o.b.'s will have a job here tomorrow! Not one!"

"T'hell with you, Little Bastard, we want Blough!" Mr. Blough was the night supervisor. His office was in the warehouse, some distance removed from the loading platforms.

"This is private property," shouted the boss, seizing on a new thought. "This is private property. Get back to work or get the hell out. You're trespassin' if you're not workin'."

"Get Blough. Get Blough. GET BLOUGH. BLOUGH. BLOUGH." The men started a chant.

Some of the fellows were getting angry, and I could see that Calhoun was becoming slightly worried.

"You'd better get Mr. Blough," I said in a loud, calm, clear voice that could be heard above the chanting.

At that moment Mr. Blough emerged from his office to see what the shouting was about. He took one glance and recognized the problem instantly.

He rushed toward the boss and waved him to silence. "That's enough," he said. "Let's be quiet."

A hush fell over the entire group.

"Who can speak for you men?" he asked. "What's the complaint?"

"I can speak," I said stepping forward.

"Fine. What's the complaint?"

"Mr. Blough, there are many complaints. We have a list. We will have to sit down and talk it over. We will have a committee from the men to discuss this with you."

"Well," said Mr. Blough patiently, "I can't get any company officials at this time of night. Suppose we set up a meeting for tomorrow or as soon as I can get some company officials together?"

"It will have to be tomorrow morning, Mr. Blough, no later," I insisted, motioning toward the strawberry crates.

"What's your name?"

"Hoffa, sir."

"Fine. All right, Mr. Hoffa, if I promise to have a meeting arranged for ten o'clock tomorrow morning, will the men go back to work and finish loading those strawberries that are spoiling in the trucks?"

"Yes, sir, that sort of promise would get the men back to work."

"It's a promise, then. Ten o'clock tomorrow morning."

"Well, sir, just to be clear: You mean ten o'clock *this* morning, today, don't you?"

"That's right, Mr. Hoffa, 10:00 A.M. today."

Sam turned to the group.

"Okay, guys," he said, in the same low, unemotional voice, "let's get back to work and get those strawberries loaded onto the trucks."

We filed past the boss, still standing on his little platform, his face now beet red.

"You'll be sorry for this, Hoffa," he hissed. "You, too, Calhoun."

"Let's have none of that," admonished Mr. Blough, and he turned and left for his office.

We didn't realize it, but we had a union. I didn't realize it, but I had taken part in my first organizing drive and had been a participant, with a slightly Machiavellian role, in my very first strike. It was symbolic, perhaps, that both adventures were highly successful from the workers' point of view.

As night gave way to a spring-pink dawn and I stretched out wearily in my bed, I felt more secure and comfortable about my job than at any time since I had started work at Kroger's. And I thought: "I have Sam Calhoun to thank for this. He showed me the way."

We had, of course, already appointed our committee, and the members had received the approval of the men. It included my future brother-in-law—Jim Langley—Frank Collins, Bobby Holmes, Sam, and myself.

We met that morning in Mr. Blough's office with several officers from the company. I handled things in a calm but extremely firm manner. I let it be known that the men had been pushed just as far as they would allow, and I took pains to point out, in detail, how improved working conditions and a more wholesome "attitude" in the warehouse would result in better and more work.

The company officials were not angry, as I had expected they might be. They had the attitude of executives who were dealing with their employees over work schedules and working conditions—which was precisely what they were doing. I listened, and I learned.

The main thing, we said, was job security. We related incident after incident of firings by our little boss and listed the wide variety of reasons selected by the tiny tyrant for sacking the men.

"All right," said Mr. Blough, "we'll put an end to that."

"Fine, Mr. Blough. But that's not exactly what we want. We want to spell out these things and put them in writing. We want exact descriptions of our duties and firm lists of things that we must do, things that we may do, and things that we cannot do."

Mr. Blough nodded. "Okay," he said. The other executives nodded, perhaps in resignation, but at least in agreement.

The meeting lasted all morning and through lunchtime. We broke off in mid-afternoon so that we members of the committee could go home and change into our work clothes and report back for work at five o'clock for the night shift. We showed up a half-hour early so that we could report on our progress to the rest of the men.

That night the little boss strutted about on his platform and grumbled a good deal. But he didn't fire anyone, and he raised his voice to holler at a man only once. When a whole group of men turned toward him and yelled, "SHAD-DUP!" he subsided and resumed his muttering.

The negotiations lasted several days. As I recall, they ran right through the weekend. When we were finished, we had formed an agreement with the management that permitted us to live like human beings while on the job.

There were specific work rules. There were rules about lunch breaks, about smoking, about using the washroom facilities, and about many other seemingly "minor" things that, added together, meant a great deal to the men.

Most important, I had exacted a promise from the management to sit down with our committee when we deemed it necessary to discuss our problems. That meant that in the future we could discuss our "waiting time" problem, and that we could talk about pay rates.

When we reported on the final agreement the night after the last meeting, the men surrounded our committee and cheered and cheered. In that moment I realized what my life's goal was to be. I would work for Labor.

7

The Other End of the Trucks

I was sixteen years old and I had a "calling." Not until years later did I realize how fortunate I was in this. I didn't have to live through the turmoil of indecision that confronts most young men as they contemplate one career, then another, never quite sure which one they wish to follow. I knew with unwavering certainty just exactly what I wanted to do. I wanted to become part of the labor movement— just as soon as possible.

I was vaguely aware, even at sixteen, of the double-barreled blessing of my choice. Realizing that it would bring me great satisfaction to serve the working men of our town and to be instrumental, in some way, in improving their working conditions and their living standards, I was not unaware, either, of the fact that in the labor movement I might quite likely move from a blue collar job to a white collar job. I was always keenly aware of my shortcomings in formal education, and I knew that in the absence of unusual career opportunities, such as those offered in the labor movement, I was likely to spend the rest of my days lugging someone else's groceries in a sweat-drenched denim shirt. In 1930 the corporate world had not crystallized its job opportunities the way it has for subsequent generations, and to my knowledge there was no such thing as a "management training program" anywhere in America for a boy who had not been able to finish high school.

Thus my mind was made up. By entering the labor movement as an activist, I could help do something about eliminating conditions such as those existing in Kroger's warehouse, and at the same time I could enter an arena that might permit me to gain a higher degree of personal success as well.

It would enrich this narrative if I could pretend, these many years later, that I played a spectacular role in the affair at Kroger's warehouse. I'm afraid my entrance on Labor's scene on behalf of the workingman was somewhat less spectacular and, indeed, much more timid. I didn't raise my hand and have the 175 workers at Kroger's fall silent to listen to my words of wisdom and then agree, docilely, to follow my lead in calling the management to account and bringing it to terms.

The truth is, I was scared half to death. I really don't know why, for I wasn't actually afraid of being fired. Being a kid, I had every confidence of landing another job if that one should be denied me, even though the depression had numbed the flow of commerce throughout the Detroit area. I guess the fear came from actively plotting open defiance. I simply wasn't accustomed to sassing back my elders or refusing to do their bidding, and an employer, even the employer personified in The Little Bastard, was the symbol of authority and the fountainhead of a discipline to which I responded instinctively, just as I "minded" my mother or the teacher at school.

I think discipline is a good and a necessary thing. When a person is young, another authority must help him discipline himself until self-discipline takes over, when he is mature. But a kid who is old enough to do man's work is old enough to make man's decisions, with a little guidance, and in Kroger's warehouse many older and wiser employees shared my bitter appraisal of prevailing conditions.

Still, I was scared.

Prior to our strawberry festival, my job with the organizers consisted of myriad little chores befitting my age and station. I was basically an errand boy, rounding up workers for meetings, dashing around the corner for coffee and doughnuts for the group, keeping an eye out for the boss when brief meetings were held during working hours.

After the boss fired the two men, it became apparent that something drastic had to be done. I didn't have to learn any speeches or memorize the points that we wanted to make, for I felt so strongly about the firings and about other injustices that had been practiced against us—including the throwing of things at us—that I'd merely buttonhole a fellow and tell him that I thought we ought to organize to protect ourselves.

I tried to do my recruiting among fellows closest to my age, for I thought they'd find me more convincing than would the older men. I learned one thing: each worker loathed the abuses practiced by the boss, but a great many of them were afraid to join a union. There seemed to be some curious notions about unionism. I noted that some young fellows responded as though I was asking them to join some secret lodge dedicated to unpatriotic and pagan rites, whose members would be expelled from society if discovered by authorities or their minions.

Then I discovered something else. If I looked a fellow straight in the eye and told him, with no baloney involved, exactly why we needed a union and exactly what a union could do for us, I generally had a recruit. Then I realized that this happened because I believed absolutely in what I was saying and knew it was, as they used to say, "God's honest truth."

It was a valuable lesson for anyone to learn upon entering the labor movement. The American labor force is com-
posed of the most uncommon collection of rugged individualists ever assembled for mutual cause. They like to do
their own griping and to solve their own problems. They
do not want outside help and instinctively resist it. They
were never "joiners"—and that included unions.

You can't fool workers for very long, and they can sense
insincerity a mile away. A fellow who approaches the average American worker and tells him he'll do something for
him will be asked, immediately, "Why? What are *you* getting out of it?" Another common response is, "Who needs
help?" Or, "Who needs *your* help?"

I have laughed many times in later years over the observa-
tions of the political pundits who attempt to predict how
the "labor vote" will be cast, in the silly belief that Labor
votes in a bloc.

Union members find it very difficult to use the democratic process of the vote to decide where to locate a water
cooler in their own headquarters; no one knowing Labor
would dare predict where such a piece of equipment might
ultimately be located. Much less would anyone who knows
the working men and women of this nation dare to predict
how they would vote in a national election.

Has it never occurred to the fanciful analysts that when
Labor does vote in something resembling a bloc—which it
does now and then—it's because individual members of the
unions have decided, as individuals, that what they're voting for is best for the nation? And those who claim that
organized Labor is the captive of the Democrats fail to realize that if this were true, we wouldn't have had a Republican president since Teddy Roosevelt, and we wouldn't have
had so many Republican governors in so many of our highly
industrialized and organized states.

It might be possible to predict how upper-echelon corporate executives will vote, or how most clergymen will vote, or how most physicians will vote. But there is no central or common ideal holding organized Labor together in a voting bloc. In a canning factory in Maine workers might believe they need improved working conditions, but in a canning factory in the state of Washington those doing essentially the same jobs might feel that their working conditions are superb. Because a man from a sea-coast town in Maine cans fish for a living, he doesn't feel he therefore has a lot in common with a fellow in Washington who also lives in a sea-coast town and cans fish for a living. In fact, he might feel a little competitive.

It would be hard to show me any great "Common Cause." Workers are workers. They are Americans. They are active participants in a hard, demanding, competitive life. They have respect for their fellow men, recognizing that most of them also work hard; they strive to keep their homes and families relatively secure; and they face innumerable problems just trying to carve out a decent living. They will listen to a fresh idea or a new thought and make up their own minds—some of them silently, some of them vociferously, depending on their individual characters. Some have extremely keen intellects; some have not. As a result, acceptance of a new idea to which all can subscribe comes harder in the world of the laboring man than anywhere else in our society.

The one thing America's laboring people will not abide is a phony. If a man is going to have anything to do with organized labor and come into contact with its members, he had better be certain that he knows what he is talking about, and that he says only what he knows to be true, only what he genuinely believes. Otherwise, he'll be ignored, or perhaps tossed out on his ear.

But I was a kid back in Kroger's warehouse. I didn't know all of these things. I was a workingman. I was surrounded by workingmen. We had a common problem. There was a common solution to be found through common action. That action began with organizing.

I must have been convincing, for my efforts were crowned with success. In fairness, I must say that The Little Bastard did everything he could, in his stupidity, to help me in my drive to enlist the support of the men, Also, I was enormously helped by the calm, quiet counsel of Sam Calhoun, who, above all, knew, understood, and loved his fellow workingmen. If I had wondered as a boy what was meant by the word "compassion," I learned its meaning from the example of Sam Calhoun.

I was not a talker, and I am to this day afflicted by a substantial degree of taciturnity that must have been inherited from my Scottish-Irish forebears. I did not rush up to Sam and declare my burning desire to serve the labor movement, nor did I hurry home to confide such thoughts to Mom. She, like Sam, had great compassion, which endowed her with penetrating perception. She, like Sam, knew the thoughts that were churning in my young mind. They fathomed my feelings and thoughts, and together they waited for me to discover my destiny.

Things followed thick and fast. As D-day arrived and the confrontation was before us, it was necessary for our company union to organize officially, draw up some bylaws, and elect some officers. To this day I am honored by the knowledge that when they elected Sam Calhoun president by acclamation, they also elected me vice-president. Bobby Holmes was elected secretary-treasurer, also by acclamation. His initial job was to collect enough contributions from the members to finance some capital investments: a desk, a chair, some pens, and some paper.

I didn't fully realize exactly how audacious I was in my activities as a union organizer. Detroit at that time was not a healthy place for union activities. The open shop was decreed by fiat, and the city and state governments backed up the tax-paying employers in their insistence on the non-union, open-shop policy. Platitudes about "right-to-work" were uttered by fat, secure executives for quotation in the press and for repetition over the air so that their words of wisdom might also be heard by the well-to-do on their Atwater Kent battery-powered radios.

The truth is, of course, that all levels of the middle class and even the upper-class owners and professional managers were just as scared about the future and as frightened of the poverty that lurked behind every shadow as were the industrial workers lower down the social and economic scale. The one difference was that those who had jobs and incomes didn't want anyone to alter the status quo, and they sicced the obedient cops like well-trained watchdogs on anyone who threatened the fragile structure of their flimsy economic world. Anyone who made waves had his head held under water until he stopped struggling.

The right to work wasn't the issue, of course, as the perspective of nearly two score years clearly indicates. The issue was the "right" to a job. But anyone who claimed that those who wanted work had a "right" to a job was branded a radical and a revolutionary.

Thus, before my beard was anything to brag about, and long before I was able to vote, I was a "radical" and a "revolutionary," for I believed sincerely that in a land as rich as ours and in a society as sophisticated as ours, anyone who wants to work should be able to find a job of some kind, and that if the existing system does not provide those jobs, even for the qualified, then something must be done about the system.

No one today would say that those are incorrect or unten-able premises. But if that is so today, why was it not so in those days? Ah, well, as my Josephine has said many times, nothing good ever comes about easily.

In Detroit in 1930 we "radicals" were destined to get our lumps—on our heads as well as on our souls. Some of our fellow men armed with nightsticks saw to the former; some of our fellow men armed with typewriters, and others moti-vated by lust for public office or desire for corporate ad-vancement, saw to the latter.

I had no comprehension of what might lie in store for me and any other Labor organizer in the area as I sought simply to eliminate the intolerable conditions at Kroger's ware-house. As I believed that men had a right to the opportunity to seek a job, I also believed that a man, having found it, had a right to be allowed to do his work under humane conditions. It was a simple equation in my mind: the owners-managers couldn't function without the men; the men couldn't have jobs without the owners-managers. Therefore, we should work together under the best conditions that we could arrange for our mutual benefit. I didn't think such an aim unreasonable; I still think it a reasonable premise. The unreasonable element in my immediate world was The Little Bastard and his tyrannical ways.

So I led in organizing the workers at Kroger's and derived much personal satisfaction from it.

Our subsequent meetings with Mr. Blough and members of the management committee taught me many other things. We hammered out many benefits for the workers in those sessions, and the warehouse was an entirely different place after the incident of the strawberries. Not one worker in that loading shed had second thoughts about joining his company union. The results were glaringly obvious and hap-pily measurable.

Fellows who once had left their wives and children wondering if they would have a job when they returned home knew for a fact that they would have one. Men who had huddled at the doorway waiting for the shift to begin, dreading the hours stretching before them, now looked forward to a nighttime of productive work. Before I quit Kroger's, I heard men actually bragging that they worked there, and they mentioned specifically that they worked on the night shift with the loading crew—*our* crew, *our* gang. And these men formerly thought they worked in the meanest hellhole on earth.

As we inched forward in our negotiations, I observed with a scientist's scrutiny the give and take between Labor and Management. I studied the sallies and parries, the thrusts and counter-thrusts, and I tried to analyze the motives behind each.

I learned that the higher up the echelon you go, the more reasonable are the conditions under which you arbitrate. I also learned that you must be specific in your demands and Gibraltar-like in your determination. In those days, Management asked no quarter and gave none. Production was nowhere near as important as sales, nor were the backroom operations of a grocery chain.

If you truly have the interests of the men at heart, you discover in each confrontation with Management that there is a time to be tough, a time to be adamant, a time to be open to compromise, and a time to reach agreement. I observed these things at those first negotiating sessions, and my mentors on either side were Messrs. Calhoun, a tough but fair man, and Blough, a tough but fair man. What a marvelous opportunity for a young man! What a profound education for a dedicated observer!

I wonder if Mr. Blough would remember me today if I hadn't become the General President and head of the International and thus garnered an uncommon amount of publicity and, in some contexts, notoriety. I would hope that he would, for his calm, careful handling of a legitimate grievance encouraged me and made a lasting impression. He also impressed me with his professional handling of our other demands, which had nothing to do with our admittedly justified complaint against The Little Bastard.

I don't mean to imply that Mr. Blough was a pushover. He was a very tough nut, indeed, and we got no more than we deserved at the time. The point is: he understood his men, he understood his management, and he was the solitary important link of communication between the two sides.

Mr. Blough was there as a fortuitous accident of hiring, but why can't enlightened managements today realize that such a person is necessary in dealing with a much more sophisticated labor movement? Someone who *understands*— that's what we need.

As our negotiations progressed in the front office, the men in the shed set about forming themselves into a formal and official union. Meetings were held to talk about bylaws and dues and shop stewards and an organizational chart.

At one such meeting a member introduced an organizer from the Teamsters Union, the most active union in Detroit and the most fearless in the face of the police opposition to all who threatened the open shop.

The Teamsters' representative made a simple appeal. Why didn't we join the Teamsters, he asked, since we worked at loading and unloading trucks? They had all the things we needed: bylaws, a dues schedule, an organizational chart. And they had much more: they had the weight of a national union behind them, and they would support us, he said, in any future demands that might be necessary and in making sure that the terms we had reached or were negotiating with the management were, indeed, carried out to the satisfaction of the men. We would pay dues to our local and to the International, but if ever a strike became necessary, provided it was authorized by the International, we would receive not only full support but full strike benefits in the form of good green dollars from the International.

I was noncommittal. I "digested" this proposal for the period of two more meetings. Then at the third meeting, a member asked me for a frank opinion. I summed it up with one question.

"Why not?" I asked.

That's the way I felt. That's the way the membership felt, too, for at the following meeting we voted ourselves into affiliation with the International Brotherhood of Teamsters. I didn't know it at the time, but the vote affected me, as an individual, as much as anything up to that date in my life.

Word of my success at organizing the men in our shed had spread beyond our own precincts—I, in my naiveté, was totally unaware of the spread of such news—and apparently a number of people knew about me at Joint Council 43, the important Teamsters unit in Detroit where policy was being generated.

Particularly interested was Ray Bennett, an Organizer.

Those who don't know about the Teamsters or about the larger unions may not know how important an Organizer is. He not only oversees on the regional and local levels, he's a genuine policymaker, a man who makes the decisions that are adopted at the top.

When Ray Bennett took notice of me, my life was destined to change, though I didn't know it.

Like Sam, like Mom, Ray, too, waited. He didn't wait for me to discover myself as Sam and Mom did. He waited for me to quit, as he knew I would. I had been too active at Kroger's to remain as the "faithful old employee." My days were numbered. I didn't know it, but Ray Bennett, whose many assignments included bringing promising young men into the movement, did. He knew I wouldn't last long, would be goaded to quit.

The Little Bastard had been eying me like a hawk ever since our strawberry festival. He had had his ears pinned back by Mr. Blough and the management, and had it not been for the fact that, to score a psychological point, the management simply couldn't give up too much, he would have been fired and kicked into the gutter where he belonged.

One of the "points" that had been won by the management in our negotiating was that the practicing tyrant of the loading shed would be able to keep score on anyone who was a chronic dropper of crates and, ultimately, to recommend his dismissal. A subparagraph of this provision was that he could summarily fire anyone who deliberately dropped or broke a crate of perishables.

The management had put this clause into the contract as protection against vandalism, and we had agreed to it. But there comes a point when enough is enough. The Little Bastard had been needling me, hovering over me, and promising to "get something on me," as a result of my organizing activities, until he was making me extremely nervous and irritable.

One night everything seemed to come to a head, and it simply became too much. He was dogging my steps, nagging me, threatening me, whispering obscenities. I was carrying a crate of perishable vegetables—I've forgotten exactly what they were—and I turned and looked at him, sizing him up for the crawling little parasite that he was. Then I threw the crate to the floor. I didn't drop it. I threw it. It split open. The vegetables spilled out onto the concrete.

His tantrum ended. He smiled. He relaxed.

"Okay, Hoffa," he said, "you did it, y'dumb bastard. You're fired!"

I looked him straight in the eye.

"You're wrong," I said. "I quit." And I turned and walked out.

Next day I received a summons from Ray Bennett.

Before the day was out I was a member of the staff of Joint Council 43. I was an official Teamster Organizer. There was no salary. I was to receive a commission, a percentage of the dues of each new member I signed.

8

Depression City, 1935

On occasion I have wondered about the trick of fate that caused Mom to move to Detroit. She might just as readily have gone to Gary or Chicago or Cleveland or any other large city of the Midwest. Had she done so, there's a possibility that things might have turned out differently for me.

The year I turned twenty-one I was appointed Business Agent of Local 299, the Teamsters' biggest problem-unit. That year, 1935, was probably the worst of the depression years in Detroit, where hard times had started earliest and lasted longest. Whole families, sheltered by worn blankets, lived in city parks, and fathers scrounged through garbage pails to find the ingredients of mulligan stews, boiled over fires made of discarded and dampened newspapers. The unemployed of Detroit were angry—at the employers, the employed, the city, the state, the federal government, the cops who harassed them and were unsympathetic to their plight, and the indifference of the temperamental elements. Most of all they were angry at themselves. Since some people *were* employed, the unemployed harbored the secret suspicion that they might have done something wrong in their own careers, and this suspicion added to the general atmosphere of anger.

Radicals and Communists filled the city. They spoke on street corners and in park clearings. They orated beside the lines that formed before the factory employment offices. They shouted their deprecations of the system or the details of their magic cures before the lines that formed at the soup kitchens and bread distribution points.

There seemed to be no such thing as a nice day. It was too hot or it was too cold. It snowed too much or it rained too little. Many believed devoutly that God was wreaking His vengeance on the world.

News from the outside was no more cheering. Drought ruined the harvests from the Gulf to the Canadian border, and those who had joined the migrant workers, hoping to earn a few dollars by following the harvests from south to north, found their journeys had been in vain.

To the east of us, the news said, there were near-riots and mass demonstrations, and to the west high, dry winds created dust storms, blowing away the life-producing topsoil off the land and filling the air with stinging, blinding, choking, worthless particles of silicate that smothered all hope of agricultural fertility in the nation's "breadbasket" regions.

The world seemed filled with despair, even to its farthest corners, and the news from overseas told of a preposterous little man with a ridiculous toothbrush moustache who changed his name from Schickelgruber to Hitler and promised his pure Aryan followers *"Arbeit ünd Brot"*—work and bread. Work and bread—it seemed to be in short supply throughout the entire planet.

In such a world, amid such an atmosphere, I was appointed Business Agent of Local 299, a unit saddled with debt and indifferently supported by a distracted and distraught membership numbering 250 workers, only some of whom had jobs.

If I had thought the little tyrant at Kroger's had watched me like a hawk, it was nothing to the way Ray Bennett watched me when I was an Organizer in the Joint Council. There was one difference: Ray had my interests at heart and was helping to shape me for future assignments; the man at Kroger's was interested solely in stamping me into the ground, along with all others unfortunate enough to work "under" him.

Ray made me toe the line. Several organizational efforts were being launched in the Detroit area, and before I learned what corner in the office was the place for me to hang my hat, he had me out in the field, talking, planning, persuading. Those who have been organized know how it goes, but for the others let me say it's usually easier to take a kid to the dentist's office than it is to get a group of nonunionized employees to join up. And the difficulty was particularly marked in those old days. Anyone who had a job didn't want to part with any portion of his paycheck for union dues. The rewards and benefits that we promised were not very tangible in comparison with a genuine silver half-dollar or an honest greenback.

We were hated and resisted by Management, shadowed, hounded and dispersed by the police, and viewed with suspicion as some variety of shakedown artists or confidence men by those whom we sought to bring into the fold.

I don't consider myself to be overly persuasive as a talker, but if I have any ability today to put across a point or to communicate clearly with my fellow man, it's because of those days of early training under Ray Bennett, when every new member was brought into the organization after hours and hours of candid discussion. Detroit was ripe for revolution, everyone said, but it was anything but ripe for unionism. It should have been a snap for us, but the workers just didn't realize how much they needed the union.

I found that, at the onset, it was most effective to talk to one man at a time and to tell him what we had done in other companies. More money was an inducement, of course, and increases in wages are basic objectives of the movement, but money was not always the major concern of every employee. Many had gripes about working conditions and valid personal grievances. Second-echelon bosses were not always kind.

Frequently, I'd tell the story of what happened at Kroger's and make the point that it would have been much simpler —might, in fact, not have come to the tempestuous strawberry festival—if we had affiliated with the Teamsters *before* instead of *after* the incident.

I was a successful recruiter, but I can't say that it was easy. If I was a bit ahead of my time in such efforts simply because the working men of America weren't quite ready for unionism, it was superb training for what was to follow, for in one way or another I have been in organizing work all of my life, and it has never been what could be described as a cinch.

Once we got the men lined up and on our side, the *real* trouble would start. Managements didn't want us around. It was as simple as that. They made no bones about it, and the police, recognizing who the big taxpayers were and responding to orders of politicians who knew quite well where the big contributions came from, seemed not only willing but anxious to shove us around.

It was, therefore, under conditions such as these that I took over a local as Business Agent. Ray had asked me to hang around the office that afternoon. The big brass of Joint Council 43 was holding a meeting behind closed doors. Finally, Ray came out and walked up to me, extending his hand.

"Well, Jimmy," he said, "you've got a local on your hands."

No one could have been more surprised than I was.

"It's flat on its back and falling apart," Ray was saying, "and we think you're just the guy to put it back on its feet. It needs a peppy young fellow in there who'll stick with it."

I just grinned and let him pump my hand.

Local 299 was having its problems all right. The office I inherited was dark and ill-equipped. The local was faced with eviction for nonpayment of rent. It owed more than the allowable number of bills in amounts that seemed staggering. I was supposed to pay myself twenty-five dollars a week from the local's accounts, but when I looked in the checkbook, I found the account was severely overdrawn and several checks had, as they said then, "gone to protest," meaning they had bounced. "Insufficient funds" was a phrase I grew quite accustomed to hearing.

The first task, and the easiest, was to get the 250 members of the local more interested in their union—interested enough, for a start, to pay their dues.

While this was taking place, my "salary" was five dollars, sometimes as much as ten dollars, per week. It required several serious talks with Mom to convince her that I had moved upward in the world. She viewed my situation from every angle possible, and to her it seemed obvious that I had happily—even gleefully—taken a drastic pay cut to do much harder work.

When the members got back on an active status, I still couldn't draw a full salary because we had so many bills to clear up. In fact, after several years of hard work—seven years since leaving school—I had less money in my pocket and was poorer than when I started.

I had never been happier.

I've read some articles about me that have said I didn't smoke or drink or date girls back in those days because I was so broke. Apparently, when you're twenty-one, you're supposed to do those things if you're to be an acceptable American boy. But it had nothing to do with poverty. I know multimillionaires who neither drink nor smoke. Smoking and drinking are always a matter of choice.

Girls were a different matter. I dated a few girls now and then in those days. But they liked to dress up and go to moving picture shows. And while I didn't mind going indoors in wintertime, in the summer I preferred the amusement park and the crazy rides.

Though I was relatively poor, I had about as much money to spend on girls as anyone else my age in my part of town. I still turned my pay envelope over to Mom, and she still gave me an adequate allowance. So I had money. And I only backed away from girls because I had not yet met the *real* girl.

I just couldn't get serious with any one girl. Yet it seemed to me that if I dated any girl more than once she began to smell orange blossoms and hear wedding bells. It wasn't that I was so overwhelmingly attractive. The girls were bored with poverty and a homelife where everything—every thought, every conversation, every act—revolved around the scarcity of money. They sought to escape, to make homes of their own, and a man didn't have to look like Clark Gable or have a bank account like Tommy Manville's to qualify as a candidate.

I had been brought up to believe that the love of a man and a woman is a precious blessing, one of the true beauties of life, one not to be taken lightly. I hadn't met a girl, at that time, with whom I wanted to spend my life, so I backed away—gracefully, I hope. I'm glad I waited. I met *the* girl later.

But I'm digressing. I just wanted to set the record straight about girls. And liquor. And tobacco. I might add that I didn't go in for pool halls or street-corner loitering, either. They seemed a prodigious waste of time. My extracurricular activities were swimming or fishing or hiking. They're still my favorite sports, and today you can add horseback riding.

Even when most of its members were paying dues and taking part in the meetings, Local 299 was still broke. What it needed was the shot in the arm of new memberships with initiation fees and dues. And to this I bent every effort.

Anyone who drove a truck and didn't belong to Local 299 was a candidate for membership. So was anyone who worked on a loading platform. I developed a program where I'd start from home at six o'clock in the morning and get to the garages by seven. I'd meet with drivers at rendezvous points around town and talk, talk, talk. Then I'd get back to the office before noon to take all of the accumulated phone calls from members, shop stewards, and, I hoped (and it did happen now and again), spokesmen from groups wanting to know about affiliation.

I spent a great deal of time at the loading docks, talking to the warehousemen and then to the drivers when they backed in. Every driver seemed interested in the fact that one day he might be paid to drive, and that helpers and warehousemen would do the loading of the trucks. Long-haul drivers, particularly, worried about their ability to stay alert or even awake after exhausting themselves loading their own trailers.

There were a number of strikes going on all over the city at the time. It was impossible to get a union recognized by Management without striking. Times were tough; the owners were too determined to maintain their open-shop policy— a misnomer, of course, for the "open shop" of 1935 in Detroit was a closed shop—closed tight against organized labor.

Every day it was my practice to spend a few hours in the afternoon or evening on the picket line somewhere, giving the men encouragement, assuring them we would win recognition and a binding contract.

My work was never finished, my day never ended, but I was doing what I wanted to do, enjoying it, and learning from the experience.

Local 299's treasury never seemed to get built up. No sooner would a life-saving batch of new members join, paying their initiation fees and their dues, than another strike or two or three would flare up, creating enormous demands for strike benefits. Increasingly, I found myself "forgetting" to draw my twenty-five-dollar paycheck. I believe a union should be totally independent and not have to ask favors from anyone. Therefore I didn't want to overdraw our account, and I wanted to keep all bills on a cash basis. If it meant that I had to forgo a salary payment for a week now and then, well, those were the breaks of the game.

But it was no game. It was a war, actually, and it was being waged in earnest by both sides, each convinced it was in the right.

There was underconsumption, said Management, and it was necessary to cut back on production. That meant cutting back on employment and wages, wherever possible. And such cutbacks helped them meet the cutthroat price competition at the retail level, the bosses said.

Consumers are real people, Labor said, and people are workers. Employ as many as possible and pay them as well as you possibly can, and they'll consume your products, and we'll all prosper. We'll make higher wages, and more of us will be employed; therefore we'll be bigger and better consumers; therefore you'll make higher profits.

Intelligent men, successful men, men who had headed big companies for many years simply couldn't understand our elemental approach to economics. Sure, they'd say, you'll create a nation of consumers if you can organize every company in every industry, but if you organize us and get higher wages for fewer hours of production, and don't organize our competitors, we'll be out of business.

But we *are* organizing your competitors, we'd tell them. We're organizing ABC Company in Cleveland, ZYX Company in San Francisco, and LMN Associates in New York.

Baloney, they'd say. We don't know about our competitors, and we don't care about our competitors. Our responsibility is to operate this company at a profit. Our business is not to "make" jobs; it's to make and sell products. We can't help it if there's a depression. We didn't cause it. Matter of fact, we kept dozens of guys working when we shouldn't have. .

When they were working, they bought your products, we'd point out. After you fired them, they couldn't.

It didn't register. It didn't get through. Polite differences in economic philosophy broadened into bitter denunciations and name-calling.

The ideological differences were paramount, of course, for we *knew* that if more breadwinners could be put to work, more goods and services would be sold, and that in this way —and only in this way—would we get ourselves back on the road to recovery. But there were many other things as well: substandard wages, lost time for going to the washroom, lost time for sickness, harsh penalties for tardiness, mass layoffs without notice, firings without cause, physical abuse by straw bosses, no compensation for injuries incurred on the job, no rest periods for "recharging" the workers' "batteries." There were many complaints.

Ultimately, the unions would have come to Detroit and to the nation even if we had never attempted to organize a single shop. But, without our efforts, they would have come, most likely, as the result of bloody revolution, not through the relatively peaceful means of progressive organizing.

When I say "relatively peaceful means," permit me to put the emphasis on the word *"relatively."* My scalp was laid open sufficiently wide to require stitches no less than six times during the first year I was Business Agent of Local 299. I was beaten up by cops or strikebreakers at least two dozen times that year. A strikebreaker wounded my own brother, Billy, while he was picketing at one plant. The business agent of one of our locals was fatally shot by a hired strikebreaker, probably not a thug or a killer, but a man so hungry and so scared and so unendowed with vision that he would fire on a fellow worker who, as they would say today, "made waves."

Within one twenty-four-hour period I was taken to jail eighteen times. We were picketing outside a plant, and the police sergeant in charge of the strikebreaking detail spotted me at once.

"Hey, Hoffa," he said, "what're you doing here?"

"What do you think?" I replied.

"C'mon." He grabbed me and put me in the paddy wagon.

At the police station the desk captain asked what I had done.

"He was going to cause trouble," the sergeant explained. "I got him just in time."

The captain released me.

The sergeant drove back to the picket line. I had to use public transportation: a street car and a bus. By the time I arrived, the sergeant was back in business.

"Hey, Hoffa," he shouted, surprised. "What the hell are you doing here?"

"What do you think?"

He clutched me by the jacket and scowled into my face.

"Okaayeh, buddeee," he said. "Let's jest hop right back into the wagon."

"Okay, Sergeant."

Again we confronted the captain. Again the sergeant was asked what I had done.

"He was just about to," explained the stalwart upholder of law enforcement.

"Just about to what?"

"He was going to start a fight, Captain."

"Had he started it?"

"Well, not exactly."

"He wasn't fighting, then?"

"No."

"Had he said anything?"

"I think so. Yes, I think he had."

"Like what? What did he say?"

"I . . . I don't know."

The captain sighed. "Okay, Hoffa," he said. "You can go. But stay away from that picket line."

I didn't answer. I was wondering if I had the two nickels for car fare to get back to the plant and the picket line. I found them in my watch pocket.

When we returned forty minutes later and the sergeant still had no complaint against me, the captain spelled it out in basic A-B-C's for him.

"You gotta wait until he does something, Sergeant. Wait until he says something or does something. Then you can charge him. But, dammit, you can't charge him if he hasn't done anything."

I waited until he dismissed me.

"Okay, Hoffa. You can go," he said.

I started for the door and stopped at the threshold. I have never liked being a smart aleck, and I wasn't particularly intending to be one then, but I realized I was running low on car fare. If I could get back to the picket line, I could borrow a couple of bucks from one of my friends.

"Captain, the wives of the men on the line brought some lunch while I was coming down here with the sergeant. I didn't have time to get breakfast and now I've missed lunch, and, er . . . a . . . I find I left my money in my other pants. I wonder if I could borrow a dime for some coffee and a doughnut?"

"Sure, Hoffa. Sure." He passed a dime across the desk.

Thus, a half-hour later, I was picked up again. That sergeant and a three-striper successor on the job packed me off to the station exactly fourteen more times before the next afternoon, and not once did they think to bring a specific charge against me. Fourteen times more I was released by that captain and the night-desk sergeant.

I should have realized then that I would be jailed many times without specific complaint, and that I would be charged in higher courts many times without a shred of evidence to back up the charge.

Later in life, when more powerful enemies with more serious intent were joined by powerful politicians and labor leaders who wanted me out of the picture, the trumped-up-charge device was used against me more often. In Detroit, in 1935, I was undergoing a toughening experience. I was learning what it's like to be treated like a criminal though no charge has been brought or, if brought, has been unproved.

I wasn't always found innocent, however; nor was I always brought before justice's bar without a specific charge. Today a labor leader is a respected member of society, and the labor activist in the ranks, the Organizer or Business Agent or field man, if not unanimously respected, is at least generally accepted.

In 1935 the labor activist was a "radical," a "Red," an "anarchist." With or without such a label, he was regarded as an enemy of the accepted system and a plotter against the status quo. He made bad waves in the placid mill pond during the dead stillness of the nation's economic doldrums.

Decent people don't kill their political, social, or economic enemies; nor do they like, really, to see them beaten up. An acceptable way to deal with them is through the legal process.

Jail is a superb solution; it removes the guy from the scene for a specific period of time. He may be carried off to the pokey on his own shield, screaming his innocence. Or he may merely be fined, preferably an eye-opening amount. Even in times of prosperity this can be hurtful; during a depression it can be disastrous. At the very least he will acquire a court record and gain some notoriety, and these indelible tattoo marks may accumulate and never be removed. But whatever the outcome, no one really challenges the majesty —or the finality—of the legal processes that are conducted under the glare of the golden eagle and the banner that symbolizes the home of the free and brave.

Of course, I had my days in court when I was twenty-one years old, to answer to the charges of "The People," my fellow Americans, the same scared, jobless, wondering people whom I had thought I was serving.

My first encounter with the blindfolded lady and her balanced scales came when I was arrested, jailed, convicted, and fined on a charge of assault and battery.

The charge stemmed from an attempt by strikebreakers to disperse a picket line. The "outrageous" demands of the union that caused the strike were for union recognition— just recognition.

This big, muscley guy came at me with an outsize billy club. He made a swing at my head that, had it connected, might have killed me. That made me mad. A few minutes later two cops were pinning my arms back, one of them most painfully, and my assailant was writhing on the ground, bleeding from the nose and mouth. I had no club, just my fists.

A third cop bent over my attacker, dabbing a clean white cloth at his injuries, and helped him to his feet. When he got up, the thug took another swing at me.

I was charged with assault and battery. He was not. He was assisted to a car and, apparently, sent home. Along with my fine I got a scolding. It went into my record—an auspicious start.

Some time later I was convicted of an antitrust law violation and was ordered to "cease and desist" from an action that we had already ceased months before.

We had been organizing some of the drivers and loaders of the wastepaper companies that abounded in the area at the time. We got the usual plea from the management: they wouldn't mind being unionized and facing the prospect of improved wages and benefits if their competitors in the same area had to operate with "the same costs."

We promised we'd organize them all at the same time and went ahead with our plans for setting up union procedures in those companies we had started dealing with first. The snag came when some of the others decided to resist us, even to the extent of facing a strike. The trouble was, we couldn't afford a strike at that time. We were spread too thin.

The result was that I suggested that we put up picket lines to slow down the business being done by those who wanted a strike while we finished our dealings with those we were organizing. Then, I reasoned, we could devote full attention to the tough ones. There was no law against such a procedure, to my knowledge. (There was no Taft-Hartley then.) But some of those tough ones had some "legal eagles" in their employ, and they charged that I was violating the antitrust laws by acting in collusion with the wastepaper dealers we had already organized.

Our lawyers advised us that it takes at least two parties to be engaged in an act of collusion or conspiracy, but in this action my government charged—and convicted—me alone. The unions' "co-conspirators" were not even tried.

Then, out of the blue, came a trumped-up charge that my unit, Local 299, was forcing grocery stores to buy "permits" from the local to show that they recognized the union of the teamsters who unloaded their trucks at the stores' docks.

We gave them permits, all right. They were signs that said the trucks were manned by members of Local 299. We tacked them up ourselves and never charged a single penny for them. But some smart guy saw them and figured he could throw another punch at the union.

When I was charged with this particular shakedown, I said it was sheer nonsense. And I denied under oath in court that I had been party to any such plot. It made no difference, though. I was found guilty and fined and again ordered to "cease and desist."

It is interesting to note that during the trial in which I faced these false charges—I swore they were false and would certainly admit otherwise at this late date if they were not —there was much emphasis placed on my previous "record."

I was learning about the labor movement; I was also learning about Justice, and its inseparable twin, Injustice. And my twenty-second birthday was coming up. I was one year into manhood.

9

Brooding Days and Gathering Storms

It was a time of great restlessness. After seven years of gloomy depression, Labor was on the move.

When I had entered the affairs of Local 299 as Business Agent, it had been placed under trusteeship by Teamster President Dan Tobin. He had received a report from Johnny English, then an International auditor (now International Secretary-Treasurer), showing a lack of financial responsibility—if not, indeed, impropriety—in the unit, and the introduction of some challengeable election procedures. It seemed some longshoremen had been brought into the unit in order to vote for the incumbents who were standing for reelection. And in those days a local could be placed under the trusteeship of the International for an indefinite period, and not merely for eighteen months as, under the Landrum-Griffin-Kennedy Act, is the case today.

It was therefore with great pleasure that at about that time I met Owen Bert Brennen, who was soon to become President of Local 337, comprised of food and beverage drivers, a local that was formed as a result of organizing efforts that he and I led together. I needed friends and help, and Owen Bert Brennen provided both. As my friend, as a sounding board, as a reliable supporter and competent adviser, he had an enormous influence on my life. Whenever

I say "I decided" something, quite often I mean that he and I decided it, for there was little I did, and not much that I thought about, that I didn't discuss with him. And it remained thus between my friend and me until his cruel and untimely death by a ruthless malignancy in the summer of 1961. I miss him.

But despite Local 299's situation, everything could not be done all at once, and the thing that interested me most in our organizing chores at first was the effort to organize the truckaway, driveaway, and car-haulers workers—the fellows who delivered new cars from the Detroit factories to the dealers' showrooms throughout North America.

It was a challenging job, trying to organize them. First, they didn't want to be organized; they were scared to death of their bosses. Second, they were rarely around town, being on long-haul jobs most of the time. Third, the employers resisted organizational efforts with every trick in the book.

I decided, therefore, that the best way to get to talk to these long-haul drivers was to meet them out on the highway. If you went far enough out, you'd find them beside the road taking a catnap. I know it's an old legend—believed by few nowadays—but it is nevertheless true that some of those fellows would light a cigarette and sleep until it burned down and awakened them by scorching their fingers. They had to rest, but they couldn't rest long. We would catch them in the short interval.

I never realized, as I drove out on the highway that first day, that I was embarking on a road that would lead to Miami Beach and the Teamsters' convention, then to Washington, where I was to serve as General President of the International, and ultimately to some *real* antagonists such as Senator John McClellan, with his special investigating committee and his chief counsel, Robert F. Kennedy, later to become the Hoffa-pursuing Attorney General of the United States.

Fate doesn't reveal itself except in thoughtful retrospect, but as I look back, I realize now that my organizing efforts with these truckaway-driveaway workers set my feet firmly in the path that led to the awesome job of being chief executive officer of the largest single union in the world.

Many an old-timer in the Teamsters today is a fellow I met and got to know on Canada's Route 2, between Detroit and Buffalo, or on old U.S. 6, on the way to Cleveland, or U.S. 112, to Chicago, or U.S. 10, where a fellow would be hauling cars to the ferry at Ludington.

I'd simply wake him up, identify myself, and tell him why I thought he ought to join the Teamsters.

For sport sometime you should go around trying to wake up a sleeping truck driver, preferably some fellow with a couple of thousand miles of hard driving stretching before him. He's not noted for cordiality and hospitality.

These were mid-depression days, and likely as not a driver slept with a spanner wrench or a tire iron beside his right hand, with every instinct primed to hit first and ask questions later if someone thunked on the cab door. On the other hand, it was a time when truck drivers were keenly aware of the troubles facing all Americans and were ready to help anyone, particularly people who were in distress on the highways. So there was a moment's hesitation before the tire iron or wrench swung toward the door, and I learned to identify myself with a rapid-fire introduction.

"Hi,I'mJimmyHoffaOrganizerfortheTeamsters,andIwonder ifIcouldtalktoyou."

Then I'd duck back.

It would take a moment for the information to sink in. These fellows had to sleep fast, and they learned to sleep soundly. More than once a driver would say, "Wait till I finish my nap, then I'll give you a lift to wherever you're going," and then drop back onto the cushions.

But when recognition came, you could actually see the

driver stiffen and freeze up right before your eyes. It was obvious that the employers had made it clear that any driver participating in organizational activities would be dismissed immediately.

"I'll get fired if I join your union," the driver would say.

"By the time you get back to Detroit, every driver who hauls cars will be organized and signed up," I'd reply.

"But I can't afford the dues."

"You'll make that up and more besides with the pay raises."

"I don't like unions. I like to be my own man, decide what I want to do—not what some union boss tells me."

"That's why you should join the Teamsters," I'd tell him. "In the Teamsters you attend every meeting, you vote on every decision. The union bosses are directly responsible to you and the dues-paying membership, and to no one else."

And on and on.

I'd discuss some of the unbelievable working conditions facing the haulaways and driveaways. I'd mention the lack of adequate overtime, the lack of incentive, the failure to provide for minimum safety standards, the refusal of the employers to recognize the danger of highway fatigue. Someone had spread the word that the state legislature would pass safety rules for the drivers, limiting the hours they could drive. That sounded fine until I explained that in the United States federal laws didn't control motor vehicles, and that safety regulations would have to be adopted in all forty-eight states in order to be effective.

I talked and talked, and gradually we—Marty Haggerty, Oney Brennan, Al Squires, and others were using the technique of meeting them out on the highways—began to sign up drivers.

Then one day I stopped beside a tractor trailer parked off the highway and went up to the cab and knocked on the door.

"Hey! Are you awake?" I shouted.

At that moment the cab door was flung open, and two burly thugs leaped out carrying "snappers," flexible rubber or leather billy clubs with lead weights in the ends. They crawled all over me. I got one, good and proper, but the other beat me to the ground with his little club. Just before I passed out, he grabbed me by the throat and pulled my face toward his. "Stay away from our trucks!" he snarled. "This is just a warning. Next time it'll be first class."

The employers had hired goons!

Back in Detroit reports began to filter into the office. Other organizers had been beaten up and given warnings. We decided we'd go in pairs, too.

War had been declared.

Then the police got into the fracas. We'd be stopped on some trumped-up motor-vehicle violation and searched. Anything that might be used as a weapon, even our tire irons, were removed. And the tickets for speeding, failing to stop at a stop sign, going too fast past a school, failing to slow down at an intersection, driving to the left of a white line, and so on, made us waste a fair amount of time in court and dip deeper into our lean union treasury.

Those same police would see a car-haul trailer snaking out of the city with three burly pugs in the cab and think nothing of it, let alone do anything about it. But if we had jack handles in our cars, they were declared to be dangerous weapons and were confiscated, even though balding and patchy tires showed clearly that they might be needed at any moment for the manufacturer's intended purpose.

Then we began to get reports of "decoy trucks," sent out by the employers and manned by whole squads of strong-arm strikebreakers. Some of the injuries reported by the organizers were serious, and more than one landed in the hospital. In some cases, even for urgent emergency treatment, we were required to pay cash in advance. We were, after all, enemies of the status quo, terrible men trying to wrest better working conditions from lovable employers who, among other things, made charitable contributions to the hospitals.

The tempo of violence built up.

Our organizing drive never ceased; it dragged on for years. Sometimes there were outbreaks of trouble, but there also were many months when the employers kept their activities against us strictly underground.

Ultimately, of course, the Teamsters won. And today this particular group of drivers is organized into a special division of the International, and I am its President.

All we knew in those early days, though, was that the Teamsters *had to* advance and grow, and that all drivers ultimately *had to* become members. There was no other way. The long progression of problems caused by the depression simply had to result in progress on the labor front. There was an imbalance in the economy, in society, and in the legislative and judicial structure.

We knew that we would not be alone in our struggle for long. We knew that Americans who had never seen the inside of a truck cab would support us, sooner or later, and that white collar men would join with blue collar men in giving the strength to the labor movement that was needed to restore balance and prosperity to the land.

We talked about this on hot nights when we worked late in the office, catching up on the record-keeping and filing and bill-paying that had to be deferred during daytime, which was filled with organizing activities.

We knew it would come. We knew that one day soon even the proprietors in America who did not own giant businesses would identify with our cause. We knew that proprietors of small retail stores, of small newspapers, of small radio stations, of small enterprises of all kinds, would come to our way of thinking, and that we would be as one, seeking economic justice.

To me, economic justice means a just return for the fair and faithful performance of duty, with reasonable safeguards guaranteed for the worker's security, safety, and seniority. I believe that responsibility is a two-way street bisecting the economy of the free-enterprise system, and that if a worker is to be totally responsible to his employer, then the employer must be totally responsible to his worker. One cannot function without the other.

I could find no way, in 1937, to equate my idea of the labor movement with the efforts being made then by the Socialist Workers party (SWP) and the Communists. And I said so. I said it, loud and clear, at meetings both formal and casual.

I had no patience with the Leninists-Stalinists of the Communist party or with the Trotskyites of the SWP. Both were Marxist; neither believed in a free-enterprise system; both failed to see that workers who leave the enslavement of capitalistic czars for the enslavement of state-appointed czars are no better off and, in fact, lose great economic and social values in the transition.

Consequently, I was disturbed by the emergence of the Trotskyites in Teamster organizing activities in Minnesota. Their emergence posed a problem, for the organizers—Farrell Dobbs, Karl Skoglund, and three brothers, Vince, Miles, and Grant Dunne—were trying to do what we had done in Detroit: organize the over-the-road and long-haul drivers, and it didn't really make sense to hobble their efforts.

The Trotskyites believed simply that the communist revolution had to be worldwide to succeed. The Stalinists or Leninists thought it could succeed in one country at a time, one revolution at a time. I don't keep up with differences among communist groups, but I imagine those same differences exist today. To me, all Communists are nuts. If there's anything wrong with our society, we can change it ourselves without destroying the system or scrapping our precious democratic process. Anyone who says otherwise has his brain shrouded in old-world mists and hasn't perceived either the trend or the goal of modern America.

Both the Communists and the Trotskyites were extremely active in the 1930s. They found sympathy in high labor councils and acceptance, if not outright support, in high political circles. And for that and other reasons conditions in Detroit were not too good for the Teamsters in the late 1930s. I've mentioned that Local 299 was under trusteeship. At least four other locals, among them the Milk Drivers, Van Drivers, and General Drivers, had soon followed us into trusteeship.

Moreover, there were other power forces at work against us, along with the employers and the politicians. The most powerful was the mighty CIO—the Congress of Industrial Organizations—the noncraft union dedicated to getting all workers under one labor umbrella that had already moved strongly into Detroit's auto and automotive-parts factories. The strong, Washington-favored CIO, with the blessings of Management, waged an incessant internecine war against the Teamsters, taking every advantage of our poverty and leaderless trusteeships.

In the circumstances, Teamsters' strategy, as I saw it, should be to restore unit responsibility to the various locals and at the same time to build up Teamster membership by bringing in the haulaway and driveaway boys. I also wasn't adverse to bringing in anyone else related directly or indirectly to the trucking industry. We needed strength, and we needed it fast.

In trying to put these plans into action, I had the total encouragement and cooperation of Ray Bennett. I have seen it written that Ray, official trustee for the trusteed locals and General Organizer for the International, supported me because of my increasing popularity among the men, and that he feared that those who opposed me would throw in with the CIO.

That is plain bunk. On file are numerous memos sent by Ray Bennett to Dan Tobin, in Boston, reporting: "Jimmy Hoffa is doing a fine job," or, "Hoffa and Squires will handle the situation all right." And why would he support me if he didn't think that I would keep the Teamsters free from the intruding union and had gained the loyalty of my men? Sometimes I wonder about the dialectical excursions of the academic thinkers who "study" the records of the labor movement and those involved in it!

One way and another, too, I was mighty busy in Detroit, busy with existing locals and busy trying to form new ones. So, if my popularity grew among the men, and if my so-called political strength in the union grew, I wasn't much aware of it. I had my job to do. I liked the men. We talked a common language. We shared common problems. That's about what it boiled down to. Still, there is no doubt that I was getting to be pretty well known among the guys.

Meanwhile, out in Minneapolis, Farrell Dobbs, who later became a noted Socialist and ran for President in 1960 on the SWP ticket, still supported by the Trotskyites, was conducting a massive organizational drive that brought nearly every truck driver in the city into the Teamsters local. Then he joined with Skoglund and the Dunne brothers in an ambitious program to organize the over-the-road drivers, not just for Minnesota, but for the entire Northwest.

I wouldn't agree with Farrell Dobbs's political philosophy or his economic ideology, but that man had a vision that was enormously beneficial to the labor movement. Beyond any doubt, he was the master architect of the Teamsters' over-the-road operations.

Dobbs had two strong arguments for organizing the long-haul drivers. First, bad working conditions among them would serve as a threat to better working conditions for all drivers. Second, they would be missionaries of trade union-ism, proselytizing and spreading the word to all corners of every state. By word and by example, Dobbs believed, the long-haul Teamsters would be attracting new members to the union and fresh support for the labor movement.

Dan Tobin didn't go for this idea wholeheartedly. He had seen the Teamsters grow along craft-union lines, with locals made up of specialists in specific fields. Some of the Teamster officials around the country weren't too happy with the plan, either, for they didn't like the idea of poaching memberships in their own bailiwicks. But Red O'Laughlin, boss of the Teamsters in Detroit, had seen what we had done with the haulaway and driveaway drivers, and he liked the idea.

Red therefore went to Minneapolis to meet with Dobbs and the others, and he asked me to go along. I was still a kid, and somehow I knew enough to listen and not talk much. I had to talk some, though, for Farrell Dobbs questioned me by the hour and in great detail about the techniques we had developed for organizing the driveaway and truckaway drivers in Detroit.

The results were very important, for me and for the Teamsters. We had been back in Detroit only a couple of days when Red O'Laughlin called me to his office.

"Jimmy," he said, "we're going to farm you out to Farrell Dobbs in Minneapolis. Give him a hand in organizing those over-the-road drivers, will you?"

Another die had been cast.

10
Josephine

It was not long after my first encounter with the forces of law and order that I met Josephine. The fate that brought us together may not have set off the greatest romance of the century, but it certainly inspired a love affair that has lasted, for both of us, from that day to this. No other woman could ever fill my eyes or my heart or my life as does Josephine, the mother of my children and custodian of my happiness.

Strike fever was sweeping industrial America in 1936, and it ran high and strong in Detroit. It seemed at times that almost every unorganized shop in the metropolitan area was in ferment.

There were grievances galore. Many employers were taking full advantage of the widespread unemployment and the hovering cloud of fear. Most of the harried employees didn't know what to do. Many wanted to strike but were unsure how to go about doing such a thing. Others wanted to send petitions to their bosses listing their gripes but feared that everyone who signed would be canned. Delegates surreptitiously called on us to come to their rescue and to help them organize.

One such delegation came from a downtown laundry. They were girls and young women, and their complaints were legion—not the least of which was the fact they were paid only for the time the laundering machines were working but were obliged to spend hours waiting for sufficient laundry to come in so that the machines could be operated.

The laundry workers were being paid seventeen cents an hour, and on some days the girls were lucky to get two hours' work. The manager would simply keep the machines turned off until he accumulated a "payload" of laundry bundles. The girls weren't allowed to go home; indeed, they weren't even allowed out of the plant.

Who would help them organize, they wanted to know. Who would advise them how to strike? Was there some fund, or something, to help them buy groceries in case the strike lasted more than a week? Could they all be fired if they went out on strike?

In those days such questions were common in Detroit and in other industrial parts of the country.

The situation at the laundry was very similar to the one that had existed at Kroger's. It was one with which I was very familiar. Possibly for that reason I was the one chosen to go to the shop and help the girls organize and get a contract with the management. Also, I suppose, the Joint Council considered the fact that I was young (twenty-three), tough, scarred, and experienced.

There was no doubt that the management was being unfair to its employees. That's the message I had committed to signs and placards. Then I had the girls form into squads and set up a schedule for picketing. We had prepared a list of grievances and had outlined formal demands calculated to end those grievances. When all was ready, we served notice on the management that unless the local was recognized as an employees' bargaining unit and the management agreed to discuss the demands, we would call a strike. I wasn't certain that all of the girls had signed up with the union, but those who had done so wanted to force the issue.

We went on strike.

We set up a conventional picket line with the girls marching in ovals—the outside oval moving clockwise, the inside oval proceeding counterclockwise.

On the second day of picketing I took my turn in the line —the outside line. As we marched around the oval, I made it a point to look into the faces of each of those young girls and smile or speak an encouraging word. All looked worried.

Then, there it was.

The brightest blue eyes you've ever seen, sparkling with some kind of excitement. Wind-tousled, shiny-blonde hair. A saucy nose. Were there faint freckles there, or was that a smudge of dust? I was going to say something, but the up-turned mouth in its happy grin was so contagious that I just smiled in response. I may have stumbled; I don't remember. Somebody nudged me from behind and said, "C'mon, Jimmy. Cut that out."

I couldn't wait until we passed again. The grin was bigger this time. It was amazing how, when this girl grinned, even the corner of her eyes turned up in a special crinkly way.

"Hi," I said.

"Hi," she replied.

I felt as though something momentous had happened. We passed again.

"Hi," I said.

"Hi," she said.

I crossed over, did an about-face, and marched in her line, directly behind her. I could look right down into that sun-reflecting hair.

I wanted to say something. I couldn't say "Hi" again. "There's a man following you," I said.

The grin radiated light over her shoulder. "Why, Mr. Hoffa," she said, "you'll lose your place in line."

"This is not quite fair. You know my name but I don't know yours."

"It's Jo. Josephine."

"Jo, and then what else?"

"Poszywak."

Old-fashioned Polish names are as common in Detroit as Smith and Jones are in rural England, and no one who has lived there for any length of time has any difficulty with them. But I pretended to be a bit thick.

"Well, Miss Jo Posie, will you have a cup of coffee with me when our shift is over?"

"I'd be delighted to, Mr. Huffa," she said.

It was like the storybooks. My heart was beating like a bongo. The whole world seemed filled with a bright, blonde, flashing-eyed, somewhat sassy girl named Jo Poszywak, who marched erect and proud and self-possessed, as though she had just bought and paid cash for all of downtown Detroit.

I endured the longest shift of picketing of my entire life, and when we were relieved, I had to waste a few additional minutes—they seemed like hours—with one of the men from headquarters. She stood on the sidewalk, waiting, a short distance away.

"Gee, Jimmy, what makes you so nervous?" asked the headquarters man.

"Nothing, nothing," I assured him and rushed toward the seemingly aloof and utterly tranquil Miss Jo Posie.

"Coffee?"

"Sure."

We headed across the street to a restaurant.

"This is it," I kept thinking to myself. "She's the one. This, Jimmy boy, is it!"

We had no sooner ordered the coffee than I made my next move.

"There's a good movie at the Orpheum," I said. "Will you go with me tonight?"

"Tonight? Gee, that's short notice."

My mind leaped about like a bass in the bottom of the boat. I couldn't endure a night without seeing this girl. I had to think of something fast.

"Well, ah, in this business you don't get nights off whenever you want them. Tonight's my night off."

"When's the next night off?"

"Uh, ah, well, um, you just never know. Maybe not for a long time." The fabrication of white lies in the name of love, I'm told, doesn't count.

She thought a minute. "Well, all right," she said. "I can go tonight."

Neither of us had ever tasted champagne, but I was sure that none could be as marvelously heady as the three cups of coffee we drank in our effort to prolong our first meeting.

She had a low, almost husky voice, sheer music that made my spine tingle, and as we talked, I knew that I had fallen in love and that, come hell or high water, this was going to be my girl and ultimately my wife. If the strike was still in progress and if the picketing was still going on across the street, I had no knowledge of it or thought for it. I was concentrating on a pair of the bluest eyes I had ever seen. Concentrating? I had been bewitched by them. I didn't know—or care—whether I was a labor organizer or a college boy vacationing on his father's yacht.

She gave me her address, told me to pick her up at seven, and went back, with a flash of teeth and slim bare legs, to resume her stint in the picket line. Oh, yes, I observed, it was still in progress.

I stood in the doorway and watched her, wondering how so much fascination and charm and loveliness could be contained in such a tiny package.

By dint of painstaking budgeting and painful skimping, I had a rather impressive car. It was a recent-vintage Chevy far superior to many of its contemporaries on the streets of

Detroit in those poverty-fraught depression years. I was proud of it.

For an hour and a half I washed, waxed, polished, and swept out that car. I spent another hour grooming myself. I was cleaning my fingernails for the third time when Mom turned from the stove where she had been preparing supper and asked: "Who is she, Jim? Anyone I know?"

"W . . . what do you mean?"

"Exactly what I said. You might as well wear a sign saying, 'Jimmy has a date with a Special Girl.' Who is she?"

"Her name is Josephine Poszywak and she works in the laundry we just organized. She's a young girl. It's her first job."

"Pretty?"

"Mom, she's beautiful."

"Umm. Well. Have a nice time."

Mom knew. She has always known things like that, things that were locked in your heart. When I was ready to leave, she said: "You must bring her to the house to meet the family, Jimmy."

She had never said anything like that before.

I got to Jo's house fifteen minutes early, so I had to drive around the neighborhood. I drove around it so many times I began to fear that some of the residents would regard me as a suspicious character.

I drove up in front of her house at exactly seven o'clock. I had set the clock in the dashboard when the six o'clock whistles blew, so I knew I was right on time, right on the button.

I down-tilted the rearview mirror to check all details. Every hair was in place; the new, faintly scented hair lotion was working fine; collar had no wrinkles; tie was on straight. After readjusting the mirror, I gave the horn two sharp taps.

I tried not to seem overanxious. I stared up the street at

folks sitting on their front porches and kids playing around the hedges. No matter how I resisted, however, my eyes kept turning toward her front door.

It remained closed.

Perhaps she hadn't heard me. After all, there was a lot of traffic around at that time of night.

I gave the horn a couple of additional taps. Well, not taps this time. Real blasts. There, she'd hear that.

Again I looked up the street at the folks on their front porches and at the kids busy at their affairs. All the adults seemed to be looking at me. Many ladies had stopped rocking. They were staring.

Again I stole a peek at the front door.

It remained closed. I could picture her behind it, scurrying around, looking for her purse, perhaps, getting a wrap from a closet. As the fantasy developed, I stared frankly and eagerly at the front door.

It was mute, sealed. It seemed doubtful that anyone was behind it.

I tried the horn again: Dum-ta-ta-ta-ta-dumm-dummm!

A kid up the street shouted an accompaniment: "Shave and a haircut, two bits!" Doors seemed to be opening all along the block. Ladies and young girls came out and stared down the street. A stillness seemed to descend over the neighborhood. I glanced in the mirror. People in the houses behind me were craning their necks to see who was tooting.

The thing to do, I decided, was to go up and knock on that sealed door before everybody in Michigan gathered to see what was going on. I was getting a little huffy about it. Didn't these people have anything else to do? Talk about being nosy!

I strode up to the door, found the bell, and gave it an authoritative push. I could hear it ringing within.

Soon the door was opened by a middle-aged lady, quite

stylish-looking yet motherly. I tried to be formal since I knew it was impossible to be casual.

"Good evening," I said. "I'm James Hoffa. Is Josephine in?"

"Good evening," she replied. "I'm Mrs. Poszywak. Yes, she is." She turned and called, "Josephine!"

I wasn't invited in, I noticed.

Mrs. Poszywak simply stood there, smiling faintly, looking me over. Soon Josephine appeared. The mother vanished. Josephine took her place at the doorway, one hand on the knob, one on the doorjamb, blocking my way.

"Hi," she said.

"I . . . hey, you look great!"

"Thank you."

"Well, shall we be off?"

"No. No, I'm not going."

"No . . . not going? I thought we had a date?"

"Well, I can't go."

"B . . . but you're all dressed up."

A crushing thought came to me. "Oh, you had another date you couldn't break?"

"No, I don't have any other date."

Now I looked closely at her, seeing *her* instead of the grand, shimmering vision. The eyes were frosty blue now. The mouth that was decorated with such a generous smile that afternoon was now firm and was maintaining as straight a line as it could manage.

"Is . . . is something wrong?"

"No. I'm just not going out with you."

She closed the door.

I stood there for a moment, dumbfounded.

Suddenly I became aware of the people on the porches all along the street and the many faces at windows across the way. I turned and, with as much dignity as possible, walked back to my car, feeling as though I were walking alone across a naked platform in a gigantic theater crowded with silent spectators.

"The last mile," I thought. "Now I know how a criminal feels when he walks that last distance from his cell to the death chamber."

I got into the car and stepped on the starter. Naturally, it wouldn't kick off right away. Finally, with a cough and a cloud of smoke, it roared to life, and I drove off as unobtrusively as possible.

I went to the office, where work was piling up. I tackled several reports. Nothing seemed to make any sense to me. Figures didn't mean anything. Memos from my superiors as well as those from the fellows working with me seemed like so much jibberish.

What did I do wrong? What was the matter with her? Why would she change her mind like that? Had I misjudged this girl?

I put the work away. There was no point in reading the same memos over and over again.

Then it hit me. I'd call her. I grabbed the phone book and searched through it. No phone. No listing. But they *had* to have a phone.

I tried the operator. Yes, there was a number.

Mrs. Poszywak answered it.

"Josephine has gone to bed," she reported and hung up—fast.

One thing was certain. Nobody liked me at that house.

Well, I couldn't work. I couldn't see Josephine. I might as well go home.

Back in the car I started toward home; then, realizing that it was what I had in mind all along, I drove back to Josephine's street. It was dark now. Most of the porches were empty.

The curtains were drawn at the Poszywak house, but the shades hadn't been pulled down. There were two silhouettes in the living room, seated in relaxed but attentive postures.

The Poszywaks, mother and daughter, were listening to the radio!

I went on home. There was pie and cheese and milk. Then cake and milk. Then a sandwich and milk.

Mom said nothing. She, too, was listening to the radio. I paced around, then went to bed.

About a week later, or so it seemed, the sun came up, and I arose from a bed in which I had not slept, looking forward to a day of hard work during which I could erase this smart-aleck girl from my mind.

That morning, though, she was on the picket line.

I fell in behind her. "Look," I said, "what happened? At least tell me what happened."

"You tooted your horn," she said.

"Tooted my . . . ?"

"Yes. You don't toot your horn for me. Not in *that* neighborhood."

"But Jo . . . Josephine. I didn't mean . . ."

"I know. I know. But that's a Polish neighborhood. Those people are quite old fashioned. There are certain things you don't do. Tooting your horn is one of them."

"I don't see what harm it does. I didn't mean to be rude."

"Oh." Her whole body showed exasperation. If she hadn't been marching, I'm sure she would have stamped her foot. "Don't you see? Everybody would have known I was going out on a date with a new fellow. You toot your horn and they all look."

"I don't see what harm . . ." I was repeating myself.

"You don't see?" She stopped and turned around. Pickets began to pile up behind us. "It looks as though I come running for any fellow who drives up and toots his horn." She swung about and resumed marching.

"Gee, Jo. I'm sorry."

No answer.

"Let's have some coffee at the break."

No answer for about five minutes. Then she turned slightly.

"Okay," she said. It sounded as though the smile was back on her face.

The coffee wasn't champagne, but it was good coffee.

"Can I start all over again?" I asked. "Will you go to the movies with me tonight?"

"I thought you weren't going to have another night off for a long while."

"Well, I went back and worked last night."

"Oh."

"Well, can I call for you at seven?"

"Yes, but don't toot."

We both burst out laughing.

"You have to come to the door and call for me properly. I will introduce you to my mother. You have to sit down for about five minutes and talk. Then we can go to the movies."

"I met your mother last night."

"Oh, no, you didn't. That didn't count. You introduced yourself. You have to be introduced by me."

At seven, with the car repolished and me rescrubbed, I parked quietly at the curb in front of Josephine's house, and silently, though not stealthily, I walked to the front door and rang the bell.

Josephine met me. Behind her was her mother. We were reintroduced.

"It's very nice to meet you, Mr. Hoffa," she said, just as though she had never seen me before.

When we went into the living room, we spoke of the weather, of the strike at the laundry, of the shortage of good rents in that part of town, and of my car.

"Don't drive too fast, boy," Josephine's mother said.

In about five minutes Josephine reappeared, bearing purse and wrap. "Coming?" she asked.

I tried to make it seem that I was leaving reluctantly. The exercise of acting didn't quite come off. Mrs. Poszywak laughed.

Gee, I thought, everybody likes me in this house. And I liked them, too. Especially the daughter.

In the darkness of the movie I found Jo's hand.

"Polish girls don't hold hands unless they mean it," she said.

"I sure *hope* you mean it," I said, "because I'm very serious about *you*."

And that's how I met Jo. Anyone who knows her can appreciate just how lucky I am.

We were married in September, 1936, in Bowling Green, Ohio.

We were married on Saturday.

I was back at work on Monday.

Jo claims she's still entitled to a honeymoon.

11

The Midwestern Council

Farrell Dobbs was a crackerjack organizer. When I joined his operation to help organize the over-the-road drivers throughout the Northwest, he had, as I have said, already signed up just about every local truck driver in Minneapolis.

Dobbs, I found, was a brilliant strategist. His plan to use the over-the-road drivers—the long-distance operators—to spread the word about the Teamsters to all parts of the nation was very successful, especially since he reasoned—most accurately, as it turned out—that improvements would follow for other drivers all along the line.

Dobbs also saw the unions as a great potential *political* force. I could not agree with him then, nor do I now. I do not believe that labor unions should involve themselves in party politics unless clear-cut social issues are at stake. It has always been my position that the labor movement is interested in *social* reforms, and that such reforms are to be brought about not by any one particular political party but rather by making our desires known and our presence felt to the whole body politic.

But politics as such, for Dobbs, was a long way off in the late 1930s in Minneapolis. His primary concern then, quite properly, was organizational and membership drives. At our first meeting I recited again the techniques we had used in Detroit to organize the truckaway and driveaway drivers.

"That's exactly what I had in mind," he said. "That's what we're going to do here. And you're going to be in charge of the operation."

I felt flattered.

In labor halls throughout America the name of Farrell Dobbs was more than well known. It was keenly respected. For him to select me to head the Midwest organizational drive of the over-the-road truckers was indeed an honor. After all, I was neither the oldest, nor the most seasoned, nor the wisest man engaged in organizing at that time.

I was well aware, as was Dobbs, that the official hierarchy of the Teamsters was of two minds about Dobbs's organizational efforts in Minneapolis. As a Trotskyite, Dobbs had attracted some headlines because of his statements to the press. His association with the Dunne brothers and Karl Skoglund was never hidden.

And, as we have seen, General President of the International Brotherhood Dan Tobin was not at all interested in identifying or affiliating with the Trotskyites or the Leninists and, in fact, wasn't very warm toward the idea of organizing the over-the-road drivers. He thought the Teamsters had enough to handle the city-based drivers.

However, Dobbs did have backers: Red O'Laughlin, in Detroit; John T. (Sandy) O'Brien, of Chicago's Local 710; Mike Healy, former President of the Central States Drivers Council; T. T. Neal, of Kansas City; and Floyd Webb, of Joplin, Missouri. Such men felt that the gains in Teamster membership and organization the Trotskyites were making were worth the risk inherent in identifying with Dobbs and Skoglund.

Then, too, Sandy O'Brien was a close friend and associate of Tom Hughes, Secretary-Treasurer of the International Brotherhood of Teamsters and a warm friend of Dan Tobin.

Presumably the word came from Tobin to Hughes to O'Brien to Dobbs that it would be all right for the latter to go ahead with his organizing, provided he concentrated on the over-the-road drivers and did not raid or challenge traditional or existing Teamster jurisdictions—or, significantly, raise the threat of a rival International.

Tobin, in common with most labor leaders of the day, was a bit apprehensive whenever a Trotskyite tried to organize in his particular field. There was the fear that a politically oriented rival union ultimately would be set up, sapping the strength of the labor movement.

When I arrived on the scene, these internal maneuvers had all been accomplished. Dobbs outlined to me his plan to form a North Central District Drivers Council. (It later became known as the Central States Drivers Council—CSDC.)

Not long thereafter, in January, 1937, Dobbs created a Drivers Council embracing thirteen locals in North Dakota, South Dakota, Iowa, Minnesota, Wisconsin, and upper Michigan. The purpose was to promote the organization of workers engaged in truck transportation and to establish uniform wages, hours, and working conditions throughout the district. Dobbs became the first Secretary-Treasurer and full-time organizer assigned to coordinating this huge and ambitious project.

By the spring of 1938 representatives of forty-six locals in eleven states had been added to the district and were attending council meetings. New states added by Dobbs (and myself, of course) were Ohio, Indiana, Illinois, Missouri, and Nebraska. Dobbs was therefore ready to negotiate a contract for all unionized over-the-road drivers in this eleven-state area.

I learned a great deal in those days, but I would have been a dunce not to have done so. I was studying at the knee of a master who understood all of the intricacies of organizational work, fathomed the responses and reactions of employers, and comprehended the many problems of his union at home base. Instinctively, Farrell Dobbs always thought ahead and planned accordingly.

Parenthetically, I might add here that though I have not seen Dobbs since he and I completed our work together in the late thirties, I have often thought of him and wondered to what heights he might have brought himself and organized Labor if he had remained steadfast to his original goals in the labor movement instead of embarking on his social and political reform movements.

In mid-career I find it fruitful to think back on all of the mistakes I have made and to ponder as well the decisions reached by other men I have known and worked with. Some of my past associates are now acknowledged to have made great contributions; others are regarded as having spent themselves. I myself find it impossible to sit in judgment. Not until the game is over and all of the chips have been counted can you calculate a man's winnings or losses. And not until he stands against the perspective of history can you correctly measure his stature.

I refuse, therefore, to make any judgment about Farrell Dobbs. The fact that his exhortations in later years left me unmoved and that his logic eluded me does not mean he has not made a serious contribution to human thinking and striving. We cannot measure with today's yardsticks matters that should be viewed through the transit of time. As a fellow labor organizer, I view Farrell Dobbs subjectively. He was one heck of a fine labor organizer. Period. On this matter only am I qualified to speak.

Toward the end of our organizational stint I began to wonder how Dobbs would swing it. We had nearly fifty locals organized in eleven states. We wanted one contract package for the entire district. Yet there was no one agency with whom we could bargain. The truckers were rugged individualists. Each went his own way. Each treated his employees in a separate manner. Each was fiercely competitive and wouldn't dream of dealing with another trucker in negotiating a labor contract.

I began to worry about the prospect of dealings with several hundred different trucking firms, one at a time.

"Don't worry," Dobbs said. "We'll get 'em to sit down with us."

Easily said, I thought. But how would he do it? I went on with my organizational chores. If Dobbs refused to worry, I wouldn't.

But when the union's negotiating committee, consisting of one representative from each state, thrashed out all of the details and came up with some solid demands in March, 1938, the American Trucking Association disclaimed any responsibility for bargaining for its members. There *was* no central authority.

Dobbs the strategist seemed undaunted by this "revelation."

"We will," he declared, "concentrate on Chicago."

Chicago was organized more thoroughly than Detroit. It was a "Teamster town." We knew we could deal with the truckers there. Not only the biggest Midwestern city, Chicago was the terminal point for all Midwest trucking routes, and Dobbs envisioned truckers in the other states scrambling to get a "Chicago contract."

The strategic significance of Chicago as a spot to launch our drive for an areawide contract was that the Teamsters would be able to remain aloof from squabbles with the truckers once the Chicago contract was signed. Truck owners would bring pressure on themselves once the program began snowballing.

After several weeks of what seeemd an endless game of shadow-boxing and feinting, the carriers appointed an Oper-

ators' Committee, and it was then that I met Jack Keeshin
for the first time. Keeshin was the truckers' chairman, appointed to undertake the basic negotiations with us and to
make the ultimate decision on behalf of the Chicago carriers,
and he had, I found, a refreshing, unusual, and totally un-
orthodox approach to collective bargaining. Though he sat
on the other side of the bargaining table from us, Keeshin
was the man who was largely instrumental in bringing enlightened working policies and labor tranquillity to that
troubled area.

You couldn't help liking Keeshin. It wasn't long before
we were friends.

Because Chicago was a key terminal city, large trucking
companies from throughout the Midwest were directly involved in our negotiations. Moreover, the principals remained aloof, leaving it to Keeshin and his committee to
handle the framing of a contract, for they had accepted the
condition that what was negotiated between the Teamsters
and the Operators' Committee would be binding on all of
them.

Without rehashing all of those old issues, what came out
of those long negotiating sessions included the following:

1. A modified closed shop in which all truck drivers had
to belong to the Teamsters.

2. Owner-operators, men who drove their own trucks, to
be paid for rental of equipment *plus* wages as drivers.

3. Elimination of "lost time" for loading, breakdowns, or
traffic delays for drivers paid strictly on a "per mile" basis.

4. Sixty percent of the Teamsters in the eleven states to
receive raises immediately. A minimum wage was set at a
level just below the rate then being received by the highest-
paid drivers in the area.

5. A grievance committee was established and recognized,
with Farrell Dobbs as its chairman.

I had received my first experience in big-league bargaining. And it was my good fortune to have been in the company of big leaguers on either side of the conference table: Farrell Dobbs and Jack Keeshin. For a man intending to make the labor movement his lifetime career, the Chicago negotiating experience was worth a university education.

I was a willing pupil.

12
The Dedicated Few

Atop my desk in my office at the International's headquarters in Detroit is a nameplate made of highly polished exotic woods; predominant among them are mahogany and laurel. My signature is rendered in duplicate in perfectly matched rare woods formed into the beautiful flowing lines of fine script. Aside from being a striking conversation piece, the nameplate is a work of extreme and rare beauty, perfect in symmetry and smoothness and mysteriously alive with a deep patina that represents untold hours of patient hand-rubbing and permits one to look into the very soul of the wood.

Its real beauty is hidden, however. It is revealed only when the piece is turned upside down. On its underside is a silver plate that says this lovely object was hand-carved by a Teamster in San Juan, Puerto Rico, and presented to me by the local there in gratitude for the material benefits that had been brought to the members of the International Brotherhood of Teamsters.

Though the gift bears an inscription to me, it is intended as a tribute to the Brotherhood itself, and it serves as a constant focal point for the International's perspective, reminding me where we have come from and where we have to go.

When we were asked to help with organizational activities in San Juan, Puerto Rican drivers were being paid sixteen cents an hour and many were driving unsafe equipment. Living standards for drivers were at the low end in the island's economy.

Today, those who pilot the big vans through the twisty, narrow streets of the Old City or maneuver the heavy diesel trailers over the steep mountains of the interior receive the same hourly pay as those performing comparable jobs on the mainland.

In many parts of Canada we have had similar successes, but vast areas of the Dominion remain to be organized, and our records bulge with appeals from drivers asking us to help them with that chore.

As I write this, our membership is reaching toward the 1,900,000 mark, making the Teamsters the largest labor organization in the world. Realizing this makes me appreciate just how far we have come. The achievements are attributable to men—dedicated men—some of whom have passed to greater rewards, but all of whom have been my close and fulfilling friends.

Without them, the Teamsters would not have grown so fast or so successfully and would not have rendered so much service to the membership and the trucking-transportation industry. The president of a trade union is not like the president of any other organization. He is an administrator, first of all, and an idea man. He may suggest policy, but he cannot set it. He may plan and chart a course, but he cannot, himself, set out upon it.

The phrase "union boss" has always seemed to me to be a misnomer. The union president is the employee of the members, each of whom has his own ideas of how things should be run. The larger the membership, the bigger the headaches. The president is a quarterback, insofar as the other officers are concerned, more than a captain. More than in any other calling, he presides over a team effort. Yet his responsibilities as the chief executive officer are magnified,

and he is more accountable to his members and fellow officers than any corporate president is to his employees and
stockholders.

The union president operates within a pure democracy,
with the rules spelled out in black and white. There are as
many monitors, umpires, and referees as there are members
of his union. And over his shoulder stands the U.S. Government, insisting that every rule be observed to the letter.

When I read headlines describing me as a "Labor Czar,"
I wondered: czar of what? The democratic process in the
union, requiring approval and endorsement for every action,
would make me grow weary and impatient. And at home
Jo, Barbara, and Jim could twist me around their little fingers. Me, a czar? I'm about as much of a czar as is a raw
recruit buck private.

A labor official's strength, if he has any, comes from the
support of the full membership. It is reflected in day-to-day
affairs through the support of fellow officers in the union.
If I have strength in the Teamsters, this support is its source,
this and nothing else. When I cease to function well and
wisely, I will lose that strength. It is really quite simple.
It is a ruthless system, but it is the best for the union.

Some of the men in the movement have been especially
close to me and extremely important in my life, private as
well as public. I have mentioned some of them in earlier
chapters—Sam Calhoun, Frank Collins, Jim Langley, Bobby
Holmes, and Ray Bennett. But there were many others:
Frank Fitzsimmons, of course, my strong right bower; Rol-
land McMaster, Dave Johnson, George Shelp, George Rox-
burgh, Otto Wendell, Pop Squires, George Stranloff, Isaac
Litvak, Bill Bufalino, to name a few from the old days, many
of whom are still on the firing line.

And there was Chuckie O'Brien—"my other son"—who
occupies a special category. I consider Chuckie one of our

family, as do Jo and Barbara and Jim. Chuckie was a tot when I met him, the son of a lady who came to Detroit from Kansas City and got a job working for the Teamsters in a potato-chip factory. As he grew into manhood, he became my friend and developed into a top-notch union official. Now my assistant in Detroit, Chuckie lives with his lovely wife and family in the house that was our first home.

Thinking about some of the old-timers brings back some of the "good old days," when being a "union man" wasn't the healthiest occupation in the world.

When I think of Morrie Cohen, for instance, I think of the Railway Express strike brought on by a jurisdictional dispute. The trucks had been idled for a full month when, on November 1, 1941, the management brought in a small army of goons, loaded about twenty of the thugs into each truck, and then encircled the picketers. The goons, carrying baseball bats and improvised billy clubs, jumped from the trucks on signal and beat up the strikers.

No one knows who hit Morrie—or with what—but suddenly a police officer, Jim Blessington, saw him lying on the pavement, bleeding severely from a huge gash in his head. He commandeered a police car, ordered a patrolman to administer first aid, and rushed Morrie to St. Joseph's Hospital.

The patrolman who accompanied Morrie—a man whose name we'll never know and whose identity we have sought for years—realized that the main artery to the head had been severed. He pressed his thumbs against Morrie's jugular and stopped the spurts of blood, holding him that way all the way to the hospital. That policeman truly saved Morrie's life. On the operating table Morrie's wounds required 180 stitches before they were closed.

I made the rounds of the hospitals later that day, Receiving Hospital and St. Joseph's and some smaller hospitals nearby, and when I saw Morrie lying there, white, waxen, struggling to hold a slim thread of life, I couldn't hold back tears.

"What kind of human beings would take money to do this to a fellow man?" I cried out aloud. A nurse rushed up, took me by the arm, and led me away. "Shhh," she said. "You must be quiet."

Sometimes it seems to me that I look back on a lifetime of cracked skulls. There was Sam Calhoun, at the Battle of the Underpass; Isaac Litvak, beaten repeatedly while he was trying to organize the laundries and, finally, with a Mafia price on his head, moving from hotel to hotel, rooming house to rooming house, for a six-month period; and the many who died on the streets, such as Louis Abrams on a bitter New Year's Eve.

Ike Litvak holds some kind of record for guts. He is no giant; in fact, he has the physical build of a waterboy on a grammar school team. Even after a lifetime in this country he is more easily understood when speaking Russian or Lituanian or Yiddish than English. But Ike has manhood where it counts.

When a half-dozen goons cornered him and began to beat him systematically for the umpteenth time, Ike held up both hands and said, "Stop already. Let me tell you something." The beating halted. "Now," said Ike, "you guys got a job. It's following me around and beating me up. Let me point out a fact: if you kill me, you'll be out of a job. There won't be anybody to follow around and beat up."

The goons looked at each other, nodded agreement, and resumed the beating, but much more gently, much more carefully. Even when the price was put on his head, the hoods figured that Ike was more valuable as a "job" than as a lump-sum rub-out.

This plucky man is a giant in his own way. He won, of course, and in time organized all of the laundries. Like all the old-timers in the Teamsters, Ike bears many scars, but he wears a smile that is reserved to a few, for it can be worn only by those who experience fulfillment and achievement.

There are many old-time Teamsters who wear that smile —and those scars.

It wasn't all hectic, though. When my income picked up a bit, Jo and I bought a "hunting lodge" on the Iron River in Michigan's upper peninsula. The description of our place as a "hunting lodge" is an affectation, for I'm not much of a hunter: I love hunting, if it means stalking game and being out in the woods; I can't say that I'm strong on the bagging of the trophy. I'm too fond of wildlife and too strong in my convictions about conservation to be much of a killer.

I do love guns, however, and marksmanship, and at our lodge we set up a target range for practicing and perfecting our aim with a .22-caliber rifle, and we also had a trap release for scaling clay pigeons into the air for practice with birdshot.

After some particularly grueling stretch of work, when the pressures had built up, I'd frequently take a group of cohorts from Local 299 or from International headquarters up to the lodge for a weekend of total relaxation. There were no phones, no problems, and it was difficult to have any contact with the outside world. The woods, themselves, were therapeutic, and I'd notice a great difference among my friends, as well as in myself, after such a visit.

Most of the fellows knew that when I said we were going hunting, what I really meant was that we were going to the cottage to rough it, do a little fishing, and take some long hikes in the unspoiled woodlands.

Cecil Watts of Local 337 was an ardent hunter, however, and he showed up with enough equipment to mount a safari. When we got to the village near the camp, a guide told us that there were more deer around that year than in a great many seasons. Cecil, we could see, was virtually boiling with eagerness to get out there and bag a deer.

Cecil may never forgive me for what I did. I took the jeep and went back into town and picked up two cases of .22-caliber shells. There were 24 shells to a box and 144 boxes in a case: a total of 3,456 shells in each case.

Then I took the cases to the target range and got everyone out on the firing line, plinking away at the targets. Within a few hours we had fired off all 6,912 rounds of .22. At the end there wasn't a deer within twenty miles.

Cecil went fishing instead—not too happily. What he had to say about Jimmy Hoffa under his breath can't be printed.

Good men. Great men. Real men. Teamsters. The International Brotherhood of Teamsters has grown and flourished and become the largest union in the world. The reason it has done so is the men—and some women, too, as well as many understanding wives—who have dedicated themselves to that task.

13

Growth: How High Is Up?

Implicit in all of the questioning at the McClellan committee hearings and in the unrelenting quest for my scalp by Attorney General Robert F. Kennedy was the fear, actual or the product of political pretense, that I, as International President of the International Brotherhood of Teamsters, held unusual push-button power over the American economy and could, by mere gesture, cause it to come to a halt.

This was implied in almost every aspect of the questioning. That the Teamsters had grown too large, and that Jimmy Hoffa had gained too much power, was what the politicians were saying in their oblique manner. More accurately, they were trying to get *me* to say it, by baiting me and goading me to lose my temper, hoping that I'd make some threat. How little such people know of the American labor union. I could no more order a nationwide strike—or any strike, for that matter—than a congressman could order use of the H-bomb.

The unasked question at the hearings was: "How did the union get so big?"

How? Solely by being the union of truckers. Governments at all levels, federal, state, and local, have poured billions upon billions of dollars into creating streets, roads, highways, turnpikes, connecting links, and bridges, and when they were done, it was economically unsound to ship the bulk of our national product any way but by truck. Shipping by truck became the least expensive, fastest, and most convenient way to move goods from one point to another. Even when ships, railroads, planes, or barges are involved in some phase of the shipment of some goods, trucks start them on their way and make the final delivery to their destination.

While the shippers turned to trucks and the governments opened more and more vehicular thoroughfares, the innovators and entrepreneurs in industry and on farms, the processors and the distributors turned out a bumper variety of more and better products and goods and sent most of them to swell the marketplaces by trucks.

What had once been a small band of truck drivers and helpers grew to a battalion, then to an army, then to a mighty force.

The International Brotherhood of Teamsters, a union of specialists, schooled in the specific needs and problems of the men behind the wheels of the nation's perpetual conveyor belt, had no choice but to grow. Either that, or it would have had to abdicate its role, and thus to betray the dues-paying members and to defile the union's courageous heroes who had fought and bled for their rights.

The union grew, and I grew with it. I grew in scope, not in power. Power has never been mine. What power I possess springs from the fear of those who either openly or secretly wish the labor movement would go away and abandon its role in the American economy. I have known many politicians, some of them my foremost detractors, who, while professing great love for organized Labor, secretly fear it and dread any confrontation with its spirit of unity.

"In unity there is strength," said the Founding Fathers,

and they were right. Whatever strength the Teamsters have, whatever muscle may be mine, stems from the fact that our union is united for common cause. United, the union has power. I, as its spokesman, wield its united power, but I wield none as an individual.

I would not remain the International President for five minutes if I set off on a tangent that was unacceptable to a solid majority of the members. Our democratic processes are more direct and less sophisticated than those that preserve the freedoms of the common citizens of this country. Union democracy, and our union is no exception, often is an exercise in quick and definite judgment, with no misgivings and no chance for recriminations.

Success is compounded of many things. For an individual it most commonly results from extremely hard work, unrelenting dedication to a goal, and the knack of being in the right place at the right time and being able to respond properly at that time.

It is clear that I was there at the right time.

Events moved me to the front rank of the Teamsters when the highway evolution caused the transportation revolution and made trucking one of the most vital industries in this mobile nation of constant consumers. I was there and I acted —and reacted. What choice did I have? Was I to say, "No, thanks. I don't want the Teamsters to grow and flourish?"

Everything in my background, everything I believed in, and everything I had worked for caused me to respond to the surge of vigor that reawakened the Teamsters just at the time I was gaining some prominence in the union.

And I was gaining prominence in the union.

Jimmy Hoffa, the kid from the sticks, the high school dropout, the young, eager guy with the unshined shoes and the bargain-price suit, had made some headway in his career. First, it was the success I enjoyed in organizing the over-the-road and the haulaway drivers that brought me to the attention of the higher-ups. Then, it was the organizing work I did in both Detroit and Chicago.

When the union began to show signs of growth, I was in a position to grow with it. And Chicago was the first step. Chicago and the Central States Drivers Council and its successor or corollary, the Central Council of Teamsters.

As an individual, I had moved ahead in Detroit, and then in Michigan, as I had helped, then led, in the organizing of locals, the acquisition of membership, and the establishment of contracts. As my area of activities broadened in the city, they also broadened in the state.

The very drive for diversification and "elbow room" that caused industry to move from the central city to the suburbs and then out into the country brought the Teamsters and me along with it.

Frankly, I hardly realized that I was becoming a statewide labor leader. Ours was a Detroit-based operation, and we considered our expansion into the countryside as an extension of our local activities. At the outset I didn't have the perspective on the whole picture.

I mention this because it's not quite the way some people would have you believe. I didn't sit there in Detroit and plot to create a nationwide union of my own.

The union was there, the only body prepared to protect the drivers (there were officials at three levels to monitor the maintenance of a truck and to inspect its parts for fatigue), to set standards of operation, and to guard against sharp practices and overloaded schedules. People made the union grow—people and necessity and circumstances. And I simply was one of the people. In a trade union leaders are neither self-anointed nor self-appointed. They are chosen by popular election. While units are being formed, however, and before they are sufficiently organized to hold an election, temporary leaders are appointed to govern and operate them.

That is the role, of course, of the Organizer. It was as an organizer that I gained popularity and strength among Teamsters throughout Michigan and, later, the Central States.

Before the war—in 1937, as I recall—the Minneapolis Teamsters set up the CSDC to organize and bargain centrally for all Midwestern over-the-road drivers.

It seemed strange to me at the time that a number of the locals opposed this natural evolution of the movement. In retrospect, though, I can see that their operations had been autonomous and that they were functioning smoothly on that basis. Thus they quite naturally resisted any tampering with the status quo.

Any regional development of that nature sets off ripples that disturb the lily pads of many large frogs in numerous small ponds. It was quite natural for them to have been concerned. I would have been.

With the citywide strength of Local 299 in Detroit I supported the CSDC and sought to encourage its growth. In this I had the full support of Ray Bennett, the local's trustee, and I was joined in my endorsement by my friend, Bert Brennan, President of Local 337 (Food and Beverage Drivers).

As the CSDC obtained areawide contracts, moreover, its influence spread throughout the Midwest. I worked actively with the council, sparing as much time as I could from my increasing duties in Detroit, employing all of the organizational and bargaining techniques we had developed so successfully in Detroit. Even so, I was flattered and honored when, in 1940, at the age of twenty-seven, I was chosen as Negotiating Chairman of the council and the following year was elected Vice-President.

The learning process continues, no matter your age or station, and I gained a great deal of knowledge about areawide bargaining from my association with the big Central States Council, techniques that I was able to channel back to Detroit, not only through Local 299, but through Joint

Council 43 as well. After all, though we had come a long way in Detroit, we still needed help. Local 299 was still under trusteeship because of its general insolvency. Milk Drivers Local 155 went into trusteeship early in 1937. Shortly to follow were Van Drivers Local 243 and Pontiac General Drivers Local 614. Through Joint Council 43, citywide Teamster problems were handled collectively. But since the largest Detroit local was—and is—Local 299, its problems, it seemed to me, were correspondingly magnified.

Experience in Chicago with the CSDC indicated clearly that there was strength, not only in unity, but in size. It seemed to me logical to look beyond the city limits of Detroit for our membership, particularly in view of the fact that the war's impetus was resulting in industrial development throughout Michigan; factories and their branches were springing up like mushrooms in midsummer.

Members of the executive board of Joint Council 43 agreed with this concept, and it was decided to start statewide distribution of a union publication to be called the *Michigan Teamster*, devoted to the discussion of programs, problems, and policies common to all locals in the state. Soon, moreover, I received permission to organize the Michigan Conference of Teamsters, a confederation of all of the locals in the state, and I was elected its first Chairman.

The next step, of course, was to persuade the locals to negotiate a statewide contract in place of the individual contracts collected in the past.

Again this made ripples. Some local officials, watching the rapid growth of hauling, trucking, and cartage activities in their areas, had envisioned little empires, grown strong by the upsurge in the economy. Their vision did not, in some cases, extend to the borders of the state. Most particularly, some of them had not entertained visions of sharing their leadership with a higher authority in Detroit.

United action, however, was particularly necessary in war-time. Forbidden to strike, we were also subject to control by the War Labor Board (WLB) when we sought any change whatsoever from Management by way of a new contract or even by supplemental agreement. In fact, in retrospect the labor movement, particularly the Teamsters, faced a major disadvantage at the bargaining table at that time.

The war followed so closely on the heels of the depression that the sudden growth of trucking caught us at a time when we had no money and were relatively disorganized. On the management side of the ledger, however, existing firms that had long since commenced their climb back into black ink suddenly luxuriated in the warmth of lush government defense contracts. Then, no sooner were we able to bring our finances under control and get ourselves launched on meaningful organizing campaigns and programs than wartime restrictions were applied. The union's "recovery" from the depression was virtually frozen at or near its Pearl Harbor levels by government fiat.

While the craft unions smarted under these restrictions, the trade unions signed on all the Rosie-the-Riveters and prospered.

It therefore was necessary for us to work together on a statewide basis, covered by one statewide contract resulting from statewide bargaining. In this way we could deal with the WLB on sensible terms. All matters thus presented before the WLB would be uniform and designed to avoid distortions between the cities and the fast-growing suburban and rural locals.

It has been suggested that it was through this device of statewide bargaining that I projected myself into a position of power in the union. Again I must say that my critics know little about the operations of organized Labor. My efforts to organize the whole state of Michigan into a cohesive unit had to be approved by the Michigan Conference of Teamsters, by Joint Council 43, by the International, and even by International President Dan Tobin.

Not only did we have to bargain with Management, we also had to deal with the federal government's wartime policies. Equally important, the powerful, rich, and fast-growing CIO's United Automobile Workers (UAW) coveted the Teamsters membership and sought repeatedly to drive a wedge into our united front for the purpose of creating a jurisdictional ·"situation." Had they succeeded, they would have placed crippling hardship on the Teamsters' convalescing treasury.

The trick, therefore, was to consolidate the organizing of the Teamsters as rapidly as possible and to centralize the union's policy-making apparatus. And if I gained strength as an individual in the statewide Teamster setup, it was simply because I was there, and because I was charged with responsibility for doing the job and melding the factions together into a united force.

When the war ended, we were in better shape than we had ever been before. We had enough trained men to do an effective organizational job, money enough to get them out into the field, and sufficient strength to bargain on an eye-to-eye level with Management. Indeed, because of the success of the organizational activities in Detroit and Michigan, the Teamsters were ready to consolidate the central states. The machinery, the CSDC, was in existence. Working through this structure, we tackled the whole Midwest and some of the Southern states as well.

It didn't happen overnight. Growth of this kind is achieved by setting high goals, then going after them, step by difficult step. By the late 1940s, however, Detroit organizers were active in cities and distribution centers from Michigan's upper peninsula to Baton Rouge, Louisiana.

I remember the night Ray Bennett stopped by my desk

with news that an over-the-road contract had been successfully negotiated in Tennessee. He went to a wall map and
stuck in a pin and, turning, said: "Well, Jimmy, you've
won."

"Won?" I asked. "Won what?"

"It's practically sewed up," he said, gesturing toward the
map. The whole central part of the nation was studded with
pins. That night I stopped and took a mental inventory.
We had come a long way. But I really couldn't get myself to
feel that we had "won" anything. I could still see many additional goals, 'way off in the distance.

I sincerely believe that to my employers—the members of
the union—I became a more valuable man during that
period. I became, I think, a top-notch programmer for organizational activities and a crackerjack negotiator. And if
this is what my detractors mean when they say I increased
my importance, they are right.

In 1943 I was appointed one of the three trustees who
examine the books of the International each year.

In the late forties, because of my success around my home
base, General President Dan Tobin offered to name me a
General Organizer, but I liked what I was doing and felt
that much remained to be won—if that's the right word—
in my familiar area of operations. I could have used that additional money, but it seemed to me that I had to do what
I knew to be right.

It turned out to be a good decision, and one for which I
was amply rewarded, for at the 1952 Convention I was appointed a Vice-President of the International. Numerous
delegates, many from the Central and Southern states, had
urged it.

My employers promoted me. It was a good, warm feeling.

14

Brother Against Brother

It is quite possible that in the entire history of man no group has ever dedicated itself to a common goal without ultimately falling into dispute about which route to follow to the goal and then, in time, engaging in internecine warfare. This appears to be the record of most ideological achievements, and it is most certainly the history of organized Labor in America.

Men who fought for the privilege of banding together to present a common front to employers and become a recognizable segment of the national economy had no sooner achieved the first plateau in their climb toward the Utopian heights at the end of the dream than they commenced to fight among themselves over how the rest of the race would be run.

The onset of World War II became the catalyst in the American labor movement. First, it caused a cleavage between the Trotskyite-oriented Socialists and the Lenin-leaning Socialists. Then, because of Russia's vacillation toward Nazi Germany, World War II rent a wider breach when the so-called traditionalists, the Americans who might be termed Laborites, broke away from the on-again-off-again Socialists.

Foreign influences on America's official policy channeled

down to the ranks of Labor and caused American blood to be shed on native soil long before Pearl Harbor. However, since this is an autobiography, I have skipped about a good deal, concerning myself with my career, and in so doing I have failed to document chronologically Labor's painful evolution, so perhaps I had better return to the 1930s.

As early as 1935 the Teamster Constitution had a clause barring Communists from membership. The prohibition was effective as a national policy, but in Minneapolis, as I have mentioned, some long-time and highly vocal Communists, the Dunne brothers and Farrell Dobbs, virtually ran the local.

In the winter of 1935–1936 Dan Tobin had tried to lessen the power of the Dobbs-Dunne combination in Minneapolis, but with only slight success. Later, by court order, Karl Skoglund was removed as local president because, as a noncitizen, he could not hold office without violating the International Constitution.

Matters came to a head in 1941, when the Minneapolis local engaged in public policy statements that were pro-Nazi, pro-Russia, and definitely anti-United States. Stalin, at the time, was proclaiming his friendship for Hitler, and Dobbs and the Dunnes were quick to condemn the United States for its softness toward, and apparent friendship with, France and Great Britain.

This was dangerous stuff for a labor union whose members represent every ethnic and national background on the globe. In the Teamsters there were, for instance, many Irishmen who had inherited no love for Britain, many Poles who felt an instinctive tug toward Mother Russia, many Jews whose parents or grandparents had come from Russia or the Ukraine, many Italians who thought Mussolini was a nut, many others who thought he had brought prosperity to Italy, and many Germans and Austrians who believed Hitler should be smashed and all the *heil*ing Nazis with him.

The tortures of soul and conscience that wracked the nation as a whole were magnified and brought into focus in the ranks of Labor.

To the average Teamster member what was involved was not a matter of economic theory, as it was with Dobbs and the Dunnes; it was tradition and instinct and perhaps some prejudice. Hitler's Wehrmacht was not the product of some economic philosophy; it was a war machine, threatening lands where parents or grandparents once dwelt, trampling traditions that are observed to this day on holidays and feast-days in mid-continent American cities.

Dan Tobin was a close friend of President Roosevelt and a loyal supporter of the President's policies. He therefore hoped to show his support of the White House by pledging the Teamsters to a full wartime preparedness program in keeping with the intensifying industrial activity of the nation. He planned to do this at the annual convention in midsummer.

In the spring, however, conditions in Minneapolis were so chaotic that Secretary-Treasurer John Gillespie called a meeting of a special subcommittee of the Executive Board of Chicago and reviewed a long list of charges against the Minneapolis leadership that resulted in a decision to place the local in trusteeship. This decision put control of the local directly into the hands of the International President, Dan Tobin.

Dave Beck was sent to Minneapolis to effect the trusteeship, but no sooner had he arrived than he ran into trouble. A general hate campaign had been raging, and before Beck could move, the membership voted to secede from the Teamsters and join the "more liberal" CIO.

It was then that Teamsters headquarters learned that Denny Lewis, head of the United Construction Workers Organizing Committee (UCWOC) and brother of the famous John L., had been working in Minneapolis. Lewis wanted to charter a local union of truck drivers and helpers in the Minneapolis area with CIO affiliation. In a wire to the Dunnes, Lewis had said, "We visualize this move on the part of the truck drivers in Minneapolis into our organization as the first step towards the complete organization of truck drivers in the United States in the CIO."

Consequently, a Motor Transport and Allied Workers Industrial Union was established under CIO auspices, and a CIO staff was sent in. Almost simultaneously, moreover, the CIO began recruiting and organizational efforts in Detroit and also in Flint and Pontiac.

Smart cookies from all over the country were brought into Detroit to work as undercover agents for the CIO. They infiltrated bars, diners, loading platforms, laundries, warehouses, bakeries, farmers' market areas, docksides, and rail yards. They sought out the disgruntled, the disenchanted, the malcontents, and the misfits and taught them to be *agents provocateurs*, schooling them in disrupting the meetings of Teamster locals and spreading rumors and fostering unrest.

Those who were strongly anti-communist, say, the devout Roman Catholics, were reminded of the loud and radical utterances of the Teamsters local officials in Minneapolis. Those who were leaning toward socialism were told how Tobin, Beck, Gillespie, and ranking Teamsters had purged the pure and undefiled Dunnes and Skoglund and Dobbs from Minneapolis and ended their good works.

It was ideological warfare at its worst.

The International Brotherhood of Teamsters, then affiliated with the American Federation of Labor (AFL), had only a shell of a local in Minneapolis (actually only what was left of two combined locals), and it was under severe attack in the key terminal cities of Michigan, where not only cars and automotive goods but also the vital output of the nation's aroused military arm were being trucked.

It seemed incongruous to me that the CIO, in its national posture, should proclaim its patriotism and its support of the Roosevelt war effort at the same time that its organizers were playing a disruptive role right at the central powerhouse of that war effort.

I had become accustomed to public apathy. I had grown used to a public that embraced the obvious and failed to comprehend the true nature of things. Never, however, was I so disturbed as when the public failed to see what was going on in the ranks of Labor at a time when, as never before, the nation needed Labor's solidarity.

The CIO activities in Minneapolis did not reflect the true national policies of that labor organization. But the fact remains that the CIO did nothing to bring an end to the fighting that went on there. And, certainly, there was turmoil: Stalinist members of the CIO in Minnesota at first welcomed the Trotsky-espousing Dunne brothers from the Teamsters and the AFL; then, when Moscow officially changed its policy, they tried to dump them. But while they were wooing the Teamsters, these alien-oriented CIO organizers brought in hoodlums, known killers, and goon squads with full intent to make the streets of Minneapolis run red with blood, if necessary, in order to effect the coup for the CIO that was deemed so necessary at the time.

Perhaps I was naive. I know I was too single-minded. I recoiled at the realization that this titanic struggle, so far removed from local ranks where I had spent so much of my adult life, had nothing to do with the enhancement of the labor movement, was not in the slightest concerned with the welfare of the workingman, and essentially was as foreign to the American ideal and the goals of American Labor as was the Kremlin itself.

When I was called to Minneapolis to help reform the ranks of the old Teamsters, I left Detroit feeling like a patriot embarking for the front, knowing that I faced certain dangers but determined to restore the democratic American principles to the foreign-dictated mess existing there.

I marched off to an unpopular war. I was appalled at how little the American press and radio seemed to comprehend what was happening. I was dismayed at the propaganda that was accepted as truth. Each utterance of a CIO official on the scene was treated as though it came from Mount Sinai.

Top CIO officials, meanwhile, were making overtures to President Roosevelt. It was apparent that Dan Tobin was being boxed into an unpleasant situation. The question was whether the wily man in the White House would see through the ploy, or, perhaps more significantly, whether the European problems, of such transcending importance, would allow him to judge separately the deeds that were being done in Minnesota—and in Michigan, too—that were so antipathetic to American Labor and so darkly linked with foreign intrigue.

It was a tough spring and summer in Minneapolis and St. Paul. There was some bloodshed, and there were many lumps and broken bones. Mostly, however, it was hard work. It was a matter of reorganizing Local 544, whose members couldn't make up their minds whether to be 544–AFL or 544–CIO. Many of the men carried two buttons. When we were around, they'd wear an AFL pin; when the CIO orga-nizers showed up, they'd switch pins. It was obvious they were waiting to see which side would promise the most. It was dirty stuff and had no place in the labor movement—but there it was, and it had to be dealt with.

The Dunnes and their friends suffered a severe setback when, shortly before the July Fourth holiday, FBI agents raided the SWP headquarters in Minneapolis and St. Paul and then three weeks later secured indictments against Dobbs, the Dunne brothers, and five other officials of Local 544 on charges of conspiracy to overthrow the government by force and violence, to engage in private military training for that purpose, and to spread disaffection among the armed forces.

From that time, the Leftist-oriented CIO raids against the Teamsters, both in Minnesota and in Michigan, lost steam. The Cause had little glamour for the rank-and-file truck drivers and helpers.

The American Civil Liberties Union (ACLU) defended Farrell Dobbs, the Dunnes, and the five indicted union officials, claiming that the FBI had been used as a political tool by President Roosevelt, who, said the ACLU, had been persuaded by Dan Tobin to bring an end to the CIO's organizing activities in Minnesota. Other liberal groups took up the cry. A *cause célèbre* was brewing, but it had no effect on Minnesota's workers.

At the time of the trial I was asked, along with other Detroit officials, to testify against the Dunne brothers, but we declined to do so. There was nothing we could say in relation to the charges that had not already been said, and, in truth, our concern was simply to get the local reestablished, not to engage in the matters of national foreign policy that seemed to take precedence at the proceedings.

To illustrate what kind of a solid man Farrell Dobbs is, and to give you an idea of why I have always liked his style and class while disagreeing with his political and economic views, I will add that he refused to hide behind the convenient shelter provided by the ACLU. He has flatly rejected the notion that the Justice Department's interference (via the FBI) constituted a payoff by Roosevelt to his friend, Dan Tobin. The raid came about, Dobbs says, because the war seemed imminent and the national mood was building toward it, and because the Trotskyite philosophy involved general class issues that were unacceptable to the American mores of the time.

I suffered torn loyalties when Dobbs and the Dunnes were arrested. I had worked with them in the old days and had learned much from Farrell Dobbs. I was hurt and saddened by the fact that they had bolted the organization, but I wished them no ill—only that they would return to the fold, stick to issues confronting the labor movement, and leave Russia to the Russians. But life is never as simple as that. Human beings rarely conform to preconceived patterns. Dobbs is Dobbs, and he had to go his own way. So, too, did the Dunnes.

At the trial that fall Farrell Dobbs and Vince Dunne were convicted and given sentences ranging from twelve to eighteen months. The sentences were upheld on appeal two years later. Miles Dunne was found innocent by the jury. Grant Dunne, during the trial period, suffered a nervous breakdown and committed suicide; Karl Skoglund, ultimately, was deported after spending much time in jail as an alien who conspired against the United States.

The collapse of CIO efforts in Minneapolis I knew to be only a beginning of a new struggle. There could be no doubt that the stronghold of the CIO was Detroit, and that if a coup was attempted in Minneapolis, it could be considered only a diversionary action: the real thrust would come in the world's auto capital.

It did—while I was in Minneapolis.

The attack centered on the haulaway drivers, the very ones I had organized using Farrell Dobbs's techniques. The reasoning of the CIO organizers was that since these truck drivers dealt with the automobile plants and since the auto industry was organized, under Walter Reuther, by the CIO, the drivers who received the cars from the CIO workers at the auto plants should be affiliates of the CIO.

I returned to Detroit to find strong-arm goons roughing up Teamsters whenever possible and spielers and spellbinders assigned to cars so they could go wherever they wanted and make a pitch to Teamster members about joining up with the "growing auto industry."

Employers, moreover, don't simply sit back and watch such internecine wars. They revel in them and capitalize on them and use them to whatever advantage comes to hand. To them it's all part of the game, and the more Labor can be kept off balance, particularly by its own members, the better off is the industrial world of employers.

The reaction was as might be expected. Employers, or at least several of them, eagerly signed up with the CIO and encouraged organizational efforts led by Denny Lewis's outfit, the same one that had sought to capitalize on the Minneapolis situation, hopeful that competition in the ranks of Labor would result in competitive bidding to see who could come up with the softest contract.

We did what we could. We boycotted establishments that signed with the CIO insurgents. We threatened to take away union cards from members who were overt in their preference for the insurgents. There was violence, violence on both sides. However, things *had been* peaceful. We didn't start it. All we sought was preservation of the status quo —which meant peace. We held, adamantly, that it was not the time to engage in interior power struggles, that our attention should have been riveted to one goal: buttressing the growing national war effort.

The biggest and most powerful CIO union was, of course, the UAW, and Walter Reuther never endorsed the raid against the Teamsters. And since Reuther did not support the CIO efforts, substantial funds were held back. Consequently, USWOC, which had hired some high-priced organizers, lost them when they drifted off because the expected rewards weren't there.

The most amusing incident of the whole affair came when Turner, head of the UCWOC organizational drive, charged that a number of his best organizers were arrested because the Detroit police secretly favored Jimmy Hoffa and wanted to help the Teamsters. Well, I have some good friends on the Detroit police force, and had some in those days, too, but I've never known those tough cops to lean over backward even for a blood brother, unless it was the official policy of the city government, much less for a rowdy labor leader such as Jimmy Hoffa, whose contact with the police, up to that point, more often than not had been at the wrong side of the desk sergeant's blotter, handing over his belt, tie, and shoelaces.

Without burdening this text with all of the details, the raid against the Teamsters in Detroit, Pontiac, Flint, and other Michigan cities ended when the Michigan State CIO Council, at the behest of the UAW, expressed the strongest opposition to all raiding tactics among workers producing and transporting defense goods.

It was only a short while before Pearl Harbor, and the edict involved probably 90 percent of our members who came into any kind of contact with the CIO unions. Almost everyone was engaged in defense work of one kind or another.

Sometimes events just seem to break in a man's direction. This time, I seemed in line to be the beneficiary. Two events, in particular, turned the tide in my favor: (1) the 1941 National CIO Convention in Detroit, and (2) the expiration of several prime truckers' contracts in the Detroit area.

The CIO convention was one of the most tense in the history of the organization. John L. Lewis was showing his strength; the Mineworkers refused to stand and applaud for CIO President Philip Murray; Denny Lewis was openly antagonistic to the CIO president. John L. was advanced by the Mineworkers as a candidate to head the organization. Steelworkers and the Amalgamated Clothing Workers closed ranks behind Murray and were joined by Harry Bridges,

Mike Quill, Phil Carey of the rubber workers, and such representatives of the textile industry as the International Ladies Garment Union and the Textile Workers Union.

Communist sympathizers—the same who had been so eager to wreck the Teamster organization in Minneapolis—now feared that Labor unrest would harm the defense program and postpone aid to Mother Russia, which had only recently been invaded by its sometime ally, Germany.

The convention broke up into numerous rump sessions, its leaders fearful of fist fights among delegates, and when it reconvened, Phil Murray was reelected by an overwhelming vote amid great ovation. Finally, Murray's speech of acceptance was directed right to the point: raiding of rival organized groups must stop!

A quarter of a century later I still feel that we were right in the late thirties in our battle against CIO raiding. So do all of the veteran Teamsters who recall those days. Labor historians, however, so openly disposed to deification of the Old-Left CIO ideas (a philosophy that it implied more than it practiced) have never taken the trouble to place the Teamsters' cause in perspective and to acknowledge that time has vindicated our judgment and our actions. But in any case, it was with a sigh of relief—no one wins in a factional war —that I turned to the job before me, the renewal of contracts.

Oh, yes, many of the contracts needing renewal were at establishments where employers had worked hand in glove with Denny Lewis, hoping to break the Teamsters. Now I'm not the kind of fellow who would delight in being handed such an ace card (it says here), but I certainly realized that I must use it to its fullest advantage.

The result was a handsome pay raise for Teamsters working in Detroit and throughout Wayne County.

There was much jubilation, particularly among truck drivers and helpers and others covered by our contracts. Any

Teamster members who had been tempted by the UCWOC flirtations snapped back to the fold, smilingly, contentedly, and, it seemed, permanently.

A short time later Denny Lewis folded his UCWOC office and moved his headquarters to Washington. This, it turned out later, was in preparation for the withdrawal of John L. Lewis and the Mineworkers from the CIO.

Then, suddenly, it was all over. We were united in one brotherhood, serving one cause, our differences forgotten, our goal clearly before us, our route to it clearly defined; for there was Pearl Harbor.

15

Ohio, the South, and the CSDC

The Central States Drivers Council, it has always seemed to me, provided the key to the growth, numerically and economically, as well as from the standpoint of influence, of the Teamsters Union. When Farrell Dobbs left the CSDC in 1940, Mike Healy of Local 710 was elected Council President. I was chosen to replace Dobbs as negotiating chairman. I didn't realize, when I accepted the job, along with a vice-presidency the following year, that it was the post that would project me into the national limelight as far as the International Brotherhood was concerned, but that job really paved the way to the General Presidency. As a rung in the ladder of my career, it provided a giant step upward.

The fundamental purpose of the CSDC was to establish uniform contractual requirements for truckers doing interstate business throughout the middle section of the continent. Only through uniformity could we prevent the big truckers from seeking out areas where they could work out more favorable contracts and make their headquarters there, an omnipresent danger to the union in the mid-1930s. Later, urban and rural cartage was included under the uniform contract concept—again to prevent maverick headquartering by employers.

To show why this uniformity was needed one can take the case of a bakery located, say, in Chicago. The bakery engaged in two types of trucking. It used large vans to move bulk loads of bread and pastries to warehouses and large supermarkets. It also used driver-salesmen with delivery trucks on home-delivery routes.

If our Chicago contract, geared to big-city living costs, was deemed to be too high, the bakers would simply move their business office to a smaller town, call in the Teamsters officials there, and ask for a local contract. Chances are good that it would be a contract with lower rates than those obtaining in Chicago. Then, even though the bakery itself remained in Chicago, and deliveries were made from that bakery, the employers would try to pay the Chicago drivers on the basis of a contract in the town where they were headquartered.

Rather than dispute this issue through the courts and federal agencies, it seemed much simpler to work out uniform contracts. In a manner of speaking, it was insurance that there would be bargaining in good faith.

This was the policy that evolved at CSDC, but from the outset it ran into snags in Ohio. In the beginning the resistance to uniform contracts was attributable to the ingrained native independence of the owner-operators and drivers in that state. Ohioans are Midwestern Yankees. The first Ohio settlers came from Connecticut, and a great deal of the New Englander's devotion to individual independence lingers in the thinking there. When a group of men in a certain community work out a contract with an employer in that community, it is, by golly, nobody's business but their own.

Except that it *was* the business of others.

In Detroit, for instance, we began to notice that some of the large interstate truckers were moving south across the state line and setting up their offices and garages in Ohio in order to avoid paying the contract rates in Detroit, which was thoroughly organized by the Teamsters. Yet at first there was little we could do about it.

Thus, in 1943 and 1945, when we tried to bring Ohio into the CSDC, we were unsuccessful. The Ohioans were too ruggedly individualistic. The same lack of success was met with in 1947 and 1949. But during our later efforts I discovered that one man, chief employer negotiator Landus O'Brien, was blocking us, and it developed that O'Brien had strong personal animosity toward me: on one occasion he even refused to sit in the same room at a negotiating table with me.

Personalities were always a factor. For example, after 1949 I found out that Frank Tobin, son of Teamster President Dan Tobin, had been working in Ohio, collaborating with some local Teamster officials in an effort to project himself into unionwide recognition so that he might stand as a candidate to replace his father, who was planning to resign in a few years.

Young Tobin's efforts were not too serious, however. For example, one obvious problem facing him was the fact that he wasn't even a qualified union member. Indeed at the 1952 convention his Dad sent him home on the ground that there was illness in the family. Whatever the reason, young Tobin's departure enabled the union to avoid what would have been an embarrassing showdown, which Frank seemed determined to bring about.

With all these setbacks it wasn't until 1952 that Ohio contracts were made uniform with those in other Midwestern states.

Meanwhile there remained the problem of the South. There weren't too many over-the-road drivers operating in the South prior to the war, but afterward, with the industrialization of that vast and fertile region, operators went into business in almost every village and town. From the

Southwest, Texas, and Oklahoma, to the Southeast, from Kentucky to Florida, big trucks began to infuse economic lifeblood into the highway arteries of Dixie.

And if separate contract provisions were needed there, they, too, had to be uniform, else there would be a repetition of the problems of the North.

The most effective way to organize the South was by leap-frogging to the largest terminal centers, getting contracts, and then pushing them out to the smaller communities. This was what we had done in the Midwest, and it had worked most successfully.

It wasn't easy, it didn't happen overnight, and it even required a series of short strikes, but by the early 1950s all of the intrastate long-line carriers of the South had been brought into the Teamsters and were under uniform contract.

However, no sooner had we acquired uniform contracts for the Southeast and Southwest than we noticed a phenomenon: a great many long-line carriers were operating out of Virginia and the Carolinas. A little investigation showed that the truckers had redomiciled in these states to escape taxes in the areas that had been industrialized longer, as well as the Teamster contracts that required living wages for their drivers and helpers.

There was nothing we could do about equalizing the taxes —and, anyway, they have a way of providing their own attrition—but we certainly could do something about getting Teamster contracts into the area.

The Taft-Hartley Act was relatively new in the early fifties, and it was being exhibited as a weapon against us by the more powerful employers. At the same time a great deal of talk was going around about "Right-to-Work" laws and considerable attention was being paid to state legislatures that seemed likely to fall for the palpable falsity of the "Right-to-Work" ideal (one person's right to work while others pay dues and undertake strikes to guarantee him a living wage and decent working conditions).

Consequently, carriers that had negotiated willingly with us in the Midwest and had finally, after hesitation, come to the bargaining table with us in the South flatly refused to sit down with us in Virginia and the Carolinas, believing they would be protected by state law, or the relatively new Taft-Hartley, or a combination of both. Indeed, there was a great pooling of carrier resources in those three states, all aimed at very neatly circumventing the Teamsters and lowering the pay levels of tens of thousands of truck drivers.

We've never been as rich a union as people have said, and we could see ahead of us a great and costly legal squabble in the Carolinas and Virginia unless something could be done.

Secondary boycotts were out of the question, of course, but there was a provision in the open-end grievance procedure that we thought might be helpful to us. Under it, the union has the right to strike if Management and Labor disagree on contract interpretation.

Soon, therefore, those carriers domiciled in Virginia and the Carolinas that did a big volume of business in the Midwest found that there were many contract interpretations that were not to the liking of Midwestern union members. It is remarkable how quickly many of these Virginia and Carolina truckers came to contract with the Teamsters.

One must use the tools at hand.

There was work to be done at home base, too. While over-the-road drivers throughout the middle section of the nation were protected by more or less standardized contracts through the CSDC, local cartage from city to city was handled by local contracts that were as diverse as fingerprints.

Though there were master agreements that in many cases applied to all companies within a single city, we found that more than four hundred local cartage contracts covering fourteen thousand employers in the twenty-two states covered by the CSDC were drawn up along different lines. Hours varied from forty to sixty per week. Wages ranged from $1.25 to more than $2.00 per hour. There were some health and welfare plans. Some contracts offered holidays, some vacations, many had no fringe benefits at all.

No one can honestly say that the more than five hundred employers involved in our efforts to make uniform the local cartage contracts were overwhelmed with joy at the prospect. They attended a mass meeting in Chicago to protest our plan, and in sparsely organized states the nonunionized truckers would underbid and undercut them in the competitive marketplace.

We were all too familiar with the practices of unorganized truckers. Obviously we had a task to perform: complete the organization job in all twenty-two states. And as we were working on the uniform contract for local carters, we also set about organizing the rest of the truckers in the region, in itself a gargantuan task.

In the process, we encountered strong resistance in Nebraska, where there were several pockets of unorganized drivers. Unfortunately, this resistance resulted in a prolonged strike in Omaha, but in the end uniformity was achieved. The CSDC had done its job well. The entire territory was brought under the jurisdiction of the CSDC in 1957.

I had played a major role in directing its operation, and though I didn't know it at the time, the following year I was to be nominated for the General Presidency of the International Brotherhood of Teamsters.

16

The Presidency

My opponent for the highest office in the International Brotherhood of Teamsters was a faction in the U.S. government. It came as a surprise to me to learn that certain elements of my own government wished me quashed. I had been "minding the store," so to speak, within the Teamster organization, albeit moving in ever widening circles, and was relatively unaware of enmity in Washington.

I entertained ambitions at both professional and personal levels. I aspired to higher office in the union, and at the same time I had ambitious plans for the Brotherhood. Many inequities continued to exist in trucking circles in various parts of the nation, and I had come to realize that only a strong, solid, large union could end them. I was arguing against racism long before the federal politicians were aware of it as an issue. In Texas, Mexican-American truck drivers were getting fifty cents an hour while drivers performing similar chores in other parts of the nation were receiving more than two dollars, plus other benefits. Negro carters in some parts of the South were paid on a par with "yard boys" who mowed and raked the lawns of the privileged. There *was* still much to be done.

Only with the strength of a nationwide union could we break down these ancient barriers of prejudice and tradition and bring equal pay for truck drivers to all parts of the country. But I must be frank: my desire to organize the South was also partly motivated by my concern for the better paid unionized drivers of the North, for the pools of poverty, the low-wage areas, in the South had a way of affecting the willingness of operators in the North to abide by their contractual agreements.

I first learned that Robert Kennedy had the knife out for me during the 1956 election campaign. Kennedy had worked as a counsel on the so-called McClellan committee, officially known as the Senate Committee on Government Operations. His brother, Senator John F. Kennedy, was a member of the committee.

One morning Robert Kennedy, who was on leave, working for presidential candidate Adlai Stevenson, made an announcement to reporters that he intended to investigate the Teamsters Union and the Carpenters Union.

Just what either union had to do with "government operations" was not asked of the young man, nor was the information offered. His statement, like so many that followed, was simply accepted without question and translated into headlines. No one even questioned the timing of the announcement. It was mid-campaign.

Strangely, both the Teamsters and Carpenters, alone among major national unions, had come out strongly in support of Republican nominee Dwight D. Eisenhower. But the reason for Kennedy's decision to investigate the two unions was not clear at first, and the explanation was complicated, to say the least.

A few months earlier Senator John Kennedy had moved to within a handful of delegate votes of winning the vice-presidential nomination for himself. None of the bigwigs in the Democratic party had thought Jack Kennedy had had a chance of winning the second spot. So when he came up with a near-miss, they, as well as the pundits of the mass media, took a second look at the young man from Massachusetts. Where, it was asked, had he found such sudden strength?

Analysis showed that it came from the conservative right wing of the Southern bloc of the Democratic party. This wing had favored Jack Kennedy over Estes Kefauver. Why?

Further analysis came up with the answer. Kefauver liked labor unions and was liked by them.

This put the issue in perspective, all right, but it also put the two political Kennedy brothers on the spot. No one can aspire to the highest office in the land, particularly a Democrat, if he is known as the fellow who receives support because he is anti-Labor. Yet, this manifestation of strength in the Southern vote not only had to be preserved, it had to be magnified.

How to accomplish this?

Obviously the Kennedys couldn't attack the major elements of American Labor, for they were four-square for Stevenson and the Democratic party. The Teamsters and the Carpenters, however, were working in behalf of Eisenhower.

The strategy therefore seemed clear. Rap the Teamsters and Carpenters and you'd accomplish two things: (1) solidify the confidence in the Southern voting bloc, and (2) please the Democratic hierarchy, which was displeased with the two unions for not going along with Stevenson's campaign. In short, the anti-union action in 1956 was, then, part of the Kennedys' long-range plans. The goal was the greatest prize in the modern world: the White House.

With Robert Kennedy's announcement to the press about the investigation of the Teamsters and Carpenters, the Kennedys cemented the support of the Southern conservatives and won the admiration of the Northern liberals—a neat trick.

Perhaps I should have expected some such tactic, and it

is to my discredit that I didn't. The Teamsters Union was ripe for just such a ploy. Under Dave Beck's leadership it was nominally Republican. With Eisenhower as a candidate it was militantly so. In addition, to make the situation ideal for aspiring politicians, the union was at professional odds not only with the labor hierarchy (now the combined AFL–CIO) but also with Walter Reuther, President of the UAW and leading spokesman for liberal causes on the whole labor front.

When the Carpenters Union regained favor with Walter Reuther, it was released from Kennedy's threat of investigation, leaving the Teamsters and Dave Beck, the International President, to stand alone against his wrath. Betimes Kennedy's inquisitorial agency had been renamed with a most awkward but carefully selected appellation: the Senate Select Committee on Improper Activities in the Labor-Management Field.

So onto the mat went Dave Beck for questioning about his alleged personal income-tax evasions—which, no matter how you view it, has nothing to do with management, "proper" or "improper," of the Teamsters Union. Ultimately, Dave Beck was removed from Kennedy's purview, convicted of income-tax fraud, and it was conceded throughout the union that I was the most likely candidate to succeed him to the post of General President.

Before I was even to stand for that office, however, Kennedy swooped down. He came up with one John Cye Cheasty, victim.

Cye Cheasty came to me on the recommendation of a mutual friend in New York because, the friend said, Cheasty had special training and experience in dealing with Senate committee investigative methods. He was a lawyer, my friend explained, who could be helpful to me in my dealings with the McClellan committee.

Kennedy, it seems, had a different version of Cheasty's origin. According to testimony Kennedy gave later, Cheasty, a man unknown to him, came to his office in the Senate Office Building and told him that I had given him $1,000 to get a job on the committee staff so that he could spy for me. More money would be forthcoming if he succeeded in his mission. The "fee," in that case, was to be $2,000 per month, or some such sum.

Now, spying is a most reprehensible practice. Stern measures must be taken against anyone who engages in spying, the government maintains. But Kennedy hired Cheasty to spy on me, and in addition ordered the FBI to maintain a twenty-four-hour watch on me. Incidentally, Kennedy took Cheasty's "fee" money, minus expenses, and turned it over to the FBI. Perhaps spying is reprehensible if *some* people do it, but not if others do it.

Kennedy sent Cheasty back to New York with some worthless documents, which were turned over to me, and Cheasty collected $2,000, which he turned over to the FBI. This agency, by the way, took motion pictures of each of my meetings with my lawyer, Cheasty.

After the first such occasion, Kennedy and I had dinner together that night, at the home of a mutual friend. The only word that described him is "condescending." He asked me numerous personal questions: How much money did I make? How did I happen to get into the union? Why hadn't I tried to go to college?

Clearly he was puzzled over the fact that a kid from a poor family, lacking education, could rise to the top of the largest union in the nation.

All the time he must have been chortling inside, figuring that he had set up a neat trap with Cheasty, and that soon he would be able to nail me good and proper.

Three weeks later Cheasty called me and said he had some

papers he wanted to give to me. I met him and accepted them. The FBI, grinding away with the movie camera behind one-way glass, decided the time was ripe. They arrested me, and sure enough there were "The Papers"—just like in one of the Bing Crosby and Bob Hope wartime spy thrillers —documents from the McClellan committee. They were worthless, of course, but identifiable as McClellan committee documents.

My attorney for the trial was Edward Bennett Williams, whose abilities before the bar of justice are unequalled. By means of direct examination of me he brought out the fact —an obvious one to all but Robert Kennedy—that I had hired Cheasty as a lawyer, and that I had hired him before he spoke to Kennedy. It was therefore clear that the McClellan committee—or was it Kennedy?—had bribed this lawyer-witness-agency-spy, not I.

I freely admitted receiving the documents. After all, they were handed to me by my lawyer. The lawyer-client relationship is inviolable. I didn't ask him where he got them. I didn't ask him if he was obeying the oath of the Bar Association. He was my lawyer; he was getting paid by me; I figured that was sufficient.

Most of all, I neglected to ask Cheasty who his other clients were. I never thought about it. I had hired dozens of lawyers by that time. I had come to regard them as highly professional, keenly ethical men, particularly the kind qualified to practice in the higher courts where I was being tried.

Lawyers take an oath that they will not serve conflicting interests. I accepted that fact. I had no reason to suspect that Cheasty could stretch his sense of ethics to serve Robert Kennedy at the same time he was serving me.

But quite clearly Kennedy, a lawyer, did expect Cheasty to violate his code of ethics and make a mockery of his oath —an obvious example of double standards. What was improper for an ordinary citizen was perfectly correct for a member of the elite corps.

E. B. Williams brought out these facts under questioning. The defense counselor was, as always, soft spoken, unruffled, deliberate. He contrasted sharply with the accusing counselor, who was jittery, obviously overanxious, and tense.

On July 19, the jury brought in its decision: Not Guilty. I was acquitted.

On the day that I was arrested for receiving the papers from Cheasty, Kennedy had issued a statement to the press. If Jimmy Hoffa wasn't convicted this time, he said, "I'll jump off the Capital dome!" After the verdict was announced, Edward Bennett Williams turned to Bobby and with a straight face asked, "Would you like me to send you a parachute, Mr. Counselor?" Kennedy turned away, clearly agitated. And he was not through.

Not having learned his lesson, Kennedy called yet another press conference to explain to the public how and why he had lost. This time he raised the racial issue!

Kennedy told the press that E. B. Williams, cleverly maneuvering eight Negroes onto the jury, had then deliberately chosen as associate counsel a Los Angeles barrister, Martha Jefferson, a Negro, and had induced Joe Louis to come to the courtroom and demonstrate his friendship to me by nodding and waving his once near-lethal hand. He added that a dope peddler, a homosexual, and a drunkard had been allowed to sit on the jury.

Suddenly the jurors were enemies of the country, too, repugnant to society. Kennedy, of course, had had the same chance to challenge the jurors as Williams had had. Yet he had approved of them, officially, as a jury of my peers (and his, too) before the trial began.

Simple truth seemed to elude Kennedy. The fact was that Joe Louis, though an old friend of mine, was brought to the courtroom by other motives than those ascribed to him by Kennedy. He was courting Miss Jefferson at the time and eventually married her.

Ex-boxing champion Joe Louis of Detroit paid his sinister visit to the courthouse in Washington for the purpose of furthering his cause with a very attractive lady lawyer whom he wanted to make his wife. He greeted me in that court-room simply because he was an old friend. It was that—and nothing more. But was it?

Robert Kennedy couldn't believe there was anything so simple to it. I suppose he couldn't believe that anyone could be a friend of Jimmy Hoffa—not anyone who is capable of being the heavyweight champion of the world.

In any case, Kennedy wouldn't let the Louis incident end there. He loosened his hounds on that poor, browbeaten man whom the fates had already treated so unkindly.

Because Joe Louis had the effrontery to demonstrate his friendship for me, Kennedy and his Select committee investigated him for income-tax evasion. Again, no one bothered to ask what possible, remote connection this investigation had with labor rackets. The investigation was, and remains, clear evidence of both judicial and political intimidation.

Kennedy explained in his book that his pity for Louis prevented him from calling him as a witness before the Labor Rackets committee. Hogwash! His fear of a coast-to-coast outcry at such highhandedness was all that deterred him. Otherwise Joe Louis, one of the nicest, most honest, totally steadfast men ever to walk the earth, would have had further troubles with his government. The tax overlords had rendered him a poor and broken man; he figured there was little more that could happen to him. He figured without Robert Kennedy. But his popularity with the people saved him. Of people, en masse, Kennedy was afraid, for they are the voters.

At that time, I, too, was concerned with the voters—the voters in my union. I was standing for the presidency. Yet in September, while I was in Miami preparing for the campaign, Kennedy called new hearings and demanded that I attend.

More than a million Teamsters read the headlines. Senator McClellan issued a list of thirty-three "improper activities" charged to me, which led him, he said, to conclude that I was unfit to hold any position of trust in the labor movement. Then, a New York grand jury indicted me for perjury in connection with an old wiretapping charge.

Next, Senator McClellan wired my Teamster leaders in Miami, who were preparing for the convention, warning them that most of the delegates who were assembling there might have been chosen illegally!

Labor Secretary James P. Mitchell then called upon the delegates to consider carefully the fact that the McClellan Committee had charges pending against me. The fact that they were unproved charges made little difference. The delegates couldn't know then that every charge would be dropped ultimately. They knew only that a member of the Cabinet, an officer of the government, was cautioning them to think twice about supporting Jimmy Hoffa!

There was more. Defecting Teamsters sought an injunction postponing the election. A federal district court in Washington granted it, only the next day to set the injunction aside. The Supreme Court took the case and turned it back to the federal court for a lack of evidence. The Supreme Court could not agree that the delegates were not qualified to vote. It said they were qualified.

Yet Kennedy persisted in his opinion that they were not.

The vote was held.

I was elected.

I became General President of the International Brotherhood of Teamsters, the largest independent union in the world, representing a group of people to whom I gladly dedicated my life, my total devotion, my maximum effort and strength.

In Washington, Robert Kennedy said he found it hard to believe that I had won. In view of what he had done to get me defeated, I don't wonder he was amazed.

17

Only the Beginning

My election was no cinch. It was nip and tuck all the way.
Someone said, in retrospect, that if the Teamsters had not
had so much outside advice, so much pressure from Kennedy and officialdom in Washington, I might have been
defeated. I doubt that, but the fact remains that the steam
generated by the Attorney General served to unite the
delegates behind me. They knew me; Robert Kennedy
didn't. They believed me; they didn't believe him. They
knew that I was ambitious and that I wanted the presidency
of the Teamsters; they began to understand that Kennedy
was ambitious, too, and had his eye on higher office; and
they surmised that I was being used as a pawn and patsy
to further those ambitions.

Given my chance to address the convention, I said:

I have no fight with the McClellan Committee, but when
a Congressional committee concentrates on a personal attack
or misuses its power, it can be dangerous for all of us.

Something is wrong when a man may be judged guilty in
a court of public opinion because some enemy or some ambitious person accuses him of wrongdoing by hearsay or
inference.

I had no way of knowing then how prophetic my words

were. Again and again Robert Kennedy accused me of sundry offenses against society, ranging wide in their scope. Again and again he garnered black headlines when he issued his charges or "planted" them with someone else to issue. Again and again my reputation was discredited by those headlines. Yet again and again I was acquitted, found not guilty of the multitudinous charges brought against me from that one generative source.

The wiretap trial, calculated to throw the election against me, resulted in a hung jury, with the vote eleven to one for conviction. When the case was retried in 1958, I was acquitted.

The point under litigation was whether or not I had hired an electronics expert to place bugs on the phones of some Teamster officials in Detroit.

Yet when the second trial came up, it was discovered that the prosecution had built its own case on wiretap evidence!

By that time I had learned about Robert Kennedy's double standards. He was perfectly willing to invade the privacy of an individual citizen to prove that the citizen had invaded someone else's privacy. His standards involved the double-think of budding anarchism.

When I was acquitted, Kennedy began to accuse me of jury-tampering. As though he couldn't conceive of defeat at the hands of a jury of his peers, he spread his accusations to cover those who had voted against him—and *for* Hoffa. However, nothing came of his mutterings. In the flurry of other charges, counter-charges, allegations, smears, and insinuations that followed, I failed to realize that Kennedy, when all else was lost, would turn on the citizens doing their duty as jurors and blame them for his failure. Whenever I proved my innocence, as I was obliged to do over and over again, Robert Kennedy's disappointment was obvious. But he had elected himself my persecutor, and he had only begun to fight. When it came to vendetta, he was the most resourceful man that any target of his wrath had ever encountered.

Make no mistake, Robert Francis Kennedy, irrespective of his later political appeal to a wide segment of the voters, had the ability to concentrate the full force of his brilliant mind and the full blast of his enormous energy on the removal of one individual enemy, be he large or small, prominent or insignificant. He sought to chisel out a spotless political career, devoid of any signs of normal political warfare. He was determined that there would be no wounded along his path of march. Enemies would be removed. They would be defeated and then cleared from the scene. There would be no survivors or compromise; no one would recover from a mere flesh wound after an encounter with Robert Kennedy.

In Robert Kennedy's book I had committed a cardinal sin: he had challenged me to the joust; I had met him in the lists; and I had emerged victorious. I had marched from the field of honor to the arena of public opinion, and, despite Kennedy's wholesale campaign to discredit me with the voters in my own union, I had again won.

My election to the general presidency of the Teamsters sealed the terms of Kennedy's vendetta with me. He would not rest until he "got" me. This he vowed to associates. This was the beginning of his much publicized "Get Hoffa" campaign. Consequently, the fact that he was also a man whose personality was such that he could not possibly abide either defeat or contradiction became of transcending significance as time wore on.

Kennedy, however, enjoyed a semi-victory over me when, shortly after my election to the presidency, the AFL–CIO voted the Teamsters out of the national organization. I was bitterly disappointed at the time. I was hurt, personally, to think that fellow unionists would so readily turn on me, but, more importantly, I was distressed, as one of the regents of the labor movement, to observe the creation of this sudden cleavage in the ranks of men bound together by common ideals and goals. I said at the time that whoever had been responsible for advising the AFL–CIO to take this step, and whoever had initiated and waged the campaign for the Teamsters' expulsion, was no friend of American Labor. Friends whose whisperings can cause wide division in the ranks of what was a united front serving a common cause are not real friends.

There is a possibility that the AFL–CIO was panicked by the crescendo of criticism directed at American Labor by Kennedy and the McClellan committee and wished to separate itself from what was the avowed immediate target, the Teamsters. But there's also the possibility that Kennedy whispered in the ear of an influential labor leader in the hierarchy of AFL–CIO, suggesting that he would be wise, politically, to initiate and promote the movement for expulsion of the Teamsters. Some mighty large unions were not really investigated by Kennedy, and that fact is surely significant.

An immediate effect of our expulsion, of course, was to save the Teamsters a great deal of money, for we no longer had to pay our per-capita assessment to the federation. But such savings were a very thin silver lining on an otherwise very large and very dark cloud.

Kennedy was even more successful in another foray against me. He persisted—despite the Supreme Court's decision to the contrary—in his claim that the convention that elected me president had been rigged. In this he was abetted by recognition among the delegates that my election had been helped, rather than harmed, by so much pressure from Washington, and some must have thought that in an open convention under no outside pressure I wouldn't have made out so well. In any case, a group of thirteen dissident

Teamsters went to court—as is their right under both our bylaws and National Labor Relations Board (NLRB) regulations—to challenge my election as president and to delay my taking office.

The court appointed a three-man Board of Monitors to hold the International Brotherhood of Teamsters in receivership, and I was given the temporary title of "Provisional President." It was a title used by the handful of dissenters; the rest of the union membership called me "General President."

Within a few months of the appointment of the Board of Monitors, Robert Kennedy issued a gratuitous statement predicting that the monitors would gather enough evidence to have me removed from office. He left open the question of whether the Teamsters would remove me, or whether I would be removed by some branch of the federal government, over which, it seemed, he was exercising increasing influence.

This kind of character assassination, coming, as it did, from a man who was only, after all, the counsel of a subcommittee of the Senate, received remarkable press coverage. It was hard to fathom the inability of the news media to get to the nub of the matter and their willingness to accept, blandly, as page-one material, such out-of-the-blue utterances of a subcommittee counselor who had never practiced law and who had obviously received his appointment because his brother was the only Democratic senator from his state at a time when there was a militant Democratic campaign to discredit a Republican administration. The Democrats could smell victory at the end of the Eisenhower tenure, and it was pretty obvious to most observers in Washington that John F. Kennedy was getting to be a lighter shade of "dark horse" with each passing day. It shouldn't have required a tremendous amount of perception to reckon that his brother, planted on a busy and vital subcommittee, was using the press conference as a means of furthering a forthcoming campaign.

Yet somehow all that went unnoticed.

Also unnoticed was the fact that Robert Kennedy was deliberately alienating the Teamsters from any possible support for his party. A national labor leader is immersed to his ears in national politics, yet he seeks to remain uncommitted. He becomes an apolitical creature who is at once multipolitical and nonpolitical. He must abide by the consensus of his membership in committing himself to an opinion about a candidate or a party—and even then he is unsure as to how effective his support or endorsement might be. Nevertheless, endorsement by labor leaders does seem to carry some weight with political candidates, and if such was the case, Kennedy was making impossible all Teamster support.

However, the analysts and pundits, having chosen not to place any political significance on Kennedy's relentless efforts to discredit me and the Teamsters, neglected to ask why the brother of an obvious presidential aspirant would deliberately flout the support of a strong and powerful labor union. No one wondered, in type at least, whether or not I might have had political differences with the Kennedys dating back as far, say, as the 1956 Stevenson campaign.

In fact, no one questioned anything very much. They were too busy listening to Kennedy predict that the allegation that "more than one convicted criminal" was getting paid his union salary while reposing in jail would be my undoing with the Board of Monitors.

It mattered little that I had just assumed the presidency —pardon me, the provisional presidency—and perforce would have had little responsibility for any policy decisions of the magnitude that were made in the past. Nor did it seem to matter to Kennedy, or to the press, that when he queried the UAW on the subject, Walter Reuther had acknowledged that his union paid the salaries of officials who were jailed because of union activities.

At the onset my relationship with the board was wholesome, one of constructive cooperation. Chairman Martin F. O'Donoghue, a Washington attorney, was selected jointly by the plaintiffs and by my group. The second member, Godfrey P. Schmidt, a New York labor lawyer, had represented the plaintiffs in their challenge to my election. The third member, Daniel B. Maher, a veteran attorney, was chosen by the defending Teamsters International.

I had known Dan Maher previously, of course, but the more close contact I had with the monitors, the more I got to know and respect him. He brought calm, level-headed judgment to the panel, and in his quiet, judicial way he soon became the board's most influential member. I cherished his relationship to the union and his friendship with me during the succeeding years when the monitors no longer existed; Dan's keen perspective on matters legal and otherwise has always been needed.

As the monitors continued their deliberations, it wasn't long before derogatory stories began to appear, all traceable either to O'Donoghue or to Schmidt. These two seemed determined to carry on the crusade by headline that had been started by Robert Kennedy. Dan Maher, in an awkward position, kept mum about it all, but his disapproval was evident in the way he ignored the slams and slanders that began to appear in print here and there. All he could do was prepare a careful record of the board's activities, a record that later resulted in the court-ordered dissolution of the board.

Meanwhile, the majority of the board demanded that I remove certain local leaders by fiat. I couldn't. Local leaders are elected by local members. There has to be more than dissatisfaction among monitors to cause an invasion by the

International. Central interference involves placing a local in receivership or trusteeship, and it's difficult to take such actions if the local is financially sound and no viable complaints are made from within it.

I'm not saying that everyone all down the line was lily-pure. What I'm saying is that there wasn't much I could do about isolated instances or wrongful action when there were no responsible complaints, when the leadership refused to complain, when the finances were sound, and when all basic requirements of the International and of the NLRB were being met or observed. And I had not put those leaders in office.

Problems with the monitors multiplied. For example, it soon became evident that they were seeking to perpetuate themselves beyond the one year of their court-appointed term. Next, it came to light that the monitors, apparently aware that the Teamsters now were a rather wealthy organization, if only because of their size, had been exacting extremely high administrative fees for performing their duties as overseers and buck-slipping recommendations to the provisional president.

Meanwhile, since I couldn't very well hire a public-relations outfit to set up a program of "Love Jimmy Hoffa" propaganda, I thought it wisest to ignore any slurs until the year was up and a new convention was held, when delegates, screened by the monitors, would conduct an election that couldn't be challenged. Patiently, the Teamsters General Executive Board waited for the year to end, then waited an additional sixty days, and then finally scheduled the convention for March, 1959. But the Executive Board was in for a surprise. They had called for a trump card from O'Donoghue and Schmidt. It wasn't long in being placed on the table, face up.

Schmidt petitioned the court to extend the period of monitor supervision (remember it was imposed by consent decree) on the ground that a fair convention was impossible until such time as the Teamsters could be purged of undesirable elements.

And what undesirable elements did Schmidt see? Why, Jimmy Hoffa. Judge Letts took a look at where Schmidt was pointing that righteous finger and, mindful of all those headlines, summarily ordered the convention postponed—indefinitely.

In the year that the Board of Monitors had served by court order it had taken out of the Teamster treasury more than $350,000 in fees. This money came from the dues of the rank and file the board was supposed to represent. In addition, Schmidt and O'Donoghue had claimed sums amounting to $210,000 as attorneys for the plaintiffs (the dissidents) plus expenses of more than $17,000.

I'll be frank. Give me a job where in a year I could take down that kind of money, and I'd be reluctant to see it end, too. I wonder if I could expect support from the courts though?

About this time Dan Maher filed his affadavit with the court to the effect that Chairman Martin O'Donoghue, who was supposed to be impartial, had stated that he intended to oust me from the presidency and the labor movement. Moreover, a little digging disclosed that O'Donoghue was using against me information he had gleaned from the Teamster files when he had represented the union.

We brought our case to the Court of Appeals.

The Landrum-Griffin Act had been passed in the meantime, and as the result of the genius—and I do mean genius—of our legislative counsel, Sidney Zagri, that law, intended to place restrictions on Labor, was used to free Labor from the supervision of the monitors.

Sidney Zagri, the Teamsters' legislative counsel, began an investigation of the monitors. Sid, who was not at that time particularly close to me, though later he became one of my dearest friends, was legislative counsel for the International, and as such he was a free agent, more or less, and not constrained to make himself accountable to a provisional president. His inquiries, however, led him to talk to numerous congressmen of his acquaintance, representatives of both parties and of all ideological persuasions.

He asked a simple question: If the Landrum-Griffin law had adequate provisions for protecting the rank and file of union membership from undemocratic practices, why should the Teamsters be denied the right to hold a convention and an election under the provisions of that law? There being no adequate answer to this question when it was whispered in several influential ears, the issue soon burst forth on the floors of Congress—in the Senate and in the House on the same day.

In the Senate two conservative Republicans—Senators Homer Capehart of Indiana and H. Styles Bridges of New Hampshire—and two liberal Democrats—Senators John Carroll of Colorado and Wayne Morse of Oregon—demanded an end to the Board of Monitors. In the House the representation was just as broad in demands for an end to the monitors, including Congressmen Abe Multer of New York, Jimmy Roosevelt of California, Elmer Holland of Pennsylvania, Frank Osmers of New Jersey, and John Shelley of California, the latter a Teamster who had opposed me in my election. Enough, they said. End the Board of Monitors.

We could only agree. For one thing the board was costing the Teamsters' treasury $700,000 a year, and this figured out as a charge of $2,500 a day. There were, at the time, 1,600,000 members of the union, each and every one of whom had a right to be upset with the way things had been managed by the outsiders.

Finally, therefore, as a result of the evidence uncovered by men such as Zagri and Maher, the Court of Appeals directed that the board be dissolved and a new convention be held. Although my term of office had not expired, I was ordered to stand again for election. We held the convention. I stood for election, or reelection. Again I won the election. This time, legal obstacles behind me, I was General President of the International Brotherhood of Teamsters.

Again, Kennedy had been betrayed—not by his peers, this time, but by one of his own "witnesses." He charged "dishonesty" and "betrayal" on the part of a New York milkwagon driver named John Cunningham who had started the law suit that resulted in the monitorship.

It seems pointless for me to insist that I had never met John Cunningham, that I had never even heard of him until his name appeared at the head of the list of the "thirteen insurgents," as Kennedy called them.

Kennedy wrote:

> By mid-1958 I began hearing rumors that John Cunningham had switched, that he was now siding with Hoffa. I couldn't believe that right under our very noses, Hoffa could take over the head of the "13" insurgents. . . .
>
> But there had been inducements. Since the middle of 1958, Jimmy Hoffa *and his union* had been paying some of John Cunningham's bills. [Italics added.]

No court case was involved. Kennedy's statements were not privileged testimony. Cunningham had been legally charged with nothing. But significantly, no one from any of the news media went to John Cunningham and asked him if the charges were true.

John Cunningham had done Kennedy's bidding. He had headed up the thirteen insurgents and had permitted his name to be used in challenging the authenticity of the election of his union's general president. This was his right. If, under persuasion, he had any question about it, it was his duty to challenge the results of the election.

Imagine his surprise when he picked up the newspapers

and read that the chief counsel of the McClellan committee had accused him of such perfidy as betrayal of the high ideals of his dozen fellow insurgents.

No one ever tried to prove the truth of Robert Kennedy's allegations about John Cunningham. Both John Cunningham and I wish they had tried to, for there was nothing whatsoever to the preposterous charge.

If John Cunningham did bolt from Kennedy's party line, it was because of widespread and mounting dissatisfaction with the monitors for their so-called administration of the International.

Strangely, Kennedy's written statement—an explanation of where and how he had been betrayed—made no reference to the decision by a federal court that the monitorship should be terminated or to the fact that thirty-one of the thirty-nine actions taken by the monitors were nullified by the Court of Appeals.

However, it is significant that Herbert Miller, who had been counsel to the monitors, was placed in charge of the criminal division of the Department of Justice and directed all subsequent prosecutions against me.

Perhaps it was at this point that I began to misjudge, to underestimate, Robert Francis Kennedy. It was foolish of me to do so. But it seemed that I had no reason to believe that the man had any degree of maturity, or that, aside from his spiteful forays, he could be considered seriously a Real Enemy, a danger to my person and my family as well as to my stewardship of a very important union.

His questioning of me in front of the McClellan committee had been painfully amateurish. It was ridiculously simple to get him to lose his temper. It was equally easy to get him to wander from the subject he was pursuing and to tie him up in knots of verbiage and dialectics.

The real danger for me lay in Kennedy's following in the press corps and among the major news and picture magazines. Though he threw out charge after charge against me, and though in time every one was proved false, he commanded towering respect among the editors and writers of such periodicals. He was an unfrocked press agent, on the grand order, and he played for the highest stakes in the land.

In time many were to join me in my analysis of Robert Kennedy as an amateur in the law. Not the least was William P. Rogers, a liberal Republican who had also served as a Senate investigator and was destined for higher responsibility. "Too amateurish to be useful in court," was his summary.

Well, Kennedy wasn't to remain an amateur for long. Before many months had passed he was in a position to hire the best legal minds in the country to do his bidding. As Attorney General he had no need to sully himself with the duties of the firing-line lawyer, or to be splashed by the mud of the investigator's quest. Yet I can make no better summary of Kennedy's type of activity than the one presented by Harold Gibbons, a member of the Teamsters General Executive Board, as a bill of particulars to the McClellan committee. *To this day it remains unchallenged.* No one has denied one single word of this statement:

It is interesting to see that in three years of investigation in connection with our union, reputed to be completely dominated by racketeers and hoodlums, one hundred and six names were mentioned.

We searched high and low for sixteen of these names and never found them among our union files or in any respect as being officials or in any way connected with the Teamsters.

Nine of these names we found to be members of the union who had never held any position other than as members. And, you well understand that if an employer hires a person we are obligated under the law to accept him into membership. . . .

We found that thirty-four of those mentioned were former

officers or employees but who were no longer associated with the Teamsters in any capacity.

We submitted the names of eight others who were officers or employees of the Teamsters who had been arrested but never convicted of a crime.

We submitted the names of twenty-six people who were officers, agents or employees, who were convicted of misdemeanors or felonies before employment by the Teamsters or election to office. Some of these [convictions] went back twenty years before the men became active in anything connected with the Teamsters.

We had thirteen who were convicted while officers or representatives of the union and were still so engaged. Among these thirteen were arrest records consisting of pleas of guilty to city ordinances relating to disorderly conduct or traffic violations. . . .

There were thirteen, as a total, who could be said to be law-breakers who were at the time we filed this report still members of the Teamsters and holding office. Out of a membership of more than 1,700,000, that's not a bad record. It seems to me that in a three-year investigation as widespread as it was, that to be able to come up with only thirteen violators [none of whom would be disqualified by the Landrum-Griffith Act] was a case of the mountain having labored and brought forth a mouse.

Perhaps a little perspective to the Kennedy exercise to which Gibbons refers might help.

Robert Francis Kennedy started as an assistant counselor during the McCarthy hearings. It was there he garnered his basic training. It was his first real job; his very first political job. When the public tide ran against McCarthy, Kennedy, at the urging of his older and wiser brother, adroitly sidestepped so that he might be free of taint.

Like so many, Robert Kennedy misjudged the public's ire at McCarthy. Kennedy thought that the public was upset because McCarthy was challenging the efficacy and acceptability of far-out liberals and Communists at a time when many Americans were unsure in their minds just how angry they wanted to be at the left or exactly how socialized they wanted to become in their own government and economy.

Instead, the public's resentment was directed against McCarthy's techniques of investigation, his inquisition-like questioning, his likeness to Torquemada, his flag-waving while denying the basic American rights to his victims.

Yet these were the very techniques that Kennedy employed against me and against the Teamsters.

I don't know how right or how wrong Senator Joseph McCarthy may have been. I was not one of his victims; I was not investigated by him. I do know this: Robert Francis Kennedy bettered McCarthy in spades, at his own game.

There was one difference: McCarthy didn't woo the masses.

18
Trial by Headline

Whether Robert Kennedy actually said that he "had the press in his pocket" is something that has never been decided. The statement was often attributed to him by people around my camp, but admittedly there was a great deal of prejudice in those precincts. Personally, I doubt that he ever said such a thing. I believe now that he was too smart to have done so. Yet the truth is that he *did* have a significant portion of the press sufficiently charmed to accept at face value many of the things he said—particularly when he made charges against me.

Kennedy had managed to convince a large portion of the public that if I was not actually a Mafia "family" chieftain, I was a Black Hand lieutenant who could, at will, command any type of mobilization from the Mafia that I wished. This would have been a humorous allegation to pin on a poor country boy of Yankee-Irish-Dutch ancestry, had it not been so widely accepted. It was accepted by many honest, law-abiding Americans as truth of Mt. Sinai quality, as though the facts pertaining thereto had been graven in granite and handed to Robert Kennedy for the ultimate benefit of all mankind.

There is, of course, small danger that anyone in the United States could so captivate the press as to become a threat to the national welfare. Most of our newspapers and news magazines guard the great American freedoms zealously. The American press, however, does love its heroes, particularly political heroes; it accords them great coverage and frequently also ascribes to them unquestioned veracity and towering wisdom.

Such a hero was Robert Kennedy. There may have been times when he wished for privacy, but since he was denied it by an ever alert press corps, he used headlines to his fullest advantage.

The American press also likes a villain. And when a Great Political Hero ferrets out a Scoundrelly Villain, it is delighted. Therefore, Kennedy, a hero, provided a villain: Jimmy Hoffa.

I would have felt easier about this arrangement had some influential quarters of the press taken more seriously the obligation of the Hero to prove the villainy of the Villain. It is one thing to throw out charges right and left; it is something else to prove them. And I submit that I was given such unfair treatment by some influential segments of the press as to throw into question the morality of the coverage. I chose at the time to believe that this biased coverage was an unwitting violation of the basic ethics of the free press. I supposed that some people in positions of influence and power, because of their connections with the press, were blinded by the reflected light of the shining armor they had placed on their hero knight. But certainly the press neglected to stand by their traditional insistence on fair and equal treatment.

Again and again, Robert Kennedy commanded huge headlines by charging me with some crime. Again and again his charges fizzled like fuseless firecrackers as soon as they reached the bar of justice. Yet when I was found innocent of the crime that Kennedy had charged me with, the headlines were much smaller. The charge would be emblazoned on page one. My innocence would be whispered on page thirty-six, months, sometimes years, later, when the charges were finally brought to court.

In this manner one clever man attempted to destroy my reputation. More than thirty times he charged me with offenses. More than thirty times I was found innocent of the crimes he ascribed to me. By the time he was through with me, most Americans believed I had been found guilty of some crime or another, and a vast majority of them were convinced I was a heel, or worse.

Few indeed, were the Americans who had never heard of Jimmy Hoffa in connection with some charge of crime or another. By the time we got to Nashville on the charges that Kennedy rigged—yes, *rigged,* and I'll prove it—it was almost impossible to select a panel of jurors that was not already prejudiced against me, if only because of the almost continuous stream of stories charging me with varying offenses over the previous few years.

In justice to the newspapers I should say that they could not ignore the chief counsel of an important Senate committee, or, as was later the case, the Attorney General of the United States, when he proclaimed that he would charge a labor leader with a specific crime. Such announcements are newsworthy and demand headlines. However, in writing what became traditional headlines, the copy editors were not always careful with the facts.

For example—one of many I could provide—Kennedy investigators uncovered evidence that some owners of Detroit laundries said that their trade association had collected some money—$17,500, to be specific—that was allegedly given to some high official in a Teamster local as a payoff to induce him to intervene in settling a labor dispute with the local.

This charge might have occupied the attention of the chief counsel of the McClellan committee charged with investigating improper labor practices. Kennedy must have been aware, however, that as many times as an investigation has uncovered a corrupt labor official who will take a payoff to settle a dispute, it has discovered an equal number of corrupt trade association officials who have *said* they need the payoff money for some mysterious, nameless person in the union who will settle the dispute and then have pocketed the proceeds.

Therefore, young Kennedy concentrated on trying to link me with the alleged crime, insisting that I had been the ultimate recipient of the $17,500. He also tried to show that I was a close friend of one Joe Holtzman, a labor-relations counselor retained by the laundry trade association and the man, apparently, to whom the money was paid. Holtzman was dead, so I faced the task of proving that while I knew *of* him, and would have recognized him, he was no particular friend.

Kennedy produced several witnesses from the laundries who all testified that they gave money to John Meissner and Howard Balkwill, both members of the laundry trade association.

On the stand Balkwill testified that the money was turned over to Holtzman. Period.

Nothing more.

"You believed that it would go to Mr. Hoffa?" Kennedy asked.

"Well, I wouldn't make that statement, either," answered Balkwill.

So let's summarize: There was not one shred of evidence, not one iota, to suggest that the money had gone to me.

On the contrary, there was testimony that it had not. *Yet Kennedy insisted that I had received the money.*

Next day, when I took the stand, this is how Kennedy began:

"There is a situation in this case, where, according to the testimony, no hearsay whatsoever but the sworn testimony of yesterday, there was a payment made of $17,500, a payoff, in order to get an intervention for a higher-up in the Teamsters Union. *Then you intervened.* Can you give us . . ."

I interrupted him to ask: "What does that mean?"

"Can you give us any more explanation of that?" Kennedy said.

I asked: "What does that *mean?* That I got the $17,500? Is that what you are insinuating? If you do, I did not get it."

"You did not get that money?" asked Kennedy in disbelief.

"And I deny under oath that I got it," I assured him.

"You did not get *any* of the money?"

"I did not," I replied.

There was nothing more that Kennedy could do, really. The laundry owners had testified they paid money to their trade association to get a dispute settled. The trade association people had testified they paid the money to Joe Holtzman, a labor-relations expert. Holtzman was dead. Not one witness even hinted that he had thought the money would have gone to me. Asked point blank if they thought the money went to me, they said they did not. Under oath I categorically denied that I had received the money.

Only one person thought the money went to me. That person was Robert Kennedy, who, again, didn't believe his own witnesses.

Given the activities in court, we were surprised, to say the least, to read the headline in the *Washington Post:*
"WITNESSES LINK HOFFA TO PAYOFF"

Here was an instance, repeated over and over again, where

Kennedy lost his case in court, even the rigged Star Chamber sessions of a special investigative committee, yet won it in the headline.

To the Americans who read that headline, Hoffa was guilty. Yet I was not, then or on other occasions.

19
Life Magazine's Role

We learned about Robert Kennedy's utilization of *Life* magazine's enormous influence (7,000,000 readers) from another whose scalp Kennedy was seeking, Roy Cohn, who, as chief counsel, had been Kennedy's boss when he was on the McCarthy committee. From all accounts, Cohn was another of Kennedy's obsessions. Cohn's conviction was slightly less important to him than the task of bagging my pelt.

In 1964, Roy Cohn was tried and acquitted on ten counts of perjury and obstruction of justice in relation to a stock-fraud case he had handled as attorney. His case, too, received bountiful headlines.

After securing an indictment against Cohn and before bringing him to trial, the Justice Department had ordered the Post Office Department to "cover" the mail of both Cohn and his lawyer, Thomas A. Bolan.

A "mail cover" is relatively unknown to the average American, who believes that his mail is his private business and that his privacy is held sacred by the government. But when a mail cover is ordered, postal clerks record the names and addresses on all letters sent or received by the subject.

Through sheer accident, Bolan learned that his mail was being covered. Further inquiry disclosed that Cohn's was, too. Bolan went to court to get the cover stopped. Federal Judge Archie Dawson issued an order enjoining Attorney Robert Morgenthau of New York, son of Henry Morgenthau, from continuing the mail cover. The judge called it a shocking invasion of privacy. But the incident served to alert Cohn to the fact that the Justice Department might resort to other tricks of dubious morality.

In thinking about some of the dirty tricks that might be pulled on him, Cohn gave some thought to an extremely unflattering article about him that had appeared in a recent issue of *Life* magazine. He wondered if the Justice Department might even have had some hand in it. Seeking substantiation of their suspicions, Cohn and Bolan subpoenaed the magazine's files.

There, filed away from what might have been its role in posterity, was a memo from *Life* staffer Henry Suydam, a friend of Robert F. Kennedy, to his managing editor, E. K. Thompson. It was marked "Personal and Confidential" and read:

> Last Saturday I got a phone call from Bob Kennedy asking if I could drop whatever I was doing and come to his office. I did, and when I got there he closed the door and told me the following: in a back room was a high official of the Teamsters, a man who had been privy to the inner workings of the organization since 1953. He was particularly knowledgeable about Hoffa. This official is honest, said Kennedy, and also quite an idealist. The man had been working directly with Kennedy and in secret for the last 2 years. He was now so disillusioned and disgusted with the corruption he saw all about him, particularly as concerns Hoffa, that he had just about decided to make a public break with the union. Kennedy said he had suggested to this man that he make his break via an article in Life in the form of a personal exposé of Hoffa. Kennedy asked my personal word that for the mo-

ment only you and I would know of this matter. Kennedy feels, perhaps melodramatically, perhaps not, that the man's life would be in danger if word leaked out of his intentions.

Who was this mysterious high-ranking Teamster official lurking in the back room behind Kennedy's office in the Justice Department?

His name was Sam Baron, a seasoned, battle- and bottle-scarred veteran of more than thirty years in the labor movement. Sam had lost his fight with whiskey. I had threatened to fire him several times because of his intemperance and subsequent irresponsibility while under the influence. I had given him notice that his only chance to remain in the union was to remain sober.

Sam was a Socialist, a sincere and devoted one. He had fought with the Republican forces during the Spanish Civil War. He had been captured by General Franco's Nationalists and been sentenced to death by the firing squad. In fact, he would have met that fate had not American Socialist leader Norman Thomas intervened on his behalf.

Sam had spent eight years with the Teamsters and had risen to the position of Field Director in the Warehouse Division. He knew that I was antipathetic to the Socialists and was inclined, rather, to be an activist on behalf of the private-enterprise system. He opposed my candidacy for the presidency, and when I was elected, he decided he had had enough of the Teamsters.

Did he resign? Did he look for another job?

No. According to Kennedy, Sam went to him and volunteered to disclose all of his intimate knowledge of the internal affairs of the Teamsters, with special emphasis on the operations of the General President.

Perhaps Sam thought he would save his job, but however Kennedy and Baron got together, *Life* was interested in the story. In another memorandum sent to managing editor Thompson a few days after the first memo was dispatched *Life*-man Suydam wrote:

> I told Kennedy of your interest and he is delighted. He makes the suggestion that the piece go into Baron's background, and philosophy somewhat, to help explain his disgust with Hoffa and his motivation for breaking with the Teamsters. Kennedy believes deeply that this is not a case of "sour grapes," but of a man acting out of conscience and principle. Kennedy thinks the break will be understood in light of his total life in the labor movement.

In other records uncovered with these memoranda Suydam disclosed to his editor that he met Baron in a back room in Kennedy's office and that Kennedy slipped them outside through back corridors and had them driven in a roundabout route to Baron's home in Virginia, where the initial interview took place. To comply with what Suydam described as a "cloak-and-dagger shift of scenery," the code name of "Brown" was bestowed on the reporter by Kennedy.

From the memoranda it is learned that Baron told Suydam that I rigged the Teamster election that won me the general presidency. Having made the charge, Baron apparently failed to provide any proof of this or even shreds of documentation that might be followed up in the hot pursuit of my scalp.

Suydam tried to be charitable to Baron and Kennedy, but his instincts as a newsman made him doubtful of the value of what he was told during the interview.

"The exposé stuff sounds interesting," he wrote to his editor, "but to me at least, pretty undocumentable and therefore probably very libelous. But the more personal stuff, on what Hoffa is like and how he behaves, sounds pretty good."

I do not intend to find fault with Suydam for believing there was a story in the situation as it was unfolded before him by Kennedy and Baron. His obligation was to his readers and to that elusive commodity called news. He smelled a newsy piece. Nor can anyone find anything sinister or improper in Thompson's decision to publish Baron's story. Like his man on the scene, he had an obligation to his readers and to the selection of a newsy, reader-attracting story.

But the fact is there would not have been anything noteworthy about the story at all had it not been for two facts:

1. Baron's "inside story" of goings-on at Teamster headquarters with its not-quite-libelous insinuations that I was up to no good appeared in July, 1962, about midway between the time I was indicted on charges brought by Kennedy that I had accepted more than $1 million in illegal payments from a Detroit trucker and my scheduled trial. (I was exonerated when the court finally called a mistrial.)

2. As Attorney General, Robert F. Kennedy had initiated the charges against me and was the chief prosecutor. Yet in his role as Attorney General he had caused Baron—by his own admission a planted *agent provocateur* and "spy" in my office—to tell his story to influential *Life* magazine when I was facing the bar of justice.

I don't ask anyone to judge my innocence or guilt—after all, the court settled that. I only ask that the reader judge for himself the conduct of the foremost legal authority of the nation and decide whether it was ethical or even legal.

Even if I was a criminal—which I am not—there is a vast army of law-enforcement officials and a mighty legal machine to bring me to justice. There are men enough and laws enough to bring ten thousand criminals before the bar when they break the law. But who is there to see that justice is done when the chief legal official of the United States of America, the Attorney General himself, stretches and bends and perhaps breaks the law?

With Suydam's memoes in our possession, we wondered what action to take. How do you take criminal action against the Attorney General? It might be possible, but such action is scarcely for a labor leader who is himself in the public eye—particularly for a labor leader who has been pictured as a scoundrel.

Nor is it very smart when you have the Attorney General, who also happens to be the President's brother, after you, deliberately to pick a fight with one of the most influential magazines in the country. Kennedy represented *Power*. Power, as most people recognize, has little concern with justice. I am willing to make reasonable gestures like a Don Quixote, but not to the extent of taking on such a combination.

Therefore, at the advice of Sid Zagri we held onto the Suydam memoranda until the 1964 Republican National Convention convened in San Francisco. Then Sid went before the platform committee and urged adoption of a plank calling for a congressional investigation of the Attorney General's tactics and denouncing "government snooping." He cited the mail cover, the wiretapping, the electronic bugging, the planting of spies, and, of course, the manipulation of the *Life* piece by the Attorney General himself, "to influence litigation against James R. Hoffa."

A month later Sid went to the Democratic National Convention in Atlantic City and repeated his request for a platform plank.

The Democrats listened, smiled, did nothing. The Republicans inserted the plank after much discussion. They called for an investigation.

No one is ever sure what will happen in an election so, when the Republican plank was publicized, the Democratic strategists decided it would be prudent to beat the GOP to the punch.

Accordingly, the House Judiciary committee voted twenty to thirteen to see if the Justice Department had invaded any constitutional rights of any citizens. It named no names, cited no possible victims.

The inquiry would be made, it was decided, by an ad hoc committee. The committee was appointed and its chairman announced: Representative Emanuel Celler, a Brooklyn Democrat, a dedicated and devoted Kennedy man. Celler had voted against holding the investigation, and his steward-ship of the committee was unblemished. There were no hear-ings; there was no inquiry; there was not even a meeting.

Not until six months later, when Roy Cohn and Tom Bolan were making a fuss over judicial invasion of their privacy, did a Senate Administrative Practices subcommittee take a look into any aspect of federal violations of the right to privacy.

During the investigation Cohn and Bolan placed in the record the Suydam memoranda and revealed how they came into their possession. When they did so, the committee's chairman, Senator Edward V. Long, a Missouri Democrat, said, "It is obvious that the Department of Justice was attempting to try cases out of court. For me this is a serious charge."

By now a senator, Kennedy appeared on the following day to state that he resented the inquiry and challenged the propriety of allowing the implication that "I had done something improper as Attorney General." He charged that he was being tried by the press.

Moreover, Senator Long, who later had his own personal troubles with the Justice Department and his problems with *Life* magazine, failed to give Robert Kennedy the senatorial club membership treatment and actually inquired into the matter.

Yet despite the evidence of the Suydam memoranda, the authenticity of which was unchallenged, Kennedy denied that the idea for the Baron article originated with him. He had merely brought Baron and Suydam together for the first interview, he said.

Then Kennedy challenged credulity by stating that the original intent—"agreement," he called it—was to refrain from publishing the Baron article unless "something happened" to Baron. This implied, of course, that those sinister forces in the Teamsters were intending to snuff out the life of this patriot who had resigned from the union and run to the Justice Department for help, and the Justice Department was worried that it would be unable to shield him from the wrath of that ogre, Jimmy Hoffa.

In vain the committee looked for evidence to substantiate this amazing statement. Kennedy had no supporting evidence to offer. He settled for an imperious "You have the testimony I have just given here." When the committee pointed out that it had only his word on a matter of conflicting testimony, Kennedy stalked out, declaring: "I have made a statement on this. I have given you full information."

So much for the national watchdog. So much for the watchers who watch the watchers.

20

The Relentless Adversary

Until the Test Fleet case—more on that in Chapter 22— came along Robert Kennedy lost his cases against me in court but won them in the headlines with frankly jaundiced copy, such as the Baron piece in *Life*. And yet the more cases he lost, the more determined he seemed to collect my scalp for his warbelt.

The frustration showed in his waspish badgering of witnesses. A lesser personage, an ordinary member of the bar, would have been before his peers for explanation, but Kennedy's tactics were seldom questioned.

An example of Kennedy's badgering technique comes readily to mind: his purely punitive treatment of Joseph F. Glimco, head of a Teamster local in Chicago. It was obvious that Kennedy didn't like Glimco, as he later indicated in his book, *The Enemy Within,* and, also, that in the hearing room he couldn't disguise his feelings (Glimco didn't help matters by persistently seeking the shelter of the Fifth Amendment). But fairness still required proper treatment of witnesses—treatment not accorded Glimco, as the following excerpt from the transcript from the McClellan committee hearing to which he was summoned makes clear:

Mr. Kennedy: And you defraud the union?

Mr. Glimco: I respectfully decline to answer because I honestly believe my answer might tend to incriminate me.

> *Mr. Kennedy*: I would agree with you.
>
> *The Chairman*: I believe it would.
>
> *Mr. Kennedy*: You haven't got the guts to answer, have you, Mr. Glimco?
>
> *Mr. Glimco*: I respectfully decline to answer . . .
>
> *The Chairman*: Morally you are kind of yellow inside, are you not?

Kennedy's actions in this respect caused Alexander Bickel, noted law professor at Yale, to write, in the *New Republic:* "The Committee . . . with Mr. Kennedy in the lead . . . embarked on a number of purely punitive expeditions." Bickel accused Kennedy of "relentless, vindictive battering of witnesses."

Joseph Rauh, the former chairman of the Americans for Democratic Action, seeking to justify Kennedy's efforts to rip the blindfold from the eyes of Lady Justice argued:

> Any abuses were not due to vindictiveness, but to his [Kennedy's] lack of experience. If it sometimes led to abuse of witnesses, it sometimes led to witnesses like Hoffa getting away with murder. . . . Far from browbeating Hoffa, it was more a case of Hoffa browbeating him.

But surely every lawyer in America at one time or another suffers from lack of experience? Never before, to my knowledge, has the immaturity of a prosecutor been deemed an excuse for throwing away the rules of ethics and jurisprudence. Even the remarkable Edward Bennett Williams was once an inexperienced lawyer, and, to my knowledge, no one granted him special courtroom privileges allowing him to abuse witnesses. Neither in surgery nor in law do the professionals make allowances for unprofessionalism.

Rauh was obviously alluding to a sequence in the transcript of the McClellan committee hearings that has since become quite well known, having been reprinted numerous times. The occasion took place when Kennedy lost his temper with me for engaging in a fencing match on the stand. He was pursuing some point about my alleged purchase of some pocket-size miniature tape recorders called Minifons:

> *Mr. Hoffa*: What did I do with them? Well, what did I do with them?
>
> *Mr. Kennedy*: What did you do with them?
>
> *Mr. Hoffa*: I am trying to recall.
>
> *Mr. Kennedy*: You could remember that.
>
> *Mr. Hoffa*: When were they delivered? Do you know? That must have been quite a while.
>
> *Mr. Kennedy*: You know what you did with the Minifons and don't ask me.
>
> *Mr. Hoffa*: What *did* I do with them? [Italics mine.]
>
> *Mr. Kennedy*: What did you do with them?
>
> *Mr. Hoffa*: Mr. Kennedy, I bought some Minifons and there is no question about it, but I cannot recall what became of them. I have to stand on the answers that I have made in regards to my recollection and I cannot answer unless you give me some recollection, other than I have answered.

The record shows that Kennedy then turned to other matters, with about the same results.

Personally I thought even more humorous was the testimony given by Barney Baker, a huge man whom Bobby sought to link with the underworld and ultimately, of course, with the Teamsters. The official transcript of Baker's "day in court" reads thus:

> *Mr. Kennedy*: Did you know Cockeye Dunne?
>
> *Mr. Baker*: I didn't know him as Cockeye Dunne. I knew him as John Dunne.
>
> *Mr. Kennedy*: Where is he now?
>
> *Mr. Baker*: He has met his Maker.

Mr. Kennedy: How did he do that?

Mr. Baker: I believe through electrocution in the city of New York in the state of New York.

Mr. Kennedy: What about Squinty Sheridan? Did you know him?

Mr. Baker: Andrew Sheridan, sir?

Mr. Kennedy: Yes.

Mr. Baker: He has also met his Maker.

Mr. Kennedy: How did he die?

Mr. Baker: With Mr. John Dunne.

It must be remembered that the chief counsel had never given anyone reason to believe he had even an ounce of humor. He was deadly serious at all times.

For all the fireworks before the McClellan committee, Chief Counsel Robert F. Kennedy's assignment during the hearings was straightforward enough and clearly understood. Yet he botched it. He was supposed to prove the need for new legislation to provide recourse under the law for all persons involved in organized Labor—employer, employee, and union member—where such recourse did not exist. Every man who believes he has been subjected to unlawful conduct has a right to his day in court and to immediate relief from the court. These are fundamentals of American law, yet Congress, in enacting its patchwork, multifaceted labor legislation—some laws designed to protect organized Labor, some calculated to protect the employer, some intended to preserve the rights of all workers— had seemingly removed the right of legal recourse from all parties concerned.

In any case, whether or not the right of legal recourse had been removed was not shown, because Robert Kennedy, pulling McClellan along with him, got involved in a vendetta with me, a political fence-building campaign with the AFL–CIO, and a vote-garnering, image-building, anti-

Labor posture for the benefit of Southern voters. The goal, the house at 1600 Pennsylvania Avenue, was more important to Kennedy and to some members of the committee he served than was the need to spend time considering the grievances, real or imagined, of thousands of employers and millions of employees.

It was of prime importance to Kennedy to "Get Hoffa" and achieve the remarkable feat of winning the adulation of the AFL–CIO, including Reuther's UAW, while at the same time gaining the endorsement and admiration of the reactionary, anti-Labor voters of the nation.

In this latter task Kennedy was successful. He did not, however, fulfill his ostensible assignment—nor, apparently, did he ever try to. Perhaps the moral of the story is that politics and the law make unwholesome and dangerous bedfellows.

Robert Kennedy was lusting for power when he conducted his investigation of organized Labor. The investigation, per se, meant little to him. The point was to win. The immediate purpose was to get Hoffa and create a reputation as a crusading leader who was so fair-minded he could endorse one segment of organized Labor while condemning another —an unbeatable vote-getting combination.

Consequently, as his prime target, pocked and scarred by the fire and brimstone he spewed about him, I dealt Kennedy a severe blow when, in mid-investigation, I was elected General President. And it was against the background of political intrigue and manipulation of the nation's laws that I delivered my acceptance speech to the Teamsters.

21

Drums Along the Potomac

I'm not sure when it dawned on me that Robert Kennedy was out for my scalp, and mine alone, and was not the slightest bit interested in ridding Labor of rackets and racketeers, even if the latter task was his professed purpose. It came more as a gradual realization, I guess. Slowly things began to add up. What conclusion could I draw from the fact that while he filled the air and the airways with accusations of wrongdoings in many areas of Labor, he used his investigative forces and the enormous borrowed power of the Senate to mount a concentrated probe of the Teamsters and myself? That while he would open a can of worms with yarns about goons and brutality and police collaboration with union enforcers, he would foul the air with such stories only briefly, then quickly close the cover and go back to the obsessive theme of getting Hoffa?

Kennedy had unlimited power of subpoena and could—by his own statements—have uncovered some sordid stories, the exposure of which would have been redounded to the ultimate benefit of the rank and file, but he did not do so unless it could relate in some way, however remotely, to the Teamsters or, preferably, to me, personally. In fact, I may state categorically that Kennedy deliberately suppressed some of the unwholesome details the inquiries disclosed in other areas of Labor.

Take the case of one employer who asked to be heard before the committee. He told of being approached by union officials who told him he had to "join" the union for all of the employers in his chain of restaurants. When he refused, he was subjected to all manner of harassment. He related tales of tacks in his parking lot, of sugar in the gas tanks of cars parked there, of his employees' being followed home and forced off the highway.

The Teamsters only entered the picture through the back door, as it were: the union with which the restaurateur had a dispute threw up a picket line, and truck drivers refused to cross it. As a result, garbage piled up, and the owner had to remove it himself. But he quickly learned that the municipal authorities wouldn't allow him to dump his garbage where the rest of the town refuse was disposed of. He had to truck it to a neighboring town.

When he asked for police help, he got none. When he appealed to the state police to protect a truckload of foodstuffs coming from a distant city, he learned that someone in the governor's office had instructed the police to stay away from the case.

Did Kennedy pursue the story? Did he subpoena the people in the governor's office who had ordered the police not to give protection to a grieving citizen? Did he bring to the witness stand the authorities in the town who had closed the town dump to a local restaurant owner? Did he even ask the NLRB for a report on the case? No, he did not.

His "broad" inquiry into organized Labor was only as broad as the Teamsters Union.

The truth is that Kennedy was afraid to probe deeper. All of organized Labor would have descended on him had he done so. And that would not have been prudent, for at the very time that the Senate Labor Rackets committee was holding hearings, Robert Kennedy's brother, John Kennedy, was formulating political plans that called for the fullest possible support he could get from organized labor— with the exception of the Teamsters, that union having been made the sacrificial lamb needed to insure support from the labor-haters of the nation.

Thus Robert Kennedy's strategy was political from the outset. Later it became criminal.

Yes, criminal, for evidence shows that the Attorney General of the United States bugged my living quarters, my meeting quarters, tapped my telephones, planted a spy in my camp, and, by eavesdropping, deliberately violated the sanctity of my relationship with my lawyers.

That is not merely unethical. That is a crime.

But the criminal aspects concerned me later. At the time only the blatant political sham of the investigation troubled me.

With hindsight it is possible to know now that the Kennedy brothers were altering course and heading from the right-wing reaction of Irish-Catholic Boston to some middle-of-the-road never-never land decreed as the only acceptable battleground for America's national candidates. As a delegate from Massachusetts, John Kennedy had been actively anti-Labor, in keeping with his background and lace-curtain heritage. When the unions, united under one flag, were battling to kill the Taft-Hartley legislation on the ground that it was a "slave-labor law," John Kennedy, a congressman, surprised no one by writing a separate minority report calling for a remarkably inappropriately named "Labor Bill of Rights," which would have made Taft-Hartley infinitely tougher on organized Labor. Of course, Kennedy was thinking only of his constituency, then, and Robert Kennedy was not yet on the scene. By 1957–1958, however, the young senator from Massachusetts had raised his sights much higher than a mere congressional district, and it became necessary not only to mend fences with Labor but to enunciate a wholly changed attitude.

In retrospect, therefore, it is not the least curious that Robert Kennedy, Chief Counsel of the Senate Labor Rackets Investigating committee, flatly refused, on more than one occasion, to investigate the UAW or Walter Reuther.

I am not saying that something could have been found had Robert Kennedy probed the UAW. I am merely commenting on the remarkable circumstances that the chief counsel for a committee charged specifically with conducting an inquiry into unlawful practices in Labor refused categorically to take even a cursory look at one of the largest, richest, and most prominent unions, the leader of which was by all odds the most politically influential man in the ranks of organized Labor.

To my mind Kennedy's constant refusal to investigate the UAW is crystal-clear proof that the McClellan committee inquiry was a politically rigged scheme, hatched, probably, at Hyannisport and brought to fulfillment by the expenditure of vast sums of taxpayers' money. In my opinion it was part and parcel of one of the grandest political coups in modern times.

When queried about the UAW, Robert Kennedy told reporters that he was convinced that the UAW was honest. Anyway, he told reporters, the UAW had already been investigated. Why do it all over again?

Some enterprising reporters answered that last question. First, when the UAW had last been investigated, there was testimony about violence, disregard for members' rights, and corruption. Walter Reuther had even published a blacklist of his enemies within the union. Second, the Teamsters, also, had been investigated before. Why "do it all over again"?

And, then, there was the matter of the Kohler Company

of Kohler, Wisconsin—closed tight in a protracted dispute with the UAW. Kennedy explained that he had sent Vern Johnson, one of his staff investigators, to Kohler to look into the matter, and that Johnson had reported back that there was nothing new to add to information already at hand. There was nothing, Kennedy insisted, to warrant an investigation.

Gradually, it became apparent to Republican members of the committee that Kennedy was engaged in a grand whitewash. Therefore, at the insistence of the Republican minority on the committee, Kennedy assigned Republican staffer Jack McGovern to make a preliminary study of the UAW.

For this titanic job, Kennedy assigned one investigator to assist McGovern. For his investigation of the Teamsters, Kennedy called on the full-time services of 91 staff employees plus 158 people from the General Accounting Office. In addition, of course, services of the Internal Revenue Service, Justice Department, FBI, Treasury Department, Department of Labor, Federal Bureau of Narcotics, and Naturalization Service were frequently used.

During 1957–1958 the committee held a total of 207 days of hearings while investigating the Teamsters. It listened to the testimony of 1,033 witnesses. It filed 35,408 pages of testimony. Yet one investigator and an assistant were deemed by Kennedy to be sufficient to probe the UAW.

Nor was the difference between the two approaches to the UAW and the Teamsters the extent of Kennedy's forging of a double standard: at the same time that he assigned Jack McGovern to investigate the UAW, he also assigned his trusted prober, Carmine Bellino, and a sizable squad of assistants to prepare a response to McGovern's expected report, designed to be flattering to the UAW.

Ultimately, try to wave it off as he could, Kennedy had

to give in to the mounting pressure for some form of
equalization in the investigation of organized Labor. Eventually, therefore, he thought it prudent to visit Sheboygan,
Wisconsin, home base of Kohler, with a brace of investigators, so that he might be able to respond, with his own firsthand report, to the snowballing criticism.

I didn't know much then about the Kohler strike, and I
don't to this day. I had read that about one-third of the 3,300
Kohler workers had voted to strike in 1954, and I had seen
the newspaper accounts of violence and terror and the
stories of goons being brought onto the scene by the UAW.
The UAW says it had about a dozen men on the scene; some
who claim to be eyewitnesses put the number nearer a
hundred. The UAW also admitted that it spent over $10
million on the strike, a remarkable sum considering its
vested stake in the local union. But as I say, I don't know
the details.

In any case, Robert Kennedy visited the scene. He found
that he didn't like the company officials he talked to. They
seemed very bitter, he said. They were very angry at the
UAW. He especially liked the union officials and the union
workers he found at strike headquarters. They were angry
but not bitter, he said.

This concluded his survey of the scene. He found nothing worthy of investigation, he reported when he returned
to Washington.

In time, of course, the UAW was brought before the
committee to answer questions about the Kohler strike and
also about the Perfect Circle strike, another UAW dispute.
And the resulting testimony is full of items that show how
Senator John Kennedy was cottoning up to Walter Reuther
and the UAW.

For example, when a UAW employee had testified that he
had had to give five dollars a week in kickbacks to the union

(over and above his dues) for a "flower fund," and that—
it was hearsay evidence, it's true—some union members had
been obliged to contribute as much as forty-three dollars
a week to the fund, Senator John F. Kennedy commented:
"It seems that if you are going to partake of the loaves and
the fishes that you have to contribute something to maintain
the organization. It seems to me that if you did not like it
you should have worked someplace else."

Now, doggone, if that isn't what *I* had said right along.
But, somehow, when it came to Teamsters, the same principle didn't apply. The Kennedy double standard was as
acceptable as oolong tea at a lawn party when applied to us.

One of the more outrageous double standards maintained
by Robert Kennedy and the McClellan committee concerned wiretapping. One of the charges brought against me
was that I had put taps on the phones of some of the officers
in the Detroit office. Indeed, it was alleged that I hired
Johnny Dio, a New York hoodlum, to do the bugging.

The first trial ended in a hung jury; the second terminated with my acquittal. But the way the Kennedy investigators learned about the bugs in Detroit, it was testified,
was by tapping my phone lines.

Thus, according to Robert Kennedy's principles, it would
have been illegal for me to have bugged phones in my own
offices—to learn, perhaps, whether my subordinate officials
of the local were engaged in any corrupt practices—yet it
was perfectly legal for his probers, as minions above and
beyond the law, to tap wherever they might wish.

I became seriously concerned, and not only about myself,
when I learned that Kennedy had tapped my phones and
had retained as a permanent staffer Edward "Second Story"
Jones, one of the outstanding experts in the installation and
use of electronic listening and eavesdropping devices.

"It's just like Big Brother is watching," I commented to

one of my associates, referring to George Orwell's book. "Only this time it's Little Brother watching," he replied.

Edward Bennett Williams wasn't amused. "You can't tap wires with one hand and prosecute wiretappers with the other," he said.

Many may have forgotten, but Pierre Salinger made his start with the Kennedys by serving as an investigator on Robert Kennedy's McClellan committee staff. Salinger's record didn't impress me. He came in with one "earth-shaker." The wife of a truck driver reported that her husband had come home with an abbreviated pay envelope each week because he was obliged to kick back some of his earnings to his union agent, a Teamster.

Salinger presented this evidence to Kennedy. Then the driver himself came in and sheepishly asked for a chance to explain. He had been keeping a mistress, he admitted, and had found her rather expensive. The story of the kickback was an invention designed to prevent his wife from suspecting where the money was really going.

At least Salinger presented Kennedy with another lead to lodge yet another charge against me. I could have been accused of contributing to the delinquency of the driver by *allowing* these affairs to go on in the union. It would have made as much sense as some of the other charges, but Kennedy missed the opportunity.

I did not spend all of my time fending off Robert Kennedy, though there was enough fending to do to take up all my days and nights. Indeed, despite the distractions created by the chief counselor, the Teamsters grew steadily in membership. This was not a good time for organized Labor. Other unions lost membership almost as steadily as we gained it. Membership in the UAW was declining at the very time that Kennedy was making his "investigation" of that union and of Reuther. Union membership dropped,

too, among the steelworkers and among the electricians—
the latter at the time that the electrical and electronic industries were growing in giant leaps.

Teamsters' wages continued to grow, too. We had some
catching up to do, and wage increases for Teamsters ex-
ceeded the rate for all other industries. Moreover, I pressed
for areawide labor contracts, working ever closer to the goal
of a nationwide bargaining agreement.

I was creating a change in the structure of one of the
oldest unions in organized Labor, as well as the largest.
The International Brotherhood of Teamsters was a sprawling, entrenched, smug, and traditionally functioning organization, and its executives in a great many areas couldn't see
where changes were going to be beneficial. What turned
the trick, ultimately, was the minimum of three dollars an
hour for over-the-road drivers. Meantime, however, much
persuading had to be done. Each contract had to win improved conditions for drivers.

It took time; it took great effort; it took much planning—
especially since, at first, I was working under the sufferance
of the Board of Monitors. And when the Court of Appeals
did away with the monitors, my problems still were just
beginning.

Robert Francis Kennedy had not been idle. His determination to bring an end to Jimmy Hoffa never flagged,
though he was, by this time, caught up in the much loftier
intrigues of getting his brother into position to be nominated at the 1960 convention.

I was fully aware that Robert Kennedy considered my
scalp as a most politically profitable talisman to bring to
the convention and, if successful there, before the people of
America. I knew this, and Kennedy knew that I knew it,
and we both girded for a fight.

You can never beat City Hall, the old saying goes. Well,

I had no choice but to try, and I feared, as the monitors were removed and I was placed on my own to be judged by my peers, my fellow Teamsters, that far from a joust with City Hall, my battle would be with the White House itself.

It was a heck of a situation for a boy from Brazil, Indiana, to find himself in. I could virtually feel, as well as see, the storm clouds gathering.

22

If at First You Don't Succeed . . .*

Three times Robert Kennedy had sought to have the federal government place me behind bars. Three times he had failed. The bribery case had ended in acquittal. The wiretapping case, when first tried, had ended in a hung jury. On Kennedy's second attempt at the wiretapping case, I had been acquitted.

These were personal defeats for Kennedy because he had made them personal issues. He had made it his personal crusade. He had boasted of his iron-clad case. If his defeats were humiliating, it was because he had staged the show.

There can be no doubt, however, that his failures, heightened as they were by his own advance publicity, intensified his bitterness against me and reinforced his determination to get me, one way or another.

Each time Kennedy dug into some situation that seemed to him to offer a chance to institute proceedings against me, he acted as though he had just caught me with my hand in the till in the dark of night. That may be why I wasn't

*Because of the complexity of the Nashville and Chattanooga trials, I have prepared a list, called "The Cast," which can be found in the Appendix. Readers who become confused by the various characters involved may like to refer to the list from time to time. If they do need to do so, they will have my sympathy; I was confused myself often enough.

too concerned when in May, 1962, Kennedy arranged to
have me indicted in Nashville, Tennessee, on charges of
accepting payments from an employer in violation of the
Taft-Hartley Act.

I had made no attempt to cover up what I had been doing
in Nashville, simply because I did not consider it illegal or
unethical. Therefore I responded with only slight annoy-
ance when the indictment was handed down. The same
matter had been investigated by a grand jury in Detroit, and
that jury had found nothing wrong. To me the Nashville
indictment was just another obstacle to overcome, another
brush with the nettles and thistles that Kennedy persisted
in planting in my garden.

But one should never underestimate his foe. I did, with
Kennedy. It was a costly mistake.

The facts of the case were these.

I and a friend and associate, fellow-Teamster Owen Bert
Brennen, had set up a truck-leasing firm called Test Fleet,
Incorporated. For tax purposes Test Fleet was jointly owned
by our wives, in their maiden names, Josephine Poszywak
and Alice Johnson.

Test Fleet leased or rented equipment to Commercial
Carriers, Incorporated, a Detroit company specializing in
hauling new cars from factory to dealer. Commercial Carriers employees were represented by the Teamsters. The
government's contention, of course, was that Commercial
Carriers *had* to do business with Test Fleet or suffer some
labor troubles. Not that Commercial Carriers had already
suffered from labor disputes or problems. The point was
that labor troubles *would* result, or *might* ensue, if Commercial Carriers didn't do business with Test Fleet.

If the government wanted to test the efficacy of this line
of reasoning, it would merely have had to induce Commercial Carriers to cease doing business with Test Fleet to
see what would happen. Kennedy, however, apparently

didn't think this course of action necessary, because his investigators told him they had found witnesses who would testify that Commercial Carriers was afraid not to do business with Test Fleet.

I'm not a lawyer, but the whole exercise in logic seemed ridiculous to me at the time. It still does. There are many other leasing firms. Commercial Carriers, if dissatisfied with Test Fleet, could have leased from another outfit. If Test Fleet was pressuring Commercial, surely one of the other leasing companies would have raised a stink you could have smelled from coast to coast. Since Test Fleet didn't do its own trucking business or in any other way become involved with the Teamsters, I just couldn't see where there was a conflict of interest. Leasing trucking equipment to truckers was no more ominous, to me, than, say, selling gasoline to truckers or selling cigarettes to truck drivers.

Can an executive in General Motors invest his savings in a gas station? I know several pharmacists and doctors who own stocks in drug-manufacturing companies, and no one complains. I even know of a doctor who owns an interest in an undertaking establishment, and it is likely that some of his patients have ultimately become patrons of the funeral parlor, but no one has ever suggested that he has deliberately created business for the latter.

At any rate, Kennedy thought he had a case. He had, in the interim, become the Attorney General of the United States, though his qualifications were not highly regarded in the legal profession. He had not distinguished himself well on either the McCarthy or the McClellan committees. He was known to be a poor courtroom lawyer, who badgered witnesses, lost his temper, and allowed himself to be sidetracked by unexpected responses from those he was questioning. As the chief litigant for the Republic, he was thought to be lacking in many qualities.

One thing, however, he had or acquired: good advice. Someone must have cautioned him about his sloppily prepared cases, as well as his need to establish himself as a man of stature in the law.

Accordingly, Kennedy set a small regiment of Justice Department lawyers to work on the case. It was said that at one time more than 150 experts were hard at work at the myriad tasks of preparing a major presentation for a federal court. The preparation, according to those who worked on the case, as well as my own lawyers who defended it, was nothing short of spectacular and meticulous. Given the tools and manpower to work with and the unlimited resources of the United States of America to finance him, plus the enormous power of his office, and bolstered by his unique fraternal superpower in the White House, Robert Kennedy proved he could present a case of Herculean proportions. Much less preparation went into the prosecution of some of mankind's hyper-enemies when they were brought to trial in Nuremberg. No traitor or spy ever tried in the United States had stood in the dock with the government so well prepared to stretch his neck.

As the trial opened, all I could think of was some of those old Mississippi River melodramas where the spoiled young scion, having lost all his cash to the riverboat gambler, places the deed to the plantation on the card table and risks his all on the next hand. The analogy wasn't quite complete, for Kennedy wasn't really risking much. Still he had an awful lot to gain if he won.

If he won. He didn't win, though.

The trial lasted two months. I've wondered recently why it took so long, dragged on so. In the end, there was a hung jury. A mistrial was declared.

There had been a vote for acquittal. Most of the jurors felt the government had failed to prove any case. The vote had been seven to five for acquittal when the deadlock occurred. Knowing there would be a mistrial with such a vote, the seven gave up their struggle for acquittal and let it go at that.

I was willing to let it go at that, too. I had had enough of courtrooms and trials and lawyers and witness stands.

I wanted to go home, to see Jo and the kids, to spend two days fishing and tramping the woods.

Then I wanted to get back to Washington and immerse myself in the affairs of the Teamsters. There was much to be done.

I honestly believed that Kennedy might feel the same way. I thought he had had enough. After all, this was the fourth case he had brought against me. It was the fourth time he had lost.

It was a big nation, I reasoned, with much to demand the attention of the Attorney General. Besides, reports had it that he was very active in White House councils, and it was proper to assume that these activities, too, would place a drain on his time and attention.

I expressed these thoughts to Frank Fitzsimmons, feeling somewhat relaxed for the first time in months.

"Don't count on it," Frank cautioned. "Remember the old saying about "If at first you don't succeed, try, try again.' "

I laughed.

Yet there was reason to be apprehensive. On the first day of the Test Fleet litigation some person unknown telephoned some of the jurors and represented himself as a reporter for the *Nashville Banner*. He asked them what they thought of the case.

The arrest and conviction of the imposter was demanded by James G. Stahlman, publisher of the *Banner,* who announced a $5,000 reward for information leading to his arrest. Kennedy had called Stahlman and asked that news of the incident be suppressed on the ground that a story about it might lead to a mistrial. Stahlman, no lawyer, but a highly moral man and a patriot, agreed reluctantly and temporarily, but his anger at what had happened plus his principles as a newspaper publisher triumphed, and the story was broken. Stahlman explained that the eighty-six-year-old reputation of his fine newspaper was at stake and that he didn't intend to have it sacrificed for me, the federal government, or anyone else—meaning, I guess, Kennedy.

Then, while the jury was being selected, James Tippens, who had been tentatively seated as a juror, reported to the judge that "a friend" had told him it would be worth $10,000 to Hoffa if he sided with him. Tippens was disqualified. Two more incidents of this nature came to the attention of Judge William E. Miller, and he replaced those jurors with their alternates.

I knew nothing of these incidents, nor did any member of my legal staff. Were there overzealous Teamsters at work, inadvertently harming my case? Or were there overzealous anti-Hoffa people involved, busily shaping a noose for my neck?

In the circumstances, then, when the jury failed to reach a verdict, I shouldn't have felt that it was all over—but I did. After all, I had not arranged those calls or those contacts.

Six months after my indictment in Nashville I was indicted on charges of jury-tampering in the Test Fleet case. So were six other persons who had varying relationships with either me or the Teamsters.

I was shocked. I just couldn't believe it. I was prepared, in one way, to expect almost anything from Kennedy, but not this, not a trumped-up charge, not a frame-up invented out of whole cloth, not in America, not in 1963. I couldn't believe that such a thing would happen in the United States. That was stuff for the movies, not for real life.

Even so, I didn't give sufficient weight to what was happening. Instead, I was concerned more with the matters at hand back at headquarters. I couldn't take my responsibilities as General President lightly. By this time I was representing nearly 1,800,000 Teamsters, hardworking men who depended on me to run their union to the utmost of my ability.

At the time for my court arraignment on this, the most serious charge ever brought against me, drew near, I began to worry about a very important problem: in the wake of Robert Kennedy's incessant propaganda campaign against me, aided as he was by many newspapers and some of the most influential magazines, would I get a fair trial? Could we find twelve good men and true who were not already prejudiced against me? I had been accused of many things but found guilty of absolutely nothing. How many ordinary citizens, brought in off the street, would realize that fact? Most, I was sure, believed that I had been actually convicted of some serious crimes, and those who read the papers more carefully probably believed I was guilty as sin and was a free man only because of legal trickery. The Attorney General had as much as said so.

There was reason for worry. There had been a rather startling "incident" during the Test Fleet trial in Nashville.

A fellow—an unemployed dishwasher, we learned later—stalked into the federal courtroom in Nashville, marched right past a dozen or so FBI men and U.S. marshals, and, drawing a pistol from his coat, fired three shots at me at point-blank range.

The guards had not been alerted to the fact that my life might be threatened and apparently sought to protect only the prosecutors, so they dove for cover behind the benches. I floored the man with a hard right to the jaw and dis-

covered, with pleasure, as he lay there, that his weapon was
an air-powered pellet pistol, so I knew my "wounds" were
superficial.

More disturbing was what he said. He revealed that he
actually thought his air pistol would kill me, as, indeed, it
might have under different circumstances. This frustrated
assassin said he came to court intending to kill me in "answer to a message from a higher power."

"I know it sounds crazy," he admitted.

Crazy, to be sure. But how many other deranged people
might be goaded into some kind of violence by the cascading
headlines generated by the Attorney General's office? And if
the unbalanced might be tipped by the deluge of propaganda, might not the sane be swayed?

Accused with me on the jury-tampering charge were
Ewing King, head of Nashville Teamsters Local 327; Larry
Campbell, Business Agent of Detroit Local 299, of which I
am President; Thomas E. Parks, a Nashville funeral home
employee and uncle of Larry Campbell; Allen Dorfman, a
Chicago insurance broker with whom I had had dealings;
and Nicholas J. Tweel, of West Virginia, a business associate
of Dorfman.

Because of the unpleasant situations in Nashville involving the *Banner* as well as some of the citizens, our defense
counsel asked for, and received, a change of venue from
Nashville to Chattanooga.

We knew that Federal Judge Frank W. Wilson, presiding
in Chattanooga, was an appointee of the real prosecutor,
Robert Kennedy, and thus owed his fine job to the Attorney
General, but counsel thought this would cause the judge to
be scrupulously fair.

However, Kennedy, who was in daily communication with
Walter Sheridan, his chief in command (sometimes thrice-
daily calls were made), had so thoroughly convinced everyone in the area of my guilt that the prosecution proceeded

with the assumption that there was no need to accord me the due process of law. And this attitude seemed to be reflected, intact, by Judge Wilson.

Skulduggery entered the trial before it began.

The "panel" of two hundred names of local citizens who were possible jurors had been sent to three local industrialists for screening. Screening for what, we had no way of knowing. Were they screened for proper anti-Labor sentiments? Or was it to be certain that there were a sufficient number from the proper economic background to weigh the decision against a labor leader?

After screening by the three local industrialists, the names were sent to the FBI for further screening.

All this time the prosecution knew who had been selected, what each panel member did for a living, where he (or she) lived, what his background was, what his philosophies were. Yet we, the defense, were kept totally in the dark.

Ultimately, it is true, we were given the names, but not the addresses, of the panel of veniremen, those who would sit on the jury. It was our right to know more about these people, but our demands were flatly denied.

We insisted that we had a right to know the jurors' backgrounds, in order to determine what attitudes they might bring to a court of justice. Our demands were refused.

The addresses, we said, were important, for they revealed economic status, hence possible economic philosophies that might be prejudicial to a labor leader. Judge Wilson ruled that we couldn't see those addresses. The prosecution could, but we couldn't.

The right to challenge jurors who might be prejudicial to your case is as sacred as the right to be heard. Yet even this right, ultimately, was denied to us. We had to interrogate jurors one by one, as they stood for selection. Knowing nothing about them, we were unable to question them intelligently, or to make any sensible judgment as to their stability, their objectivity. Moreover, before we really began questioning of jurors, Judge Wilson lost his patience and insisted on handling the interrogation himself. Whenever we raised objections to questions put either by the prosecution or by the judge, we were overruled. We were silenced.

When it was too late for us to do anything about it, we learned that this was a "blue-ribbon" jury made up mostly of upper-middle-class people, most of them with fine, comfortable backgrounds and average to above-average educations. It was unlikely that many of them would be overly sympathetic to a man with my harsh origins, my imperfect and careless grammar, and my labor-oriented view of life.

You must be able to identify with a defendant in order to understand him. To most of the members of this panel I was as strange as any creature that might have stepped into their midst fresh from a flying saucer just arrived from outer space.

On the second day of the trial Cecil Branstetter, the Nashville attorney who represented Larry Campbell, noting that not until the day the trial started, when it was too late to do anything about it, was the defense allowed to know the occupations and addresses of the veniremen, put it squarely to Judge Wilson that upon examination of the first one hundred names on the list he found the panel weighted with types that could hardly be expected to be impartial toward me.

On his list, Branstetter said, he had found seven merchants, fourteen women whose husbands were insurance men or bankers or executives in industry, fifteen retired persons, including a retired rear admiral and a retired colonel, seven electricians employed by the Tennessee Valley Authority, four maintenance engineers, six supervisors or foremen, fifteen salesmen, sixteen executives, two bankers, two government officials, one city employee, and nine farmers. As possible counterweights on this list, Branstetter said, he found six clerks, one restaurant employee, and two truck drivers. The list did not, said Branstetter, "even come close to representing a fair cross-section of employment categories in this community."

That statement remains unchallenged.

When Attorney Jacques Schiffer, representing Thomas Parks, reported to Judge Wilson that he had gone to the clerk's office and sought copies of the questionnaires filed by the one hundred additional jurors who were to be on hand the next day but was told they were not available, Judge Wilson ducked the issue, saying that he understood the defense had been furnished a list of all jurors.

The defense *had* been furnished such a list—the day before, the first day of the trial! But it had been denied access to the questionnaires giving information about the jurors.

When Judge Wilson prohibited the defense lawyers from questioning the jurors and insisted that he do it himself, Branstetter protested that the judge's examination was weak. The judge was not making it clear, said Branstetter, that the burden was on the government to prove guilt and that there is no duty on the defendant to prove himself innocent. The judge's instructions on this point, he said, were being given in "negative form," and he urged—again—that counsel for the defense be permitted directly to interrogate the jurors. Yet Judge Wilson flatly refused to allow this normal and established procedure.

Thus with the trial yet to begin, we were denied our basic rights to know who our jurors were to be, and Judge Wilson had usurped our right to interrogate them.

We were off to one helluva start!

The prosecution opened its case with three witnesses who were called to give evidence of jury-tampering.

Even under direct examination the witnesses' stories were flimsy and wouldn't have stood up before an austere schoolmarm. On cross-examination they refuted their previous testimony, trapped themselves in lies, and wound up disavowing what had been testified to. Before their testimony was ended, the trio had confused everyone in the courtroom, including the prosecutor, who, it turns out, had threatened his own witnesses with indictment or other punitive retribution if they did not testify as he expected.

Does this stretch the truth? No, I write boldly, fearing no libel, no contradiction, for it is all there in the transcript of the testimony, with officers of the court, attorneys for the U.S. government, and a justice of the federal court being witnesses and tacit parties to it.

I still seethe at the obviousness of the frame-up arranged by Robert Kennedy, and I boil at the cowardly, vile, un-American acceptance of the violation of the judicial system by professional men supposedly endowed with some grain of honor. A judge who would be party to such a deed should be impeached and disbarred and drummed from his community in dishonor, and I hope I live to see the day when it happens.

Manifest at Chattanooga was the danger that motivates me to write this book. A corrupt Jimmy Hoffa is no great danger to the United States of America. There are police forces and law-enforcement agencies to take care of a Jimmy Hoffa, courts of law to try him and jails to incarcerate him, if he truly violates the laws. The real menace is a vindictive cabinet officer with power over the courts, who by threat or coercion can force weak men to do his bidding and thus make mockery of the forces of law and order, the elements that hold us together as a nation and provide us with our safeguards against each other and from tyrants in high office.

The government sought to show that in Nashville there had been an attempt to influence a juror named Betty Pas-

chal through her husband James Morris Paschal, a Tennessee State trooper, by means of an intermediary named Oscar
"Mutt" Pitts, a trucking firm employee.

It was alleged that the fixer was one of the defendants,
Ewing King, then president of the Teamsters local in
Nashville.

Pitts testified that he was known to both Paschal and King,
and that King knew that he, Pitts, had been a long-time
friend of Paschal. Late in October, Pitts said, King began to
sound him out on his opinion of what kind of man Paschal
was—meaning to find out, Pitts implied, whether or not
Paschal could be bought, and whether or not he could or
would influence Mrs. Paschal, who was a member of the jury.
Pitts didn't *say* this; he *implied* it.

Pitts testified that he informed King that Paschal was a
"good boy," and that since both Paschal and his wife had
some money, the offer of cash would be no inducement to
them.

But, Pitts said he told King, there was one thing Paschal
wanted above all else, and that was a promotion in the State
police department. King was said to have expressed confidence that the Teamsters' political influence would be able
to arrange a promotion for Paschal. Then King, according to
Pitts, suggested that Paschal might be induced to speak to
his wife about the Hoffa trial, and he inquired what kind of
woman Betty Paschal was. Pitts replied that she was a girl
who "could stand on her own two feet anywhere."

Pitts took pains to explain that King never mentioned
specifically what Paschal might talk to his wife about in
reference to the Hoffa trial. King never suggested that she
might be induced to vote for an acquittal, Pitts stated.

Then, Pitts said, he set up a meeting between King and
Paschal, at a lonely spring off River Road on the rainy night
of November 17, 1962.

Pitts related that at this meeting King told Paschal he felt certain he could get him a promotion. Then, Pitts testified (under direct examination), Paschal brought up the subject of his wife, mentioning that she was on the Hoffa jury. Paschal was the first to mention it, Pitts said. At this point, according to Pitts, King asked if Paschal would be willing to talk to his wife, but Paschal replied that they weren't getting along very well and that, because of their differences, he couldn't do a thing with her.

Then it was time to cross-examine. Harold Brown, Chattanooga attorney for King, asked Pitts some questions and the entire testimony was altered!

1. Pitts now agreed that he was the one who approached King, and that King had not approached him.

2. Pitts said he had backed a loser in the gubernatorial election in Tennessee while King had backed the winner, and that he approached King knowing he had influence and hoping he could help Trooper James Paschal.

3. Pitts, being confronted with a transcript of an interview he had held before a court reporter, admitted that the testimony he had given at the time in the office of Z. T. Osborn, Jr., who had been my counsel in Nashville, was true and accurate.

According to the transcript, Pitts had said that after King and Paschal had discussed the latter's promotion, Paschal first brought up Hoffa's name, asking, "What are they going to do to Hoffa?" King replied, according to Pitts, "They would do nothing if he could get a fair trial."

Pitts testified at my trial that he had told the truth when, in Osborn's office, he had said: "Ewing King did not ask James Paschal to help Mr. Hoffa in any way." And he added the gratuitous information that Ewing King had asked Paschal not to tell his wife about their conversation, and that King had assured Paschal that her being on the jury had nothing to do with their conversation about his, King's, possible intercession on behalf of Paschal's promotion in the State police department.

As a witness, Pitts was twitchy, nervous, and fidgety, and he seemed harried. He admitted at one point: "I'm scared to death."

Under cross-examination, Pitts said he had been questioned so often that he couldn't remember how many times it had been, and he spoke of being interviewed by William Sheets, the FBI man who, it turned out later, was in charge of the round-the-clock surveillance over me and my attorneys; James F. Neal, the U.S. attorney in charge of the prosecution; Walter Sheridan, the chief investigator and Kennedy's friend; and several other federal attorneys or officials.

Then Pitts made the startling revelation that one of the government officials "got disgusted" with him and told him: "If you don't tell me the truth, I will get you and your wife both indicted."

This incident took place, Pitts said, on the Sunday before he testified before the grand jury.

Who was this who intimidated witnesses? Further cross-examination brought out his identity: Walter Sheridan, mastermind of Kennedy's "Get Hoffa" squad.

Defense counsel continued to question Pitts. Why, he wanted to know, had Sheridan made such a threat?

Then the incredible story came out:

Pitts had insisted that events happened just as he had related them in Z. T. Osborn's office, and just as they appeared in the transcript of that interview as recorded by a court reporter. Pitts had said that King had said to Paschal that they should not be talking about Betty Paschal's service on the jury. But Walter Sheridan, Pitts now testified, wanted him to change his testimony to indicate that King wanted Paschal to intercede with his wife on behalf of me.

When Pitts had balked, Sheridan, according to Pitts, had

insisted that Pitts "tell the truth"—meaning Sheridan's version of the story—or that he would get both Pitts and his
wife indicted.

Which of Pitts's versions was the right one? Even I was
wondering, though I believed King when he said that he had
not even hinted that Mrs. Paschal might be useful to the
cause, but that he figured the Teamsters could use as much
friendly public relations as possible in the State police department, and that another State trooper well disposed toward truck drivers wouldn't hurt matters any.

So everyone waited for Paschal to testify. The issue rested
squarely with him. He could clear the questions up and
prove Pitts's story, or disprove it.

Paschal started by confirming the details of the rendezvous
of November 17 by the spring off the River Road. Then he
gave testimony that was damning to King, making him out
to be the instigator of a vile plot.

Trooper Paschal declared unhesitatingly that it was King
who had brought up the fact that Mrs. Paschal was serving
on the jury.

"He asked me if I could talk to her," Trooper Paschal related. "I told him no, that I couldn't talk to her, that we
weren't getting along too good."

Then Paschal quoted King as saying: "You talk to her. I
will get you the promotion."

Finally, it was time to cross-examine Paschal.

First of all, Attorney Brown wanted to know why Paschal,
a trooper, an officer of the State police department, had never
reported this jury-fixing attempt. Well, Paschal said, he
should have done so, but he hadn't. He admitted also that
he hadn't testified to this same effect when he was questioned
by Judge Miller on the day, in Chattanooga, when his wife
was thrown off the jury.

Indeed, Paschal admitted, he had signed an affidavit to the
effect that he hadn't known King was connected with the

Teamsters, that King had never even mentioned Betty Paschal's connection with the jury, that there was never any conversation "about me talking to my wife."

He had given this version in his own living room, with his own lawyer present, and had signed an affidavit prepared by an official court reporter. He had also given this version in his first interview with the FBI, he said.

What made him change his testimony to the incriminating version he had just given in court?

Well, said Paschal, he had changed it after several sessions with the FBI!

"They didn't tell me they were going to indict me," Paschal said, but "they told me I could get in trouble and maybe be indicted."

Who had said this? Paschal identified Sheets as the man who had informed him of what might happen to him if he didn't "tell the truth."

Sheets also told him that he could lose his job, Paschal said. An FBI man giving this kind of information to a nervous-in-the-service State trooper must have been impressive, to say the least.

However, Paschal said, they always told him just to tell the truth. But the truth, it became apparent, was not necessarily what happened; it was what they wanted to hear.

Paschal said he was also called into sessions with his immediate superior, a former FBI man, the latter's chief, and the commissioner of the State highway patrol. The way he related these interviews made them sound like the inquisition of a suspected molester by the Ku Klux Klan.

"They told me," Paschal said, "that they wanted me to do the *right thing* and if I knew anything other than what I had stated, they wanted me to tell it."

The chief told him he had been a good officer, but then the chief said something else: "He [said] he wanted me to do the right thing and that they couldn't have anybody in the department that didn't."

The man who had been hoping for a promotion now was worried that he'd have no job at all. Worse, there was the possibility that he would be drummed off the force.

Many men would have given in and agreed to say whatever was wanted. As it was, Paschal, at best a shaky witness, testified to the effect all of this had on him. The effect "on my mind," he said, "is that it would be a lot easier on me— I would come near not losing my job and everything would be better."

It would be better if he testified the way Mr. Sheets of the FBI wanted him to.

Trooper Paschal, so ill at ease in the stand, informed the court: "I knew that I was deliberately perjuring myself when I was in the U.S. District Court and questioned by Judge Miller and Mr. Neal. I knew that there is a penalty for perjury. To my knowledge, there has been no indictment returned against me for perjuring myself. I don't recall the Federal government has threatened me with a perjury indictment—they may be going to. I am still wearing the uniform of the Tennessee Highway Patrol."

I felt sorry for Paschal. I also felt sorry for that lonely lady atop the courthouse wearing the blindfold and holding aloft justice's scales. I felt sorry for America, to think that our courts of justice had come to this.

With its case in shambles, the government sought to prove another jury-fixing attempt—one of the most fantastically involved plots ever unfolded—concerning a high design to influence the sole Negro juror on the Nashville panel, a man named Gratin Fields.

The plot is involved, the names unfamiliar. It might be necessary to check "The Cast" in the Appendix to refresh your memory of identities. After sitting hour after weary hour in court, listening to the names over and over again, even I found myself getting confused. However, since details bear heavily on the incredible events in Nashville, I must go through them all.

The prosecution produced a star witness. He, too, was a policeman, a patrolman in Nashville, James T. Walker. James T. Walker knew Thomas Ewing Parks, the funeral parlor employee in Nashville who was the uncle of Larry Campbell, Business Agent of Teamsters Local 299 in Detroit, my local.

friend in the funeral parlor, called him one day in Novem-
Officer Walker took the stand to testify that Parks, his
ber while my trial was in progress in Nashville and later came to his home that same day between 5:00 and 6:00 P.M. They sat in Parks's car, Walker said, and talked. Parks asked Walker if he knew anything about the Hoffa case. Walker replied that he knew only what he read in the paper. Parks asked Walker if he knew Fields, who lived up the street from him. Yes, Walker said, he knew Gratin Fields.

Walker said that Parks asked him if Fields needed money, and Walker answered that he didn't know.

Thereupon, according to Walker, Parks said the "big boys" wanted to talk to Fields because they needed one more man to hang the jury, and they would be willing to pay $10,000, at least, to talk to him.

A couple of days later Parks called Walker, who in addition to serving as a city patrolman also ran a small printing and stationery business, on the phone to talk to him about printing some handbills. Parks explained that he was opening a dry-cleaning establishment and that he needed Walker to print the handbills. He also needed someone to work for him in the dry-cleaning place, Parks said, and asked Walker if he knew of any neighborhood youths who might like a job. Yes, Walker said, he knew two of them, Carl Fields and Walter Jackson.

My goodness, was Carl Fields the son of Gratin Fields who was on the Hoffa jury? Parks asked. Yes, Walker said, he was. That, said Parks, was his man, and he asked James Walker to get in touch with Carl Fields.

Patrolman Walker, who put in a day's work for the police department and moonlighted with his printing business, still had sufficient time to do favors and run errands for his friends, it appears, for he looked up Carl Fields and arranged for a meeting with Carl and Parks in his printing shop that very night. They met at the shop and then went out to Parks's car to talk, Walker related, but unfortunately he, Walker, couldn't hear anything that was said.

Later, according to Walker, Parks called up and asked him to find out what Carl Fields intended to do. Walker called Fields, and Carl told him that he hadn't done anything, that Walker then said that when he had obligingly transmitted he was afraid to talk to his father and wouldn't talk to him. this information to Parks, Parks came up with an outlandish response.

"Parks wanted to know what Mr. Fields was going to wear—the type of necktie and that was what he wanted Carl Fields to find out for him," Patrolman Walker testified in court.

"He said he had given Carl Fields some money and that he thinks he would come through," Walker continued.

Carl had discussed "the matter" with her, she told Walker, said, so Parks contacted the patrolman again and asked who wore the pants in the Fields family. Walker said he guessed that maybe Carl's sister, Mattie Leath, wore the pants.

Here Walker related how he drove Parks out to a housing authority site where Mattie Leath worked, and while Parks stayed in the car, he, Walker, went in to see the girl.

Carl had discussed "the matter" with her, she told Walker, according to the latter's testimony, and then she added: "I don't want any part of the government or anything of that particular type." Whereupon, Walker testified, he told her she was a fine girl, that this was what he had expected her reaction to be, and that if anyone bothered her again, she should call the FBI and the police.

Walker relayed this bit of information to Parks. That was all, except that Parks, when taking his leave of Walker, promised him: "We will take care of you." No amount was mentioned, Walker said.

Now Walker, by his own testimony, knew that a jury-fixing attempt was being plotted, and that a $10,000 bribe was in the offing. Yet he did not notify his superiors on the police force; he did not notify the FBI, despite the fact that he himself had been promised a reward of some kind, according to his own testimony.

Under cross-examination by Jacques Schiffer, attorney for Parks, Walker said he did not consider there was anything unlawful about the "conversation" he had had with Parks, and that he had not agreed to try to influence Gratin Fields.

"It is the truth, the whole truth and nothing but the truth that when I introduced Carl Fields to Mr. Parks, the defendant, there was only one purpose in my making the introduction and that was the purpose of securing a job for Carl Fields; there is no question about that," proclaimed Walker.

There remains to this day the mystery of the identification of Gratin Fields by his attire—his necktie. The whole idea stretches one's imagination a bit, for Gratin Fields was the only Negro on the jury, and certainly Parks would not have had to know the color of his necktie to be able to recognize him sitting there in the jury box.

Moreover, it seems self-evident that if Walker was innocent of any wrongdoing, so, too, was Parks. On the other hand, if Parks was guilty of an attempt to fix the jury, so, too, was Walker.

Then Carl Fields came to the stand. He described his meeting in Parks's car.

"He asked me was my father on the Hoffa jury and I told him yes," Carl testified. Parks then said, according to Carl, "Well, you know Bobby Kennedy is out to get Mr. Hoffa." Then Parks is reported to have asked Carl if he thought he could talk to his father as far as voting for acquittal. Carl had said he couldn't.

If he could influence his father, Carl said Parks told him, it would be worth $10,000—$5,000 for him and $5,000 for his father. But Carl insisted his father would have nothing to do with a deal like that.

"Then he [Parks] took five twenty dollar bills and laid it on the seat of the car," Carl declared under oath. "He said, if you can just tell me what kind of suit he would be wearing or what kind of coat he would be wearing tomorrow and give me that information before nine o'clock, I will give you another hundred dollars."

Carl was distressed by this crass offer. He didn't want the money, he said. But Parks insisted it would be a great favor to him, so Carl "obliged him" by taking his money. It all boiled down to the fact that later that night Carl called Parks (after his checkup call from Walker) and told him he couldn't ask his father what tie he was going to wear next day. So he asked Parks if he wanted his money back, and Parks is reported to have replied, "No, you can just keep that for your trouble."

Carl also testified he had given a statement to Z. T. Osborn that was not true, "because I didn't want to become involved in it." He had also talked twice to the FBI, he said. The first time he lied to them, but the second time he told them the facts, he said.

On record, of course, was the sworn affidavit Carl Fields had given to Osborn and an official court reporter. This completely contradicted the testimony he had given on the stand. He had also given the same kind of statement, originally, to FBI Agent Sheets, he said, but Sheets didn't believe him.

Sheets had taken notes both times he talked to Carl. Called to the stand and asked to produce these notes, Sheets testified that they had been thrown away. He explained that after his interview he dictated notes to a tape recorder, then destroyed his notes. Customary FBI procedure, Sheets explained.

In his original statement, Carl Fields had said he was not acquainted with Parks and had never talked to him. He said no one had ever asked him to influence his father's vote on the jury.

But this was, said Carl, a "pack of lies." He had "deliberately lied" to Osborn and the FBI.

So much for Carl. He was under oath when he gave his account to Osborn and again when he gave it to the FBI. He was also under oath when he testified in court. Which version is the right one? Which is the truth? Is there room for reasonable doubt?

Parks, who testified he didn't know a single one of his co-defendants until the very moment he was indicted, said he was walking down a Nashville street one day, during my trial in that city, when he happened to encounter Patrolman Walker. Walker asked him, Parks said, if he wanted to make a little extra money, and when Parks asked how that could be done, Walker asked him to come out to his print shop about 5:00 P.M. that day.

Parks did go to the shop, he said, and asked Walker what he had in mind: "He said he had an assignment from the Federal government," Parks testified. "He wanted me to help him out on a little detail."

The assignment, Walker said, was this: He needed some information from a young fellow Parks would be meeting there at the print shop office between 6:30 and 7:00 P.M. Walker said he needed to know what type of clothing the young man's father would be wearing each morning when he left home.

Hereupon, according to Parks, Walker peeled off $125 in bills and said that each time the young man gave Parks the details about his father's clothing, Parks was to pay the young man $100 and keep $25 for himself.

The name of the young man? Carl.

Parks said he met Carl that night, and, he says, at Walker's suggestion they went out to Parks's car to talk.

Here Parks testified: "I got in the car and I said, 'I suppose Mr. Walker told you just what he wanted *did*. I have to give you my phone number where you can call me and then I will contact him in turn and give him your message —and he wanted me to give you this money.'"

About eight-thirty that night, Parks said, Walker called and asked if he had received any message from Carl. Parks said, no, he hadn't. Walker then gave him a number where he could call Carl, and Parks called.

Parks asked Carl what message he had to relay to Mr. Walker.

"He [Carl] said," Walker reported, "'I have talked this over with my mother. She thinks I shouldn't get involved in it because I don't know what it is he is really trying to find out.'"

Parks continued, "I said, 'You know Mr. Walker is a policeman and it wouldn't be anything illegal, I don't think.' He said, 'Yes, but it involves more than he evidently told me. I think I better give you the money back.'"

Parks said he told Carl to keep the money or return it to Walker, that it wasn't his to take back. He testified that he never saw Carl again. He also testified that he never knew his full name until he was indicted. Parks reported all of this to Walker, he said, and the policeman said, "Well, just forget it."

About ten days later, Parks related, Walker asked him to drive him to South Nashville. Parks drove Walker where he wanted to go. Walker left the car, disappeared for several minutes—during which, presumably, he saw Mattie Leath —then, Parks said, he drove Walker back to the city, let him out of the car, and drove off, never knowing what it was all about.

When a federal grand jury began investigating the alleged jury-tampering charge, Parks was subpoenaed. He telephoned Walker to seek advice.

Walker told him, Parks said, that the best thing he could do was to plead the Fifth Amendment. If he did that, Walker is alleged to have told him, he couldn't possibly get into trouble.

So that's what he did, Parks said.

Not much later the federal government impaled Parks on the other horn of the dilemma he ultimately found himself in. It indicted him for not having filed a 1961 income-tax return.

His gross income for that year was $1,568.17. And it was after this indictment had been handed down against him that Parks had his first encounter with Walter Sheridan—a remarkable coincidence, it would seem.

Parks met Sheridan when he went to the courthouse to plead to the income-tax charge. As he entered the building, a U.S. marshal stopped him and told him Sheridan wanted to see him. Parks testified: "He told me if I could cooperate with him I could forget about the income tax thing if I would just go along with what he had in mind for me.

"I said if I cooperated in any way I would have to be lying because I don't know a thing about these people's affairs no more than I read in the papers. He asked me if he would not indict me, would I go along and cooperate with him.

"I said, 'No, I wouldn't.'

"He said, 'Suppose I take Larry out of it?'

"I said, 'It's still nothing I could tell you but a lie.' "

For two hours he and Sheridan talked, Parks testified, and, if Parks is to be believed, Sheridan spent the entire time trying to convince him to lie so they could bring a charge of jury-rigging against me. Sheridan offered him immunity, Parks said, from what loomed largely as a trumped-up indictment about his income tax. Sheridan offered to move him to any city of his choice. Sheridan offered to let Parks's nephew, Larry Campbell, off the hook, if Parks would only lie as Sheridan wanted him to, Parks said.

"He told me if I would cooperate with him I wouldn't have to stay in Nashville," Parks said, "that I could take my choice of any city or state in the United States that I wanted to live in under government protection. I wouldn't have anything to worry about."

Sheridan asked him to call Larry Campbell and arrange a meeting so that Sheridan could "make a proposition," Parks said.

Parks said that Sheridan told him that he wasn't interested in Parks or his nephew Larry: "It was Mr. Hoffa he was interested in, so if we would cooperate with him, it would be a direct link to Mr. Hoffa."

Parks reported that he said it was impossible, that he knew nothing and couldn't help Sheridan without lying.

"I said I couldn't lie for anybody," Parks said.

So he was indicted on the income-tax charge.

It is worthwhile pointing out, I think, that when Parks was cross-examined, his testimony was unshaken. Nothing was brought out then, or subsequently, to provide any kind of proof that he was wrong in what he said in court.

On the other hand, each of the witnesses against him completely recanted under cross-examination, confessed that they were lying, at one time or another, and left it up to the court to judge which one of their stories was a lie and which was not.

It does seem strange that Parks, who was said by Carl Fields to have had "a fat wallet" when he paid him his $100, had an income of a little more than $1,500. And it does seem too much of a coincidence that Parks was indicted for income-tax evasion at a time when he was wanted as a witness by the federal government. Moreover, it scarcely seems right that Walter Sheridan, Kennedy's chief investigator and, as such, an agent of the U.S. government, should use Parks's income tax to bargain with, telling him his failures to file would be forgotten if he'd cooperate.

Even to one totally uninterested in the outcome of the trial, the testimony of these witnesses creates a horrifying suspicion that the U.S. government, through its agents, used this poor, unsophisticated man, Thomas Parks, as a patsy to set up a situation to frame me on a trumped-up charge. And that I was framed there is no doubt.

The testimony given by the government's own witnesses, of which I have omitted nothing that bears on the issue, is clear.

To those of us who sat, stunned, in that federal court of law and heard these details unfolded from the witness stand, it seemed as if we were involved in a nightmarish play concerning high courtroom intrigue in one of those imaginary countries "somewhere in Middle Europe." As the pieces fell together in the great puzzle, and as it became obvious to us what had been going on, we found it harder and harder to believe that this was actually taking place.

Bill Bufalino, my lawyer, leaned toward me and whispered, "I'm worried. This is a kangaroo court. They're framing you."

"Why don't they take me out to a wall and have me shot by a firing squad, and be done with it?" I asked bitterly.

"Well, maybe it's not as bad as it seems," Bill said, trying to find some glimmer of hope. "We'll wait and see."

But it was bad. For example, it was just about that time that we discovered that our quarters were bugged and that every conversation we had held regarding the trial had been known, instantly, by the prosecution.

The blindfolded lady still held aloft her scales. Though she should have thrown them away and permitted her hands to be bound behind her back, she couldn't, for she remained the symbol of the land that once boasted the finest judicial system in mankind's history. Besides, she was made of granite. In this respect, she differed from Kennedy's victims. They were not statues; they were living, breathing creatures, made of flesh and blood and endowed with many other values that Kennedy, from his high office, ordered trampled.

23

No Ethics, No Honor, No Law

The suspicion that we were being constantly watched, spied upon, and listened to mounted with each passing day. After several incidents during which the prosecution, in court, effectively dealt with some strategy that we had planned the night before in my quarters, some of us became convinced that we were being bugged by the prosecution. Some of my lawyers refused to believe any such tactic was underway, reminding me that the lawyer-client relationship is held to be one of the most sacred and sacrosanct tenets in law. No lawyers—officers of the court—would ever violate that relationship, they said, particularly lawyers affiliated with the Department of Justice, the highest legal arm of the government.

Yet evidence continued to mount that we were living in a goldfish bowl that had been wired for sound.

It's a frightening experience to those who have never been subjected to the government's surveillance procedures, and, of course, most of the legal counsel in our party, being free from political persecution, had never been exposed to the techniques. We became increasingly jittery. Every time the phone rang, it was viewed with the suspicion with which one would regard a ticking bomb. More and more we recognized the telephone as a worthless instrument, of value only for

ordering a pot of coffee from room service. Our conversations became guarded, whispered. We kept looking over our
shoulders, as if expecting to see large ears poking around
corners or old-fashioned microphones dangling from behind
pictures on the wall. It became impossible to discuss fully
or in any detail the slightest matter relating to the trial.

Even less did we at first suspect that the Justice Department had also planted a paid spy in our midst, a Judas, who
was pretending to be my friend yet was reporting daily to
the lawyers who were trying my case in court. We could not
guess that this man, in a manner not dissimilar to that used
on Parks, had been put into a position where he was happy
to escape charges from the federal government in exchange
for the betrayal of a "friend"—said friend being me.

The bugging of my quarters began to catch up with us, I
recall, late in the afternoon of Friday, January 31, 1964.
Most of the lawyers of the defense—whom the press described
as "Hoffa's large battery of legal experts"—were meeting
with me in my suite, Room 914, in the Patten Hotel in
downtown Chattanooga, a handy walking distance from the
courtroom in the new Federal (and Post Office) Building.
We had been meeting there almost every afternoon after
court had adjourned since the trial began on January 20.

It was late. I was pacing about the room, glancing out the
window at the lemony sky of the fading day. I pace. People
think I'm nervous. I'm not. I'm restless. Sometimes I feel as
though I can't possibly get enough exercise. I do push-ups
every morning and night. I do isometrics. I exercise as much
as I can, but somehow the sedentary aspect of my job always
bothers me.

Sitting in court all day really affects me. I watch the
cigarette smokers grow woefully twitchy as they anxiously
wait for the reprieving words of the judge: "We will take a
ten-minute recess here." I can sympathize with them, for
though I don't have the tobacco habit, I feel a great need to

move about, breathe fresh air, look at the empty sky, stretch, move, move, move. My muscles demand it in the way, I suspect, nerves can learn to demand the intake of nicotine. I seem to think better on my feet. I will always be that way. Weight on the seat of my pants slows down my brain, I guess, and that may be why I had to work so hard back in school. I hope someday they will let a defendant (and a plaintiff, too, if necessary) walk about in a courtroom if it helps him to think more clearly. I know it would have helped me. No doubt the same privilege should be accorded prosecutors, but to tell the truth, my prosecutors had more privileges than they were entitled to.

Seated around Room 914 on that afternoon were most of my "counselors," though, of course, many of them actually represented the other defendants. Since I was the key defendant, the prize after which every resource of the Justice Department was in hot pursuit, they naturally gathered at my private wailing wall, or war room, or strategy center, or whatever you want to call it.

They were tense men, rapt, intent, preoccupied. One was making notes on a yellow pad ruled with blue lines. Another was reading some kind of report. One of the heavier members of the legal staff was sitting Indian-fashion on the floor, his coat rumpled around his shoulders and his vest bulging threateningly as he searched the compartment files of an important-looking black briefcase.

Nobody was saying anything. This disturbed me, for I wanted them to talk. I wanted to hear some of this expert opinion about how the trial was going; I wanted to know what these keenly trained men thought of the obviously conflicting testimony we were hearing. But they were mum, and these fellows you don't order around. Some are prima donnas. Some are richer than any client they'll ever have. Most are portly, dignified, unorderable. With lawyers you have to be polite and circumspect, even if you're hiring them at handsome fees and they're not doing, at the moment, what you expect them to do. A fellow like me has to remember that he's not dealing with some representative of Management who thinks of you as a sweaty representative of Labor and expects you to holler.

Morrie Shenker was looking out of the same window that I had been staring through. He was sprawled in a chair, though, and he was looking at the reddening sky. If he had strained a little he could have seen Lookout Mountain—and I could have told him that the effort was well worth the making—more. Where I was standing I could see lights begin to pinpoint the premature winter dusk in the city's downtown neon-splashed canyons. I was beginning to feel hungry. I hadn't eaten much at lunch because of the way the trial was going. When I get hungry, I feel a sharp pinch where an ulcer would be if I had one.

I turned back to the room. There had to be some redeeming feature to all of this courtroom production.

"They're pushing too hard," I said to Morrie. "They act as though they haven't got a good case. They haven't, of course, if they have to invent witnesses."

He nodded, acknowledgment that he had heard me, but a gesture that conveyed nothing, either affirmative or negative.

"Let's eat early tonight," I suggested. "I'm hungry."

"Okay."

"What are they going to try to do tomorrow?"

Buff, squatting on a hassock, made a hissing sound, waving his hand palm out, like a fan, and shook his head. "Shhh." He put his index finger to his lips. "Not here," he whispered.

The atmosphere in the room changed. Everyone began to glance around—at the walls, the ceiling, the furniture, the floor, the corners, the magazine rack, the ashtrays, the television set, the door, the transom, the desk, the draperies, the wastebasket. No telltale wires. No protruding microphones.

But of course not. If only it were that simple. It's not like the old days. The thicknesses of several walls means nothing to the skilled eavesdropper these days. No wires, no actual contact—nothing tangible is needed.

Buff shrugged his massive shoulders. We were being bugged. We were all convinced of it. We were also being shadowed, tailed, twenty-four hours of every day, day in and day out. There was abundant manifestation of that. Wherever we went, two men followed us, whether afoot or in cars, even in taxis. Whenever we used the phone, we were aware of that telltale hollow sound, a vague ringing in the ear, like what you hear when you hold your breath too long.

"Awwww . . . hell!" somebody exploded.

It was getting to be too much.

Counsel had already informed Judge Frank W. Wilson that we had reason to believe that our rooms were bugged, our phones tapped, and our persons under surveillance. Judge Wilson took it upon himself—I note it for the record —to relay our complaint to the prosecutors, and he asked them if this were true.

Of course not, they replied, entering a categorical denial of any such dastardly plot. They had no knowledge of any such nefarious activities.

So Judge Frank W. Wilson let the matter drop. In fact, he still ignored the matter when, much later in the trial, the FBI admitted that it had had us under constant surveillance, when, later still in the trial, it was proved beyond all doubt that our phones were tapped and our quarters bugged.

Suddenly my room seemed terribly confining. I was fed up with the whole situation. The disgust that was building up in me crystallized, and I wanted to strike out at something.

"Let's call Spindel," I said.

Somebody—I forget who—leaped up and shouted, "Shhhh!"

"Never mind that," I said. "Let's find out. Let's find out,

or let's make 'em stop. Call Spindel. Get him on the phone and get him down here as damn well soon as you can."

Morrie Shenker made a gesture. The lawyers near him huddled toward him, and he whispered to them. There was a muttered discussion with numerous gestures. At length he turned to me. "Okay," he said.

Fine. I'd call Spindel myself, I decided.

Bernard B. Spindel, who lives in Rome, New York, near Utica, on the old Erie Canal, is one of the foremost experts in the nation on the subjects of wiretapping, bugging, and electronic eavesdropping, but he prefers to be used defensively rather than offensively—that is, he likes to track down other people's bugging devices or other surveillance gadgets.

Bernie had worked for me before, and we had become fairly good friends, not only because he's a nice person, but also because he inadvertently found himself ensnared in the government's omnifarious efforts to nail me. He had been indicted with me, and acquitted with me, on that charge of tapping phones in the Teamsters' office in Detroit. We had shared a laugh to think that the government had brought its case against us on the strength of information the Justice Department had learned by tapping those same telephone lines. It had been our first experience with the Justice Department's double standard when it comes to observing the law.

Now, if things went right, Spindel would be able to find out for me what these fellows were doing, and perhaps we might be able to bring the same charges of wiretapping against the same people in the same department of government as we had brought in the Detroit case.

Spindel chuckled when I called him and told him my story. He said he'd come. I told him to do it as fast as possible.

"It's not that easy," he warned, "I have to pack and ship more than a thousand pounds of equipment."

"Pack it and ship it," I said. "Start right away."

He promised he'd ship it air freight and have it in Chattanooga in a dozen hours, and that he would appear on Monday. Figuring his logistical problems rapidly, he said he'd ship the equipment from New York on Saturday and would take a plane on Sunday night, so he'd be in Chattanooga on Monday morning.

Bernie did have the equipment shipped on Saturday. It arrived on schedule. If he'd thought, he might have stopped by the passenger terminal and bought his own ticket and confirmed his reservation. He didn't do it, however, and that turned out to be an important detail.

Sunday night Bernie couldn't get a plane. When he tried to fly to Chattanooga on Monday morning, he still couldn't get a seat. Time was pressing, so he decided to take a plane to Nashville, on which one seat was available, and hire a car there to drive to Chattanooga. In New York, therefore, he asked the car-rental agency to reserve a car for him in Nashville.

When he arrived in Nashville, two FBI agents were waiting for him.

It was easy enough to check with the car-rental agency in New York to find out where he was going. But the big question was: How had the FBI known Spindel was going anywhere?

Had someone overheard my telephone conversation with Spindel on Friday, a phone call that was made by me from the phone in my room in the Patten Hotel?

There is little doubt about the truth; for example, the two men who met Spindel in Nashville were men who were on duty with the FBI in Chattanooga and were assigned to maintain surveillance over me and other members of the defense team.

This information we learned later, and it was admitted to be true by the FBI.

The two agents in Nashville observed Spindel getting his rental car and then, in their own car, followed him all the way to Chattanooga. As they approached the city, they used their shortwave radio to alert other agents in other cars to intercept Spindel at the city line.

Spindel did not know, of course, as he drove toward Chattanooga, that he was being tailed by the FBI in the car following him, or that the FBI agents were covering every access into Chattanooga, waiting for him, ostensibly to confirm that he had officially arrived and that he was, indeed, going to the Patten Hotel. In all, a total of twelve agents were used on that assignment at the scene. More must have been involved in New York.

From the command post of the FBI headquarters across the street from the Patten Hotel, as a dozen agents converged on the helpless Spindel, the scene must have been strikingly reminiscent of a war movie as the Gestapo mobilized to catch the downed airman who was taking The Papers to The Underground Hideout. But this was no movie.

Then, after all its secrecy, the FBI staged a big public display. As Spindel drove into the city, the agents converged on his route and followed him, en masse, like the entourage of a sultan, all the way to the Patten Hotel. The agents made no effort to disguise their identity or their activities. It was obvious that they wanted Spindel to see them. He did. Apparently this was calculated to be a grandstand play, intended to frighten him off, and twelve FBI agents tailing one man is, indeed, an impressive sight.

When Spindel left his car to enter the hotel, two other agents took over and followed him on foot.

All of this the FBI admitted later in federal court, before Judge Wilson. Yet, under oath, the agent in charge of the detail denied flatly that there was a tap on the phone of Room 914. The FBI would never explain its phenomenal clairvoyance in knowing that Spindel had been ordered onto the scene and exactly when he would arrive, so the defense urged Judge Wilson to inquire further into the matter. He did not do so.

If the FBI could say honestly that it did not have a tap on my phone, it seemed natural for us to inquire as to whether some other agency had a tap on the phone, say, the Attorney General's office, which could have alerted the FBI to Spindel's planned arrival. Judge Wilson did not deem it of sufficient importance to press the inquiry in that direction.

The official position, then, as exemplified by Judge Wilson's conduct, was that the FBI had amazing powers of perception, at least extrasensory in force, and that it could do what mere mortals cannot do. The FBI can know the intentions and whereabouts of any private citizen at any time that it wants to. If it does not eavesdrop or bug telephones, supernatural power is the only other conclusion.

Spindel set up shop in a separate room and installed his elaborate equipment. It would, he said, track down any electronic eavesdroppers in the vicinity. As soon as he turned the thing on, he located some strong radio waves in the vicinity of the Patten, and tracing them, as well as recording them, he learned that the FBI had two radio-equipped lookout posts in nearby buildings.

One of these lookout posts, Spindel reported after listening at length and making extensive recordings, was a communications headquarters. There agents kept in contact by radio with a veritable fleet of agent-manned cars. Spindel recorded the entire "broadcasting day" of the FBI's transmitters in Chattanooga, to which we gave the call letters of WHOF, since the broadcast dealt almost exclusively with Hoffa.

Those tapes are still in existence. I have never heard them. No jury has ever heard them. It would have been a violation of federal communications law for Spindel to make public, even in court, those broadcasts or any others that were intercepted, unless the presiding judge ruled that they were important enough to be submitted in evidence.

The tapes, plus a transcribed copy of what was on them, were handed to Judge Wilson by Spindel in a sealed envelope.

Judge Wilson did not open that envelope. He was told what the envelope contained. The defense then requested him to examine the contents of the envelope and pass judgment on their admissibility in court. Judge Wilson declined.

The seal of the envelope remained unbroken, the contents undisclosed. The judge did not rule on the admissibility of the contents since, technically, he didn't know what was in the envelope.

Is this suppression of evidence? No. Not if the case before the court concerns charges of jury-rigging. Neither the FBI nor the Justice Department was on trial. But . . .

24

The Spy Who Came to Dinner

Forget about decency. Forget about privacy. I ask only that the principles of American justice and democracy be considered, as I tell the tale of Edward Grady Partin.

It was Edward Grady Partin who volunteered the testimony that sealed my doom in the Chattanooga court.

You may have read about him. Thanks to government sponsorship he was portrayed as something of a national hero. He somehow looked the part, too: a rugged, firm-jawed man with slightly wavy hair and the appearance of sincerity and honesty that would have made him a successful salesman. Ah, you'd say upon meeting him, there's a true-blue American, a churchgoer, no doubt, a man who contributes regularly to charity, a fellow who devotes much time to community-service groups, a chap who turns over most of his paycheck to a devoted wife.

There was a serious attempt to portray Partin in the press as a slightly too exuberant American boy who was just a little too red-blooded. And again, *Life* magazine, either through too much reliance on the word of the Attorney General or through too little research, was guilty of complicity in spreading the whitewash.

Life pictured Partin as having been involved only in some inconsequential brushes with the law when, in the cause of democracy and so that justice might be done, he agreed to work for the Justice Department as an undercover agent and informer. He was in jail, *Life* wrote, "because of a minor domestic problem," and in addition, he had been indicted "on charges of embezzling $1,600 in union funds."

These things seemed mighty insignificant when one considered how noble the man was, how much he had done for justice and his country. *Life* quoted Walter Sheridan as saying: "I've dealt with a lot of informers, and until this guy, they all wanted two guarantees: nothing traced to them, and never call them as witnesses. Ed asked for neither one.

"But," Sheridan went on in *Life's* article, "asking him to take the stand in open court meant exposing him as an informer, jeopardizing his job—maybe much worse."

Yet when Sheridan put the brutal issue squarely to Partin, *Life* recorded, the latter merely shrugged and philosophically declaimed: "I've come this far. Whatever you say."

This is the Edward Grady Partin whom the jury got to know. It is the Edward Grady Partin who, according to *Life* and other informational media, had the courage to stand up and be counted in the struggle against the forces of evil. But there's another Edward Grady Partin, one the jury never got to hear about.

This Edward Grady Partin is mentioned in criminal records from coast to coast dating from 1943, when he was convicted on a breaking and entering charge, to late 1962, when he was indicted for first-degree manslaughter. During that twenty-year period Partin had been in almost constant touch with the law. He had had a bad-conduct discharge from the Marine Corps. He had been indicted for kidnapping. He had been charged with raping a young Negro girl. He had been indicted for embezzlement and for falsifying records. He had been indicted for forgery. He had been charged with conspiring with one of Fidel Castro's generals to smuggle illicit arms into communist Cuba.

This paragon of virtue, then, was the government's star witness against me. I claimed his testimony was false. I claimed, in short, that he was lying. He told one story; I told another. It boiled down, really, to the reliability, the veracity, the credibility of the witnesses.

Judge Wilson ruled literally dozens of times that Partin's character and his burgeoning criminal record had no bearing in the evaluation of his word against my word. Though we sought time and again to introduce testimony or evidence indicting the unreliability and instability of the witness, Judge Wilson flatly refused to allow such evidence or testimony to be heard by the jury. The jury retired believing Partin to be not only an excessively courageous man but also an extremely honorable man. It's not for me to say that he isn't both of those things. But I think that Partin's record did have some bearing on his credibility as a witness.

To the best of our knowledge, Partin's first encounter with the law occurred in December, 1943, when he and another man were arrested in the state of Washington for breaking into a restaurant. Partin pleaded guilty to the charge and was sentenced to fifteen years in the state penitentiary. Twice he broke out of jail.

When he was freed he joined the Marine Corps, from which he was dishonorably discharged.

When Partin began to attract the attention of federal law-enforcement agencies he had been boss of the Teamsters local in Baton Rouge for several years. Some rebellious members of his local accused him of embezzling union funds. They also charged that he had gone off to Cuba and consulted with a Castro deputy about a gun-smuggling deal.

At about the same time and just before federal auditors arrived on the scene to see if there was anything to the charges made by the union members, a six-hundred-pound safe containing all of the union's records and books disappeared from the union hall. It was found sometime later in the Amite River—empty.

Then, in November, 1961, Partin was involved in a mysterious shooting. A pistol was discharged. Partin was wounded in the abdomen. Partin insisted to authorities that he had been handling the weapon and that it had gone off accidentally.

Leading the union criticism against Partin were two rank-and-file Teamsters, A. G. Klein, Jr., and J. D. Albin. In company with other Teamsters from the local, the two men testified before a grand jury in East Baton Rouge that indicted Partin for forging a withdrawal card—a form of resignation card—that, it was alleged, effectively removed one of Partin's other critics from the union.

Subsequently Albin and Klein were brutally beaten up by a group of six men, allegedly Teamsters from Partin's clique in the local. And soon thereafter Klein was killed when a truck loaded with sand "fell on him" in St. Francisville, Louisiana.

There was, therefore, sufficient activity going on in Partin's vicinity to arouse some official curiosity. District Attorney Sargent Pitcher of East Baton Rouge began an investigation and was soon joined by not only the FBI but also by special attorneys of the Justice Department.

As a result, the East Baton Rouge grand jury, on June 27, 1962, indicted Partin on twenty-six counts—thirteen of falsifying records and thirteen of embezzlement. He was freed on $50,000 bond, but these offenses, which seemed to *Life* to be minor, could have resulted, upon conviction on all counts, in fines of $260,000 and sentences totaling seventy-eight years in jail.

Six weeks later, Partin was again embroiled with the law when he was named a defendant in the first of a series of accident suits that were soon to total $400,000.

Airman Leo D. Paris of Haverhill, Massachusetts, stationed at Lackland Air Force Base, Texas, charged that at 12:30 A.M. on Christmas Day, 1961, a sports sedan driven by Edward Grady Partin struck his car, drove it off the highway, and rolled it over several times, in the vicinity of Cuba, Alabama. Paris and a companion, another airman, were seriously injured, the complaint said. A third airman, William Andres Halas, of Milwaukee, Wisconsin, was killed.

The suit, a civil matter, apparently sparked an investigation by Alabama authorities, and on September 26, 1962, Partin was indicted in Alabama on charges of first-degree manslaughter and of leaving the scene of an accident.

On the day before the Alabama indictment was returned, on September 25, 1962, Partin had surrendered himself to Louisiana authorities on another major charge—one of aggravated kidnapping, the outgrowth of that "minor" domestic problem *Life* referred to.

The charge involved the domestic problems, not of Partin, but of a friend of his. The previous June, two children, one of them two years of age, the other ten months, were kidnapped from a motel where they were staying with their mother, who was separated from her husband, one Sidney Simpson, a friend of Partin.

The mother had legal custody of the children, and after investigating the matter District Attorney Sargent Pitcher secured an indictment against Partin and Simpson on the aggravated kidnapping charge. Partin was jailed.

The tots remained missing for three more weeks. Then, on October 4, 1962, the youngsters were turned over to authorities in the basement of the courthouse after having been missing for five months. Partin, who had not been eligible for bail, with the return of the children again became eligible.

There was the question of money, however. Partin's original $50,000 bond on the federal indictment for embezzlement had been revoked by the bonding company when Partin had become embroiled in his other legal troubles. But then suddenly, as if by magic, the sun shone through the dark clouds for Partin. With ease he obtained another $50,-000 bond, plus $5,000 bail on the Alabama manslaughter charge, plus another $5,000 for bail on the Louisiana kidnapping charge.

Curiously, this bright new day dawned for Partin after he had had a formal conference, while in jail on the kidnapping charge, with William "Hawk" Daniels, an investigator for the district attorney's office; District Attorney Sargent Pitcher; and A. Frank Grimsley, an attorney for the Justice Department assigned to my case.

Partin was released from jail on October 7, 1962. On October 8, 1962, he telephoned me in Newark, New Jersey, and told me he wanted to see me.

Unknown to me, federal investigators were recording the conversation—as was later admitted in court.

Partin, this wholesome and dedicated American citizen, was on his way to effect his greatest coup of them all, as a spy in my camp. I should have known better than to listen to him. I never seem to learn that a fellow who plays with viperous critters is likely to be bitten.

25

The Sergeant-at-Arms

Only when it is viewed in perspective can one fully realize how gigantic was the case that the government was preparing against me. An elaborate scheme for my entrapment had been devised in Washington and was being carried out by Robert Kennedy's "Get Hoffa" squad, said by the Attorney General himself to number, at times, as many as five hundred men.

It is significant to note the remarkable coincidence that Partin was approached by Hawk Daniels, the district attorney's investigator, at the same time that I was facing the start of my trial in Nashville on the Test Fleet case. Probing the coincidence, we came up with sufficient evidence to warrant lengthy examination in court, and the examination disclosed some other remarkable facts.

The defense was never permitted to establish just what Hawk Daniels and Partin discussed in the Baton Rouge jail. Partin did acknowledge that my name might have been mentioned "casually," but he insisted that Daniel's purpose in visiting him in jail did not concern the Nashville trial. However, though Partin admitted that he, Partin, did have a plan for discussing the Nashville trial, the defense was never allowed to ferret out the nature of this plan, even though Partin said it concerned the trial.

Grimsley, the Justice Department lawyer, admitted under oath that he met Partin "at least two or three times . . . probably three." These meetings took place in late September, Grimsley said, or early October.

Grimsley also said that Partin was working as an informer "probably late in September" and admitted that when the much-indicted man called me in October 8, he was a full-fledged agent.

Partin made an amazing somersault, turning from legally pursued to pursuer, from accused to accuser. And, naturally, one raises the question as to what inducement was used to persuade Partin to align himself with the forces of law and order, to say nothing of the company of angels. Perhaps a clue lies in the fact that Partin was not brought to trial on his recent indictments. All the cases, except one, were dismissed, and the one remaining case has been postponed with monotonous consistency. Partin's status with respect to the law, as of this writing, is indefinite, for the charges have been allowed to gather dust and lapse into a legal limbo of convenience.

Certainly, subsequent testimony, as we shall see, disclosed that the government had engaged in an elaborate scheme to channel sums of money to Partin's wife, though, under oath, Walter Sheridan and A. Frank Grimsley had denied making any payments whatsoever. Their statements have gone unchallenged and remain in the transcript of the testimony.

Partin called me a second time on October 18. This conversation also was recorded by investigators working for the Justice Department.

The theme of these calls was that Partin, in trouble with his union, was also being persecuted by the federal investigators because he was "such a loyal Hoffa man." At this point, I was certainly willing to believe that the Attorney General's vendetta against me could spread to others in the Teamsters as well, particularly to a fellow such as Partin, who struck me as being not too alert and definitely trouble-prone.

Knowing that the Nashville case was coming up, Partin asked me if it would be all right to join me there so he could discuss his problems with me, some personal, some involving the union.

In later testimony Partin insisted that I was the one who had invited him to Nashville, and that he did not ask to come. Judge Wilson permitted this discrepancy to become a large issue in the case, and he ruled, ultimately, that I was lying when I said Partin invited himself, and that Partin was not lying when he said that I had invited him. On the basis of this ruling, Partin was allowed to testify before the jury. However, when the wiretaps were later exposed, it was revealed that Partin had initiated the telephone calls and had invited himself. The jury did not hear that revealing bit of testimony, though, nor did it hear Partin admit, finally, under oath, that he was planted as an undercover agent.

Partin also testified that before he left for Nashville, he was rehearsed and briefed by Grimsley and was furnished with Walter Sheridan's telephone number in Nashville.

What was Partin to look for in his undercover role?

Grimsley told him, Partin said, to report immediately to Sheridan "if I saw evidence of jury tampering or other illegal activities."

Thus, sworn testimony from Partin shows that the Justice Department was discussing the matter of jury-tampering even before my trial in the Test Fleet case had started. Nowhere in the records, nowhere in any testimony, nowhere in any transcript is there indication that the matter of jury-tampering had been discussed prior to that briefing of Partin by Grimsley. We are asked to believe, then, that through powers of magnificent perception, the Justice Department was alerted to what was to come and accordingly provided for it by employing an undercover agent.

Surprisingly enough, the valiant Partin experienced no difficulty at all in fulfilling his assignment. In fact, he accomplished his mission the very first day he arrived in Nashville. He found his jury-rigger. At least, that's what he said.

He arrived in Nashville on October 22, 1962, and just about the first man he met—one he had never seen before —told him that he was working on a plot to fix the jury. The first jurors were not to be selected until the next day, incidentally.

According to Partin, he had just arrived and was hanging around the coffee shop of the Andrew Jackson Hotel, waiting for me, when he struck up a conversation with a man who introduced himself as Anthony Quinn, a man in the "vending business," presumably meaning he owned vending machines. Partin, in turn, introduced himself as what he was: a Teamster official from Baton Rouge, Louisiana.

Later that day, according to Partin's testimony, when Partin was still at the hotel, Quinn came up to him, laughed, and confessed that he really wasn't Quinn at all. He was Nicholas J. Tweel. He had lied to Partin, he said, because he didn't know him, but since meeting him that morning, he had checked with me, and I had assured him that Partin was okay and a member of the team. Whereupon Tweel, according to Partin, confided the story of my plot to fix the jury.

Tweel told him, Partin said on the stand, that Allen Dorfman, a friend of mine, had called him from Chicago. Tweel himself was from Huntington, West Virginia, and, according to Partin, he had business dealings with Dorfman, an insurance broker.

Tweel then went on to tell this perfect stranger, Partin said, that Dorfman had told him it would be a personal favor to him if he would "come down to Nashville and help him set up a method to get to the jury."

Partin, of course, zoomed off to the nearest phone, dug out the number that Grimsley had given him, and called Walter Sheridan with this block-busting tidbit of information, as the government's star witness later testified.

After leaving Quinn-Tweel, Partin came to see me to tell me some stories about his troubles, but I was up to my ears in my own problems at the time, with my trial getting underway, so I told him we'd have to discuss it all at a later date. Partin hung around, anyway, waiting.

The next day, October 23, a juror named James C. Tippens, a Nashville insurance man, was tentatively seated. Subsequently, Tippens testified that when he returned to his office he picked up a message saying that his friend and neighbor Lawrence "Red" Medlin had been trying to reach him. When he contacted Medlin, Tippens said, Medlin told him it would be worth $10,000 to throw the case by voting in favor of me. The next morning Tippens reported the incident to Judge Miller, who dismissed him from the jury.

It is worth noting that Medlin never appeared at the jury-rigging trial in Chattanooga. Instead, he was tried in Nashville. He was found guilty of trying to bribe his friend, but the government failed to produce one shred of evidence or testimony linking Medlin to me or to the Teamsters. Medlin, in fact, swore that he had never heard of me.

It's also worthy of note, I think, to point out that when Tippens was seated he was selected *tentatively*. The jury was not completed until two days later, October 25. Though a tentative juror is seldom removed, at any time Tippens might have been challenged and thus removed from the jury, right up until the moment the jurors were sworn in. It therefore seems a lot to expect that someone would run the risk inherent in offering a bribe to a tentative juror, for he might not be on the jury by the time it is sworn. But these things we are asked to believe.

Twice more during the course of the trial there were reported attempts to approach and influence jurors. Each time the juror in question was dismissed and replaced on the panel by an alternate.

The jury was not sequestered. Its members left the courthouse each day and returned to their homes, there, if they chose, to read the newspapers, listen to the radio, or watch television.

Surely these jurors must have believed as did most of the rest of the citizens of America, that, caught at last in a charge I couldn't beat, I was fighting a last-ditch battle to buy off the jury. Yet when it came to a question of my guilt, seven of the twelve jurors steadfastly voted for my acquittal! And they voted for my acquittal in spite of the fact that during most of the trial and until the day that he revealed himself as an undercover agent, Edward Grady Partin frequented my quarters almost constantly, participated in our discussions and plans, and reported daily to Walter Sheridan.

But though the government lost its case in Nashville, Edward Grady Partin had provided the prosecutors with sufficient grounds to seek yet another indictment against me —one of jury-tampering.

Thus it was on May 9, 1963, another federal grand jury indicted me and five others on the jury-rigging charges, and thus it was that I wound up in Chattanooga facing Judge Frank W. Wilson on January 20, 1964.

In Chattanooga, my *raison d'être* was Edward Grady Partin; he's the fellow who put me there. He shows up again. But, meanwhile, we can return to the trial, to the point following the appearance of poor Gratin Fields.

26

The Frame-up and the Voodoo Man

Some of the following seems beyond belief. Yet it is sworn testimony and appears in the transcript of the Chattanooga trial, though a great deal of what appears here did not reach the jury, for Judge Wilson forbade it.

First of all, we were able to produce an undercover agent of our own, Frederick Michael Shobe, who had come to Bill Bufalino and revealed his role as an *agent provocateur*— his own description—in the Teamsters.

Shobe, one of the government's very active informers, was paid to spy and to cause trouble in the union by the Justice Department and had worked for two years for Walter Sheridan's special unit. During that two years, Shobe testified, he ranged the country, causing trouble for the Teamsters. He incited riots, he said, and fomented dissatisfaction wherever he could, his salary and his expenses the meanwhile being paid for by the U.S. Department of Justice by direction of the hand-picked investigator of the Attorney General.

How did Shobe get such a job? He explained in court. Like Partin, Shobe, too, had fallen into the toils of the law.

Shobe had been convicted for burglary, forgery, and armed robbery and had served a term in Michigan State prison. When he was released, he was put on probation for four years. But when Shobe looked around for employment, he found none to suit his capabilities—he was a college graduate—so he took a job on the docks.

It wasn't long before he was picked up. By working on the docks, Shobe was informed, he was mixing with ex-convicts and known criminals, thus violating the terms of his parole. He therefore faced return to the state prison. But, he was told, there was one way to redeem himself and to keep his freedom: he could go to work for Walter Sheridan in his special investigative unit.

To Shobe the prospect seemed a heck of a lot better than jail, so he took the job, which, as I have indicated, lasted for two years, according to his testimony, and concluded with his complicity in setting up a carefully planned government frame-up in Nashville.

Not long after beginning work on the Nashville case, Shobe discovered that time had removed the bondage of his parole, and he figured he had had enough of the Sheridan-directed job. He therefore asked the Justice Department to free him and help him find employment elsewhere. He needed the Department's help since, with his record, he might likely wind up again on the docks, again working in company with ex-convicts, and again finding himself in trouble. He had his eye on a job as a computer operator and was hoping to be given a chance to train for it.

He got no response for several months, but, finally, he was informed that there was a job with the government awaiting him in Japan. The way Shobe looked at it, the Attorney General, having used him in one of the most distasteful roles possible, was now anxious to get him out of the way where he could cause no embarrassment.

After all he had done for Sheridan, Shobe thought this was very shabby treatment. He thought it over at length and then, in a rebellious mood, sought out Bill Bufalino and told his story.

When Shobe took the stand in Chattanooga, he sought to prove his close relationship with Walter Sheridan by reading into the record Sheridan's office telephone number in Washington, his unlisted home phone number in Bethesda, Maryland, and the number in Nashville through which Shobe maintained daily communication with Sheridan.

In June, 1963, Shobe said, on instruction from one Thomas McKeon, a federal official in the Justice Department, he had been dispatched from Detroit to Louisville and then to Nashville with orders to put up in Brown's Tourist House in the latter city and to hang around Joe's Palm Room and to remain in daily communication with Walter Sheridan at Nashville 242–2106.

Shobe offered in evidence a slip of paper detailing this information, and he said it was in Thomas McKeon's handwriting. McKeon, he said, gave him this slip of paper, along with $250 in cash, and he departed that night for Louisville.

His assignment was to try to locate "someone who would state that Larry Campbell or Charles O'Brien had made incriminating statements about their interest in the Hoffa trial."

My indictment by the federal grand jury in Nashville had preceded Shobe's assignment by only a few days. The government, obviously, was baiting yet another trap.

Shobe testified that as soon as he reached Nashville he had a meeting with Walter Sheridan. But as he stated this, the prosecution jumped to its feet, shouting, "Objection! Objection!"

When Judge Wilson sustained the objections, it was impossible for Shobe to relate in court what he and Sheridan had discussed. However, Shobe did manage to get into the record the fact that Sheridan wanted to get Parks to collaborate with the government. Parks, the funeral parlor employee, it will be remembered, had been a reluctant government collaborator who had ended up being indicted for income-tax nonpayment and charged with five counts of jury-rigging. Sheridan, said Shobe, "was primarily concerned at that time with getting Mr. Parks to come into the government and at that time our plans were directed toward that end."

The prosecution was on its feet almost constantly, and the shouts of "Objection! Objection!" drowned out almost everything that Shobe said.

The prosecution objected to having Shobe testify to anything specific or involve anyone in particular. Judge Wilson sustained just about every objection, almost succeeding in muzzling Shobe and successfully preventing him from testifying before the jury.

Consequently, it was with a change of pace that Attorney Jacques Schiffer asked Shobe if he had ever met Patrolman Walker. Shobe said that he had, that as he was leaving Nashville for Louisville, Walker approached him.

At this point the prosecution objected again.

Judge Wilson then decided to dismiss the jury, ruling that Shobe would be examined in *voir dire* hearings—by judge alone, with no jury.

Schiffer was joined by every defense attorney in the courtroom in protesting this, but the judge was adamant. In fact, the *voir dire* hearing was practiced again and again by Judge Wilson, who admitted, in his own court, that 60 percent of the record of the proceedings was compiled in the absence of the jury.

In other words, the jury reached a decision and based its judgment on only 40 percent of the information that was brought before the court. The trial transcript contained many typewritten lines of strong objections from defense attorneys who protested that this procedure deprived them of the chance to present their cases properly.

In the *voir dire* hearings, Schiffer presented what seemed

to me to be a compelling argument on behalf of the admissibility of Shobe's testimony.

The defense, Schiffer said, had not only a right but a duty to "expose any attempt by the government to do something wrong or illegal." He said it was a "sign of weakness in their case when they attempt such activity and when such attempts are made to frame the defendants and Mr. Parks in particular."

Where it could be shown that the government had attempted to fabricate testimony and suborn witnesses, Schiffer argued, "it is for this court to take such testimony and for the jury to hear it directly because it bears very materially upon all of the credibility of all of the testimony of all of the witnesses put in here up to this point by the government."

Judge Wilson didn't see it that way, however, and he categorically ruled that what Shobe had to say should be prevented from getting to the jurors.

There is no question in my mind that Shobe's testimony was some of the most important offered in the case for the defense. It went into the transcript, but no one on the jury heard it, or knew about it. Yet Shobe said that Parks was set up for a frame-up by the government!

One of the things that bothered Sheridan, Shobe said, was the fact that Parks, known to have a low income ($1,500 a year), was to be cast in the role of offering a considerable sum of money—up to $10,000—to Gratin Fields, as well as the other substantial amounts to be offered to Fields's son. Some explanation of how the bribe money came to be in Parks's possession should be provided, Sheridan is said to have told Shobe.

Shobe said he was assigned to produce this evidence, to provide this missing link in the story. Accordingly, he went to Detroit and approached a man named Harry Ellis, a numbers operator with several charges against him as well as a fat record of previous violations.

Shobe testified: "I arranged for Mr. Ellis to have a con-
ference with the U.S. District Attorney, William Merrill, in
Detroit, in order that he testify that a man named John
White, of Detroit, Michigan, had brought bribe money to
Nashville during the early fall of 1962. Mr. Ellis refused to
do this."

Failing in this respect, the government then turned to voodoo in an effort to bring Parks into the fold as a witness
rather than as a defendant.

Shobe said that, on assignment, he then returned to Nashville and began to shadow Parks. (Here the testimony is a
bit confusing even to me—and you can be sure that I had
a keen interest in what was being said and what it meant to
my case.) Shobe said that Sheridan had given him a list of
names of Parks's associates, and that he had got in touch
with these associates, and "I guess you would say I had
threatened them to a certain degree."

The remainder of what Shobe was trying to say was not
brought out, because of prosecution objections.

Shobe then testified that he sought out a locally renowned
practitioner of voodoo known as Bishop St. Psalm to see if,
through incantations or other persuasive measures, Parks
might not be brought into line.

Shobe said that while he personally didn't really believe
in voodoo, Sheridan told him that as long as there were so
many superstitious persons in Nashville, it was worth giving
Bishop St. Psalm a chance to try to change Parks's adamant
ways.

Therefore, Shobe said, he introduced Bishop St. Psalm to
James Durkin, the special assistant district attorney assigned
to the case. Bishop St. Psalm, though he may have had access
to powerful spirits in black magic, apparently had no way to
quell the needs of creditors and others who require money,
so he pointed out that he published a small magazine on the
arts of voodoo and such and suggested that if he was going to

help the government by working a spell on Parks, the least Uncle Sam could do would be to buy some advertising in his publication. He was told, Shobe said, that this might be arranged.

It will be recalled that Parks worked at a small cleaning business, or at least tried to. When Bishop St. Psalm was given the assurance about the advertising, Shobe said, he left Durkin's office and went directly to the shack maintained by Parks, called Tom's Cleaners, where, Shobe testified, St. Psalm picked up "some object" belonging to Parks and quickly left.

Shobe and St. Psalm went straight to the bishop's house, where the voodoo man set up a little altar and began to burn black candles and intone incantations.

The testimony of Frederick Michael Shobe was certainly as credible as that of any witness to appear before the court up to that time. Therefore the following, taken directly from the transcript, is of paramount importance:

> Q. Let me ask you this now: As you sit here now can you tell us whether you had discussed with Walter Sheridan a plan to frame Mr. Hoffa?
>
> A. We had discussed Mr. Hoffa, Mr. Bufalino and Mr. Fitzsimmons and various Teamster officials at different times. As a matter of fact this was a constant topic. It was my understanding that the only reason for the existence of the particular department that Walter Sheridan headed was to get Mr. Hoffa.
>
> Q. I see. Was that made plain to you by Walter Sheridan— that the purpose was to get Hoffa?
>
> A. That is correct.
>
> Q. And was it indicated to you that it made no difference whether he was—[whether] they used legal or illegal means?
>
> A. Well, preferably if there was something found that incriminated Mr. Hoffa, well and good; however, if there wasn't, the feeling in the department was that Mr. Hoffa should be in

jail anyway, and that we—if we had to resort to unfair tactics, well, that's where a person like myself came in.

Q. I see. And that is why they called you into service—because they wanted you—like you described—"That's why they wanted me in the service, to frame Hoffa"—is that correct?

A. Well, to get him by any means, fair or foul—that was my understanding of the matter.

Q. And you were directly told that by Walter Sheridan?

A. That is correct.

Shobe left the stand unchallenged. After all, it made little difference to the prosecution, for Judge Wilson had seen to it that the jury did not hear this. None of it was known to a single juror.

But that isn't all, by any means, for Schiffer then brought the questioning back to Shobe's encounter with the Nashville cop, Patrolman Walker—the point at which Prosecutor Neal had succeeded in "persuading" Judge Wilson that the jury should be removed from the courtroom so as not to hear the testimony.

According to Shobe, the encounter took place in the Greyhound Bus Terminal in Nashville. Walker, Shobe said, approached him and stated he was working for the same man as he was.

"Of course I feigned ignorance because I had never spoken to Walker and I had no orders to contact him from Mr. Sheridan whatsoever, and—'Walker'—I said—'Well, whom do you work for?' "

"He says, 'Well, you know Mr. Sheridan,'" Shobe testified.

According to Shobe's description, he "brushed off" Walker, but later, he said, he checked with Sheridan and learned that Patrolman Walker was working for the government. Shobe also testified that Walker had told him he had been on the case since it started.

So there it was: testimony that absolutely incriminated the government and involved it in a specific plot to frame a witness. But there is yet more—material even more startling and certainly more revealing.

The government, testified Shobe, was so anxious to force the defendant, Parks, into becoming a witness for the prosecution that at one time Sheridan discussed a plan with him, Shobe, to abduct Parks and to scare him into submission.

According to his testimony, Shobe devised the details of the plot, though one may infer from what he said that Sheridan conceived the idea. If Sheridan didn't, he certainly appeared to be an agreeable bystander, according to Shobe's direct testimony.

Shobe said he had noticed that in the evenings Parks sat in front of Tom's Cleaners either on a milk crate or on a half of a chair. He suggested to Sheridan that it would be "comparatively easy" for him and a couple of companions to drive up and "arrest" Parks.

They would then drive him to the big parking lot behind the Federal Building. Then, suddenly, they would end the pretense, handcuff Parks, gag him, blindfold him, and drive him out to a park in East Nashville.

There, according to Shobe, "we would take him out into the woods and, well, we had a couple of shovels and we were just going to start digging a hole. And Mr. Parks being an undertaker, I imagine he would get the message."

After they had scared Parks "to within an inch of his life," they would remove the gags and reason with him, pretending they were strong-arm men sent by Hoffa and assigned to get rid of Parks.

If Parks responded to all of this by being scared enough to cooperate—and one would imagine that there would be no trouble in convincing him that he should cooperate under those circumstances—fine, the plot would proceed. If, however, Parks refused to be scared sufficiently to capitulate, then Shobe had an alternate plan. He would signal with a flashlight, and men waiting in the woods would come charging into the parkland to "rescue" Parks. Shobe and his companions would melt away into the darkness.

A great idea, but why wasn't it carried out?

"Simply because," said Shobe, "I felt that with the feelings against the government in Nashville and their part in the civil rights, and I don't think the local authorities would just say release Fred Shobe if they caught him with this man bound and gagged in a car or else out digging a hole."

Basically, Shobe said, he was afraid that some local policeman would accidentally happen on the scene and ruin the plot.

And there was another dissuader: the penalty for kidnapping in Tennessee is death.

Well, this wild tale was about plans that never were carried out, yet, in the light of what went before and in conjunction with events that really did take place and pressures that really were brought to bear, who's to say it was not seriously considered? A government that can use voodoo to try to change a defendant into a witness for the prosecution is really not to be considered as being above a little friendly kidnapping.

The jury, however, knew little of this. For example, it knew nothing about:

1. Any of Shobe's conversations with Sheridan.

2. How much money the government paid Shobe to work as an informer.

3. Any of the details of the plot to terrorize Parks into joining the prosecution.

Shobe was permitted to relate to the jury only that:

1. Patrolman Walker had worked for Walter Sheridan since sometime in 1962.

2. Walker and some other detectives on the Nashville police force visited him at his motel to check on whether Sheri-

dan would keep his promises to them. (Nashville police were under investigation at the time. Presumably, the investigation was one of those devices used to frighten cops such as Walker into collaborating with the Justice Department in unethical and illegal practices.)

3. Walker told Shobe that Sheridan had promised him immunity in the sweeping investigation of the Nashville police department.

The prosecution seemed content that it had kept from the ears of the jurors the most damaging testimony in the entire trial up to that point. It did not challenge one statement made by Shobe. What he said remains undisputed in the transcript—a matter of record. Yet Shobe positively identified Patrolman Walker as a secret agent of the federal government, after having identified himself as a man playing the same role.

With his testimony unchallenged, unassailed, unimpeached, how significant was the remainder of the case against me and the other defendants?

But we hadn't yet heard from Edward Grady Partin. It is interesting to compare how much of the testimony of Partin, undercover agent for the government, reached the ears of the jurors, against the amount from the defense's undercover agent, Shobe.

When Shobe had finished, I flagged Jacques Schiffer, a crackerjack lawyer frustrated by the court.

"Jack," I said, "they'd never dare make a movie out of a plot like this."

"It's too damn complicated for Hollywood to use," he grunted.

It's a pity, but what he said was true.

27

Tippens and Partin

It is clear that the testimony of Trooper Paschal and Carl Fields was a disappointment to the prosecution, even if it was accepted on its face value and apart from the recanting that was done under cross-examination.

It was admitted by the prosecution that neither Paschal nor young Fields talked to either Betty Paschal or Gratin Fields about the trial or their role as jurors.

Both Mrs. Paschal and Gratin Fields had stated that they knew nothing of the alleged plot to approach them about their vote until they were summoned before Judge Miller and dismissed from the jury.

The testimony of Paschal and Carl Fields can only mean that the jury wasn't tampered with. Even if you believe the part of testimony they gave before their later denial, it means only that there was *discussion* about tampering with the jury. In fact, James C. Tippens, the Nashville insurance man, was the only juror to whom a direct approach had allegedly been made.

Under these circumstances, it was natural for the defense to expect that Tippens would be the big gun in the prosecution's arsenal. Here was an actual juror who had said he was definitely offered a bribe. But, in fact, the prosecution was not able to make use of the Tippens affair.

The story of the alleged offer of a bribe to Tippens has already been recounted. Tippens had gone to Judge Miller in Nashville on October 24, 1962, to tell the judge that on the previous day, October 23, after having been tentatively seated on the jury, he had been told by Lawrence Medlin it would be worth $10,000 to Tippens to vote for me.

To say the very least, this story raises some questions:

Who was putting up the money? Who was behind the bribe attempt? Who induced Medlin to approach Tippens? Who was close enough to the situation to know that Tippens was one of the very first jurors selected to be tentatively seated?

The way it turned out, however, Medlin was not in court, and he could not be produced. As it happened, Medlin had been indicted when all of the defendants in the case were indicted, but when the rest of us had asked for a change in venue, Medlin had refused to join in the action. He wanted to stand trial in Nashville, he said, without offering a reason for his decision. So his case was handled separately.

Consequently, when it came to Chattanooga, the prosecution faced a major legal problem. Medlin was not on trial there. And thus the government was prevented from trading the alleged offer by Medlin back to me or to anyone else.

Nothing about Medlin could be used in the Chattanooga trial. In fact, it was not until nearly a month after my trial ended that a jury in Nashville on April 3 convicted Medlin of offering a $10,000 bribe to his neighbor, Tippens.

But consider these facts:

1. The government produced no proof to link the alleged offer to me or to any other member of my organization.

2. The case was based entirely on Tippens's testimony about his conversation with Medlin.

3. Medlin admitted a conversation had taken place but denied making an offer of money.

4. Medlin insisted he had relayed to Tippens, a friend, details of a conversation he had overheard. He did not know, he said, the identity of the persons conducting that conversation but thought it interesting enough to relate to Tippens, who, he knew, had been called up for jury duty.

5. The government offered no hint as to whom Medlin had overheard.

6. Medlin insisted—and swore under oath—that he had never heard of Hoffa and knew nothing about him. His statement is in the record unchallenged. And heaven knows I had never heard of Medlin until Tippens's testimony.

When Tippens was slated to appear in Chattanooga to repeat the story he had given to Judge Miller in Nashville, without the supporting testimony of Medlin, defense counsel presented a strong argument against his appearance. There is ample legal precedence as well as venerable custom to support a ruling against Tippens's appearance, but Judge Wilson at first decided that Tippens should be heard.

After heated arguments, however, Judge Wilson did stipulate the subjects to which he would allow Tippens to testify, and on the surface these seemed sufficiently limited to assure some degree of fairness—except for two things.

First, Judge Wilson ruled that Tippens's testimony should be accepted only to the degree that it might tend to corroborate details of Partin's testimony regarding statements made to Partin by me. We were reluctant to agree that Partin was a reputable, credible witness, or that any of his testimony was corroborative or indeed, corroboratable.

Second, though Judge Wilson ruled to restrict Tippens's testimony, he then seemed uncommonly slow in stopping him when Tippens rambled off into a recitation of prohibited testimony.

The court decreed that Tippens would be permitted to testify only to the following: that he had had a conversation with Medlin; that he had reported this conversation to Judge Miller; that he felt the conversation was of such a nature as to disqualify him from serving on the jury.

Specifically, the court said, Tippens could not say what he and Medlin discussed, and he could not relate what he had reported to Judge Miller.

This sounded fair enough, and the defense indicated its agreement, but Tippens seemed determined to violate both the letter and the spirit of the court's ruling, much to the delight of the prosecution.

At one point, despite repeated admonitions by defense counsel as well as some warning from the bench, Tippens stated flatly: "I told Judge Miller that I felt disqualified to serve on the jury due to the fact that I had been offered a sum of money!"

Berke leaped to his feet, objecting. Branstetter demanded that the remark be stricken from the court record. Judge Wilson turned to the jury and instructed it to ignore the remark—to disregard it. Easy to say, but the damage had been done.

Tippens made such excursions repeatedly, and the transcript of his testimony is studded with objections from the defense, which tried to interrupt him as he boldly ignored the court's ruling and thrust into forbidden testimony.

That transcript also reveals clearly that the prosecution was egging Tippens on, hoping to drive the unmentionable testimony into the minds of the jurors, even though the court record might show that it had been expunged. Take, for example, just one example of Tippens's testimony: "I went into Judge Miller's office and told him that I felt that I should be disqualified as a juror due to the fact that I felt like that I could not serve under the conditions that existed in which were, namely, I had been offered . . ."

Berke shouted an objection.

Judge Wilson instructed the jury to disregard the remark.

But the remark had been made. Unless it was collectively daydreaming, the jury heard it. And there's one thing certain about human nature: if any juror hadn't caught the remark and then was told to disregard it, he was certain to ask other jurors what it was he was supposed to disregard. Thus the point was driven home more forcibly than had the judge said nothing. In fact, once Tippens had made his point, there was no way to undo the harm he had done.

Tippens testified that after having held his conversation with Judge Miller on October 24, he again met with Medlin, near the latter's horse barn in the country (it was in the country that Medlin and Tippens were neighbors; in town Medlin ran a sandwich-packaging company). At this point in his testimony Tippens seemed about to repeat what he had said in the judge's chambers, and when the defense protested loudly, Judge Wilson dismissed the jury while he listened to legal arguments.

Yet even this dismissal appeared prejudicial to the defense. Quite clearly we were being portrayed as a guilty-as-sin group clutching at every legal straw to keep an earnest and cleancut citizen from testifying about a crime.

But the fact was that it was the prosecution's duty to establish that the alleged $10,000 bribe was linked to me or connected with me in any way. And this it failed to do. This, in fact, it couldn't do.

There were substantive doubts about the testimony given by Pitts, by Paschal, by Fields, and by Patrolman Walker.. There is on record conflicting testimony for each one of these witnesses. Now there was the testimony of Tippens. And Tippens's testimony had to stand alone, for Medlin swore it was not as Tippens said it was.

In view of the fact that Tippens seemed extraordinarily *eager* to get in some damaging testimony in spite of the court's ruling, is not the credibility of his statements placed in doubt? I say there is strong doubt.

It was not up to me to prove my innocence. And, presuming my innocence, none of the testimony revealed thus far had been at all damaging. Indeed, the evidence presented was quite insubstantial.

Now comes Edward Grady Partin with his extraordinary story.

It will be recalled that on the very first day that Edward Grady Partin arrived in Nashville he had stumbled upon the exact evidence he had been assigned to unearth. His extreme good fortune in accidentally bumping into Nicholas J. Tweel, alias Anthony Quinn, and having Tweel spill the whole story of my plans to fix the jury may seem a little bit far-fetched. The whole thing, of course, was, to say the least, implausible—despite Partin's insistence that his testimony was true. But how did Tweel and Dorfman remember the incidents?

Tweel, one of the defendants, testified on the stand that he and Allen Dorfman, another defendant, had been involved in many business deals. Dorfman, a Chicago insurance man, handled some Teamsters Health and Welfare insurance.

Under examination Tweel went into considerable detail of the business relationship he had with Dorfman. Tweel said that he and Dorfman had planned to meet in New York to discuss some business transactions, but when, at the last minute, I asked Dorfman to bring some records to Nashville that I thought might be needed in the trial, Dorfman had telephoned Tweel and suggested that they meet in Nashville instead of New York.

Tweel testified that he and Dorfman were sitting in the coffee shop of the Andrew Jackson Hotel when Partin came up and introduced himself to Dorfman, reminding him that he had met him previously. Dorfman introduced Partin to Tweel.

Who, then, was Anthony Quinn?

He was a figment of Partin's imagination, Tweel said. There never had been any Anthony Quinn, he said.

Shortly after the introductions Dorfman left, Tweel testified, and Partin engaged Tweel in conversation, telling him, a total stranger, all about his legal troubles in Baton Rouge and finally asking Tweel if he knew a good lawyer whom he could recommend.

Tweel said that by coincidence he did know a good lawyer in Baton Rouge, but he couldn't think of his name. He said he'd try to look it up in case Partin might wish to get in touch with him later. Then they parted.

And that was all there was to the entire incident, Tweel testified. Partin never had called him later to find out about the lawyer in Baton Rouge. In fact, said Tweel, he had never seen Partin again. Tweel said he had met some acquaintances, had had dinner with them, and had gone nightclubbing on the town until about two o'clock the next morning—a statement that was supported by independent testimony.

The next day, Tweel said, he and Dorfman had gone over to watch the opening of the trial at the courthouse. When the morning session of court was ended, Tweel said, he and Dorfman had gone to lunch and conferred on their business matters. Then Dorfman had caught a plane to Chicago, and he, Tweel, had caught one to Huntington, West Virginia.

Tweel said he had never before been to Nashville, and that he had never returned. More, he testified that he did not meet me, that he had seen me in the lobby of the hotel and again in court, and that was all.

"I never had any occasion to meet him," he said. "The next time I saw Mr. Hoffa we were being arraigned together in Nashville, Tennessee. I don't know how I got involved with him. . . . I didn't even meet him on that occasion."

The upshot of his testimony was that the jury acquitted both Dorfman and Tweel—which, in effect, means that Partin's testimony was disbelieved.

Consequently, we felt justified, as soon as Partin had taken the stand and commenced this tale about his alleged conversations with Tweel, when my attorney, James E. Haggerty, former president of the Michigan State Bar and a director of the Detroit Bar Association, entered a motion to suppress Partin's entire testimony. Haggerty argued that Partin had been planted with the defense as an undercover agent and had remained one during the period covering my previous trial in Nashville. Partin's intrusion, Haggerty stated, was just as much an intrusion on my right as if the government had bugged my rooms or tapped my phones.

Partin was present during our discussions with my lawyers, Haggerty said. "He had had discussions with me during the trial of the case and, to my knowledge, discussions with others. He was constantly hanging around, I never knew for what reason," Haggerty told Judge Wilson. "He was in court nearly every day. He was at the hotel and Mr. Hoffa's suite where the lawyers conferred at night."

Harvey Silets, Chicago lawyer and Dorfman's counsel, declared that the snooping and spying on the defense in the midst of its trial was illegal, and that consequently illegality "taints everything this man touched."

"It is as if Your Honor's law clerk should all of a sudden turn out to be an informer and a spy for the defense," Silets said. The judge appeared unmoved by this zeroing-in of the espionage.

The Judith Coplon case was cited by Cecil Branstetter, Larry Campbell's lawyer, who reminded Judge Wilson that the prosecution's case was dismissed because the FBI eavesdropped on Judith Coplon's conversations with her attorneys (via taps on her wires). The identical principle was involved,

Branstetter said, in the eavesdropping done in person by Partin.

U.S. Attorney James Neal countered this argument by conceding that if I had been *convicted* in Nashville, the verdict might have been tainted because the government had planted an informer in my camp. But this, Neal went on, had nothing to do with the *new case* in Chattanooga, which was built upon information that had been gathered since then, by informers.

By admitting this much, however, Neal had made an error. He had admitted that there had been spying by a planted informer in Nashville! Silets leaped to his feet.

Silets recalled that in July, 1963, Federal Judge Frank Grey, Jr., had listened to defense arguments that the jury-tampering indictment had been based on illegally obtained evidence, and that Neal had categorically denied any such thing. Silets then told Judge Wilson: "I can remember it as if it was said a moment ago. Mr. Neal in great pain and anguish, saying to Judge Grey, 'Your Honor, there was no eavesdropping; there was no wire tap; there was no illegally-obtained evidence.' At that time, Mr. Neal must have known that such a thing as what has been perpetrated on this court was in fact in existence because that is the basis that this indictment was returned upon."

As the point was argued back and forth, it boiled down to this single fact: the court was asked to accept the fact that during the Nashville trial the government had listened to Partin's information about alleged jury-tampering and any other law-breaking plots involved but had learned not one word from this spy about the defense's tactics and plans and strategies.

When Partin was put on the stand to be questioned on this issue, he could remember in detail and with clarity every conversation he had with the defendants about their alleged jury-tampering activities, but he couldn't remember a thing about trial strategy that was discussed in his presence.

He explained all this by saying he was capable of writing down in his mind things that he wanted to remember. He didn't write anything in his mind about anything else pertaining to the trial—just the jury-tampering stuff. Partin admitted that he dined almost constantly with me and members of the defense, but he denied on the stand that the case ever came up as a topic of conversation around the dinner table.

Moreover, Partin had another explanation for not listening to discussions among the lawyers or between the lawyers and me.

"I wasn't interested in the case," Partin said.

What could anyone do with a witness like Partin?

Every member of the defense staff was certain that Partin had reported on our discussion of the case in the privacy of our rooms, and there seemed only one way to prove it. One by one the defense attorneys from the Nashville trial took the stand as witnesses, and one by one they reported on unusual coincidences where the prosecution seemed to have been informed of what was about to be done in court by the defense.

Bill Bufalino, for instance, testified that in our room on the night of December 4 he had interviewed several witnesses, truck drivers from Detroit. He had asked questions and then made notes of their responses to those questions, he said, and later they were typed up in question-and-answer form.

"They were typed, and Ed Partin helped me staple them," Bufalino said. "He [Partin] was carrying copies back and forth from one place to the other."

On the next day, December 5, Bufalino said, "When Mr. Neal was interrogating the witnesses, he asked, 'Isn't it a fact,' or words to this effect, 'Isn't it a fact that—or were you supplied with questions and answers as to what your testimony should be?' "

Bill Bufalino testified to another remarkable coincidence that took place that same day, December 5. On the night of December 4, he related, five or six defense attorneys had been sitting around a large table in my room, discussing trial strategy. Partin was sitting with them, shuffling a deck of cards, as was his habit, as Bufalino outlined an approach he planned to take the next day when he put a certain truck driver on the stand.

On December 5, when Bufalino reached the area that he had discussed the night before he was faced with another strange "coincidence."

"When I got to this particular area," Bufalino testified, "I started, now, and this is the language, 'Now, witness, I bring you back to 1953,'—and that is all I had to say and Mr. Neal jumped to his feet and said, 'I object, Your Honor, they are getting into a different area.'

"I said, 'How do you know where I am going, what I am going to ask?'

"He answered, and he said, 'Your Honor, I suggest, may I request, that the jury leave this room and I want to argue this particular case in the absence of the jury.' The jury left the courtroom.

"I said to Mr. Neal, 'How do you know what I am going to ask—all I said was 1953?'

"He said, 'I am psychic.' That's in the record."

As Bufalino testified to this in Chattanooga, Neal stood and listened. He made no answer, offered no rebuttal, let it go unchallenged in the record. It seemed as though he had been forced—albeit through his silence—to admit that the government had, indeed, used in its case material gained by eavesdropping on defense lawyers and their clients.

Walter Sheridan reinforced that confirmation. Called as a defense witness, he testified as to the manner in which Partin had kept him informed.

Asked if the information passed to him constituted matters pertaining to the lawsuit then on trial, Sheridan answered: "Occasionally."

The "comings and goings" of people constituted most of the information he received from Partin, Sheridan said, and it dealt with matters that were "at least unethical and improper," if not, in fact, illegal.

This information, Sheridan said, he passed along regularly to Neal. Then, when, under direct questioning, he was asked if on December 4, 1962, Partin had informed him that witnesses were being interviewed and that they had written questions available, he answered: "There was an occasion when Mr. Partin told me that witnesses were being interviewed by Mr. Bufalino and that they had questions and answers and he was going over them."

Q. He did advise you of that?
A. Yes, sir.
Q. Did he tell you who they were?
A. I knew who they were, I think.

We considered Sheridan's to be highly incriminating testimony, coming, as it did, from the man who was the chief strategist for the entire operation. We thought it was particularly significant because we knew that we could testify to the fact that Partin not only had been eavesdropping on our defense plans but had deliberately tried to get us to approach a juror who, he had said, was known to him—and that we had turned him down!

28

When You Peel an Onion, You Cry

We did not know that Edward Grady Partin was a spy in our midst. As soon as he revealed himself as one, however, we recognized instantly that he was intent on involving us in some form of entrapment. It would be impossible to prove that the government, through the Department of Justice, had tried to play the illegal game of entrapment. It is easy to prove, however, that Partin, as an agent for the Justice Department, had tried to entrap us into jury-rigging.

At one point in Nashville Partin mentioned the name of a particular juror. He said that he had known him in military service, and he suggested that he contact this former buddy and rambled off into some discussion of joining the juror when he went on vacation, or some such. Partin, moreover, had said all this in the presence of Bill Bufalino, who responded not merely with displeasure but with anger.

"Lay off that," Bufalino said, and he testified to this statement in Chattanooga and put it in the court record later. "I want to have absolutely nothing to do with any such discussion. . . . We have a cinch case here. This case is absolutely nothing."

Bufalino lectured Partin, telling him that he had better forget "anything like that." Partin took his lecture sullenly, remaining silent. But why shouldn't he remain silent? He knew what was in store for us.

When Partin took the stand, Judge Wilson, it will be remembered, would not allow us to question him about his array of indictments or even about his past criminal record. So far as the jury knew, Partin was an ordinary clean-living citizen who, as a Teamsters official, was so disgusted by the conduct of the Teamsters' General President that he had voluntarily turned witness for the prosecution.

Stymied in his efforts to have Partin reveal himself for what he was—a man with a serious criminal record who was employed by the government in an unethical, if not illegal, assignment—Attorney Silets tried to have Partin disclose the nature of his secret talks with Hawk Daniels and Frank Grimsley when he was in jail in Baton Rouge.

In a courtroom crowded with lawyers there was an audible gasp when the witness turned to Silets and declared, "Well, sir, that is a matter not related to this here at all."

Partin had ruled on the relevancy of a question!

Normally some remonstration from the bench might be expected, but Judge Wilson concurred with Partin, declaring, "I have difficulty in seeing how it is material to the issue that is now before the court."

It was perfectly clear that the defense was trying to establish the fact that Partin had been a hired agent of the government before he had called me. Since burden of proof of guilt is on the prosecution, this certainly seemed to us to have some bearing, for if "proof of guilt" is rigged and the result of a frame-up, just how valid is it? For hours, however, the defense found that its task was not one of pursuing the truth but one of getting past the legal barriers erected by Judge Wilson.

In time, of course, the testimony of both Hawk Daniels and A. Frank Grimsley, of the Justice Department's staff, revealed that Partin had become an undercover spy for the

Justice Department in late September or thereabouts and was serving as an undercover agent when, on October 8, he had made his first phone call to me.

It was even admitted that before Partin made his call, a recording device was brought from the district attorney's office in Baton Rouge and attached to his phone by experts so that a recording of what was said in Partin's conversation with me could be made.

But none of this information ever reached the ears of the jury. And at this point in the trial, when it was vital to the defense and to the direction and course of the trial that this information be made available to the jury, Judge Wilson would not let defense counsel pursue these facts and get them into the record. As far as the jury was concerned, Partin had stayed in Nashville for two and a half months during the course of the trial on "union matters and personal business."

Silets asked Partin if he had been paid by the government. Partin said he had not.

Silets asked Partin if he had been promised anything. Partin said he had not.

Yet, of course, both Partin's statement were lies, as subsequent evidence and testimony showed.

After Partin had denied receiving either reimbursement or promises from the government, however, Silets quickly asked a question that evoked an incriminating answer.

Silets asked: "Will you tell me, please, why did you want to take the assignment from the FBI to come to Nashville to do what you say you were going to try to do for the FBI?"

"I don't know," answered Partin, as Neal thundered an objection that Judge Wilson sustained.

At this juncture, when the cat had just about been let out of the bag, Judge Wilson decided that he would take over the questioning of the witness.

Partin reiterated for the judge his statement that the government had not sent him to Nashville. Under Judge Wilson's questioning, he denied that the government had provided any transportation for him in Nashville, that there was any arrangement by which the government would pay any of his expenses or compensate him in any way while he was in Nashville, that he came to Nashville not at the government's request but at my request per the phone call of October 8.

Over and over again Partin, along with various representatives of government in sworn testimony, denied that he had ever been compensated in any way by Uncle Sam for his activities as an undercover agent and *agent provocateur*. Indeed, when he was on the stand later, Walter Sheridan gave the following sworn testimony:

> Q. Have you ever authorized any payment to Mr. Partin?
> A. No, sir.
> Q. Has there been, to your knowledge, any money paid to Mr. Partin?
> A. No sir.
> Q. Has any promise been made to Mr. Partin?
> A. No, sir.

Yet all this testimony notwithstanding, subsequent evidence indicated that Walter Sheridan could well have perjured himself by making such statements. But though the evidence finally found its way into the court records and transcript toward the end of the trial, no juror ever heard of it.

At the very moment that Sheridan was denying on the witness stand that any payment had ever been made to Partin, there was in existence in government files a memorandum from Walter Sheridan to S. A. Andretta, administrative assistant to the Attorney General, dated July 3, 1963, setting up the secretive, circuitous method of paying $300 a month to Partin, a "confidential source." There was also proof that this money was handled by Grimsley and that it was paid to Partin's wife. But the jury was to know none of this.

What appeared to be the perjury of the two government employees remained unchallenged at that time, and even when it was exposed later on in the trial, it evoked no special reaction from the court or, more specifically, from Judge Wilson.

Of course, the responses of Sheridan and Grimsley might have been accurate technically. As they stood, though, they were misleading. The prosecution was extremely clever in the area of technical accuracy, and we had the feeling sometimes that they were playing games with us and with the court.

There was the matter, for instance, of Sheridan's "notes." Asked if he took notes when Partin relayed information to him, Sheridan said yes, he did, and he had them on file.

Naturally the defense demanded that these notes be turned over to Judge Wilson so that he could rule if they contained information helpful to the defense.

Neal took over the questioning of Sheridan, however, and it was revealed that Sheridan took down "cryptic notes," in which one word might represent "five minutes of conversation." The notes were in no way "verbatim," Sheridan said.

The law provides that such notes, if they are to be examined by the trial judge to determine whether they are of material value to the defense, must be "essentially verbatim" or signed or acknowledged by the witness. Therefore, since they were not verbatim, Judge Wilson didn't get to see the notes.

Eventually, Judge Wilson ruled against the defense in the matter of Partin. He ruled that Partin had not been sent to Nashville by the government, that he was in Nashville at my request: "I would find that there has been no interference by the government with an attorney-client relationship of any defendant in this case. I would further find that the government did not place this witness, Mr. Partin, in the defendant's midst, rather that he was knowingly and voluntarily placed in their midst by one of the defendants."

In other words, the jury was going to have to listen to Edward Grady Partin, no matter what! Understandably, I think, I was very upset by the ruling.

Partin's testimony, if taken verbatim from the transcript, would fill a volume by itself, interspersed as it was with objections, arguments between counsel, and the methodical insistence of Judge Wilson that Partin be heard. It is, however, sufficient merely to set down the damning and damaging testimony given by this witness.

Partin testified that:

1. I was desperate, worried, intent on rigging the jury in Nashville.

2. I was infuriated when Tippens didn't respond to the bribe offer, saying, "The dirty bastard went in and told the judge that his neighbor had offered him $10,000," and adding, "We are going to have to lay low for a few days."

3. I told Partin I would "pay $15,000 or $20,000—whatever it costs—to get to the jury."

4. On November 5 he overheard me raging at Ewing King in the corridor of the Andrew Jackson Hotel because King hadn't been doing what I had instructed him to do. Later I told Partin, "King keeps telling me he can get the patrolman, but he doesn't get him."

5. Two days later I told him I had Gratin Fields in my "hip pocket."

6. I explained that I had Fields in my camp because—and this is a direct quote from Partin on the stand—"One of my business agents, Campbell, came to Nashville prior to the trial and took care of it."

7. One week after that I berated King to Partin calling

him "a stupid S.O.B. for thumbing around and not getting the job done."

8. Five days after that I expressed disgust to Partin over the fact that the "highway patrolman didn't take the money."

That is the essence of what Partin had to say about me, and certainly it was incriminating in the extreme. But three things stood out as the defense undertook cross-examination.

1. Partin said that with the one exception of the instance when I was hollering at King in the hallway of the hotel, all of my conversations had taken place when no one else was present. This placed full weight on Partin's credibility as a witness.

2. Larry Campbell had incredible extrasensory perception in knowing, before the trial started, who the jurors would be and in getting to Gratin Fields.

3. The highway patrolman, Paschal, claimed he wanted a promotion, that he was not lacking money, but Partin said I was angry because he "didn't take the money."

Attorney Harry Berke got Partin to reiterate that he had quoted me as saying Campbell had come to Nashville prior to the trial and then followed up with an unanswerable question.

"How could he fix the jury," Berke asked, "prior to the time when he didn't even know who was going to be on it?"

Neal, however, immediately objected on the ground that Partin was merely repeating what I had told him, and Judge Wilson sustained that objection. Jacques Schiffer protested that the question went right to the roots of the testimony and complained to Judge Wilson.

"Every time we reach that point in cross-examination where we come to a crucial question," Schiffer protested, "we are not permitted to receive an answer."

The defense then tried to get into the record some reference to Partin's friendliness with Fidel Castro. It sought to

introduce a letter from a Cuban general thanking Partin for
help in training Castro's militia. It tried to show that Partin
had been trying to lease freighters to run arms into Cuba.
But, needless to say, Prosecutor Neal's objections blocked
every effort to bring this out.

Judge Wilson turned to Schiffer, saying, "You will not be
permitted to introduce charges for the purpose of attempting
to degrade a witness. We're not here for that purpose."

Schiffer argued that we were there for the purpose of
evaluating Partin's credibility as a witness, and that an evaluation of his character was necessary in order to make a judgment. He charged that the court was unfairly limiting the
defense, a charge that, repeated over and again, always fell
on deaf ears.

Silets then strove to get onto the record some reference to
Partin's indictment-packed past. Partin, however, professed
that he was unable to recall that he had been convicted in
Bremerton, Washington. He couldn't remember, either, that
he had been dishonorably discharged from the Marines.
However, when Silets began to read from the record, Partin
interrupted.

"It wasn't a burglary charge. You said it was a burglary
charge. I said it wasn't," he said, to justify his statement that
he wasn't arrested for burglary.

A further difficulty arose when, as a study of the transcript
shows, it became clear that Partin wasn't responding to the
questions. He seemed loquacious on many subjects, including, at one point, coon dogs, but when faced by pertinent
defense questions, he was evasive.

Schiffer, fed up, protested that the witness wasn't answer-
ing questions and a few moments later called for a mistrial.
Finally, Schiffer, frustrated by Judge Wilson's refusal to
make Partin respond to the questions, asked the judge to allow him to withdraw from the case and "put Parks under

the protection of the Court and let Your Honor defend him because I am being prevented from defending him."

Partin, Schiffer said, "defies the order of the court. But the court idly does nothing with this witness, and this is prejudicing my man."

"Just make a note of this in the record," retorted Judge Wilson. "We will take it up at a later time."

Silets then resumed questioning Partin about a breaking and entering charge and the conviction that brought him a sentence of fifteen years, and he alluded to the fact that twice Partin had broken out of prison. Dim stirrings of memory began to come to Partin. He remembered that he was "confined in the reformatory school for something. . . . I don't remember the name of the place or who was there or whatever it was."

"I don't remember—I certainly don't," Partin said over and over. Silets observed that this was remarkably strange for a man who could remember in such exact detail every conversation he had held with me, Hoffa.

Couldn't a man who was possessed of such a remarkable memory recall his own arrest and confinement in jail? No. He just couldn't.

Finally, Partin declared, "I have never been convicted of but one felony in my life."

"You have pleaded guilty to other offenses, haven't you?" Silets asked.

"Minor fighting or something."

"And one of those was assaulting a Mr. Colotto which you pleaded guilty to on December 2, 1955?"

Judge Wilson interjected: "Sustain the objection!"

"I didn't hear one, Your Honor," protested Silets.

"Well, counsel stood up," said Judge Wilson, sustaining a nonexistent objection and silencing forever in his court any information about the assault on Colotto.

It was only a short time after that, with the jury out, James E. Haggerty, former President of the Michigan State Bar, charged Judge Wilson with mishandling the trial.

Haggerty said: "In my forty-one years of experience, mostly in federal courts, I have witnessed an exhibition this morning up to date that leaves me clearly puzzled and somewhat disgusted." The witness had refused to answer questions, Haggerty said; he had rambled off into extraneous subjects; prosecution lawyers were smiling at the jury, grimacing, shaking their heads. Such deplorable conduct, Haggerty declared, should never be allowed in a court of justice.

Then Haggerty threw his bombshell. He declared that the defense was ready to present positive proof of the surveillance by the government of me, the other defendants, and the defense attorneys.

"We have photos taken last night," declared Haggerty. "We have photographs of an FBI agent by the name of Sheets and we will present that proof this afternoon."

While Haggerty was telling the court that the surveillance was most active and constant and that it "hamstrings the defendants and the defendants' counsel," James Durkin, the special assistant attorney general who was linked with the Bishop St. Psalm incident, got up from the prosecution's table and hurriedly left the courtroom.

Branstetter, noting Durkin's departure, asked the court to instruct Neal, as head of the prosecution, not to discuss with Sheets the information that had been given to the court. Neal protested that he hadn't sent Durkin out for that reason. "The purpose I sent that man was to get a subpoena to a well-known wire-tapper who was indicted and tried with the Defendant Hoffa, who came to town the other day, *Bernard Spindel!*"

Silets leaped up: "How do you know that, Mr. Neal, unless you have been surveilling the premises?"

The issue was now joined, and Silets, boiling from the frustrations of trying to defend a case that seemed to him to have been rigged, in a court that seemed to him to favor the prosecution, asked the court to put Neal on the stand to say under oath that there had been no surveillance in the case. Silets said he wanted a flat denial under oath, not anything to the effect: "I know of none."

Neal offered to take the stand and testify "to the very best of my knowledge and belief there have been no surveillance of any counsel." Then, he, too, joined the fray: "I would expect, however, the court to hold Mr. Schiffer in contempt," Neal declared.

That did it for Schiffer.

"For what?" he demanded. "For telling the truth? That is the type of tactic of the government. As soon as defendant gets up and talks about the malfunctions of justice in this court by these prosecutors, they run to the court and they say, 'Throw Schiffer in jail, hold him in contempt, but leave us alone, Judge. We are the select fellows; we are the masters in this case. The Attorney General appointed us. He hates Hoffa, and we will get Schiffer, too.' "

Soon after this outburst, court recessed for lunch.

At 1:30 P.M. Schiffer stormed back into the courtroom, raging. He had returned to his hotel room, he reported, and discovered that while he had been in court that morning his files had been stolen. He said he had been told that a government investigator had been seen in the hotel about noon, and that a federal marshal had been observed near the door of Schiffer's room.

Schiffer said he had spent many months preparing the case to defend Parks and that all of the documents representing that preparation were missing.

"This has never happened to me before," he said.

A chill ran through us all. This was a horrible violation of the lawyer-client relationship, and it seemed to many of us that this invasion of privacy was exactly like the Gestapo's tactics.

We waited for a roar of indignation from the bench as Schiffer related this sickening story to the court.

Judge Wilson heard Schiffer out, then ruled that we would continue the trial. He did note, however, that we would take up the surveillance issue later.

Aghast, we sought to pick up the thread of the trial, to bring our minds back to the crucial matter before us, that of exposing Partin as a fraud and liar. Schiffer sat down, breathing heavily, shaking his head in disbelief.

29
Reimbursement Without Pay

It is apparent that Judge Wilson was encouraged in his decision to permit Partin to testify before the jury by his belief that Partin had in no way received pay from the government for his activities. Indeed, Partin himself had sworn that no payments had been made, and Walter Sheridan had testified under oath likewise.

Since the defense could produce no evidence that any payments *had* been made, Judge Wilson, at that point in the trial, had no reason to disbelieve the two sworn witnesses.

In one part of his direct examination, however, Partin had described various trips he made to contact government agents. He went to Alabama, Tennessee, New Orleans, and other points on these assignments, he related. Moreover, when he was cross-examined on the matter of these trips and asked if he had been paid either directly or indirectly for his expenses, surprisingly he admitted that he had. The money, he said, had been paid to his wife. He also said that some money was still owing him.

Silets pursued the issue. He wanted to know how the money happened to be paid to Mrs. Partin.

A. Because I wanted my children taken care of, that's why.

Q. Well, how did that arrangement come about? Did you ask the government to do that?

A. I think they asked me did I have any outstanding things that had to be taken care of and during the course of the conversation I told them I was interested in that.

It turned out, under this questioning, that Partin was divorced and had been in arrears in his alimony payments to Mrs. Partin. He wasn't sure how much she had received in this manner from the government, but he thought it might be around $1,000—maybe more, maybe less.

Partin's abrupt denial of his previous testimony and his belated admission that in a manner of speaking he had really been reimbursed by the government was sufficient for Silets to demand that the government produce all vouchers and checks involved in the transaction.

Prosecutor Neal, contending that the payments to Partin's divorced wife weren't really payments, but expense money, argued against producing checks on the ground that they weren't relevant. In the process of doing so Neal also denied to the court any suggestion that the prosecution had had anything to do with the pilferage of Attorney Schiffer's files, and he let it be known that he thought that Schiffer had made up the entire story. The latter was an uncommon charge for a government attorney to level against an officer of the court, but it illustrates the degree of bitterness between prosecution and defense as well as the absolute arrogance with which the prosecution handled its case.

Judge Wilson, meanwhile, ordered that the government vouchers be presented.

It turned out that there were four items: two checks for $300 apiece and two for $150 apiece. But here again the government asked us to believe in another remarkable coincidence.

These checks, Neal had insisted, were for "expense money," and it turned out that Partin ran up *exactly* $300 per month in expenses, three months in a row.

Schiffer appealed to the reason of the court. The checks,

he said, obviously represented payment for testimony, and
he reminded Judge Wilson that under the law it is a crime
to pay witnesses to testify.

Neal shouted that what Schiffer was saying was an "un-
mitigated lie," and he charged that the defense, too, was
paying witnesses.

Schiffer admitted that it was: mileage expenses and standard one-day witness fees, as spelled out in the law.

Silets, who had been examining the checks, then reported
to the court on what the cancellation marks disclosed.

"I am flabbergasted by these documents," Silets told Judge
Wilson. "Apparently the check was issued to Mr. Grimsley,
then Grimsley used the check to go to the First National
Bank of Atlanta, and with this check having been endorsed
by him he has a cashier's check issued by the First National
Bank of Atlanta, payable to Mrs. Partin.

"Now," continued Silets, "if this is not an attempt to cir-
cumvent the meaning of this act of Congress [making wit-
ness-paying a crime] then what is?"

When A. Frank Grimsley was called to the stand, he testified that, starting in July, 1963, he had channeled $1,200 to
Mrs. Partin via the device of getting cashier's checks. He
said Uncle Sam still owed Partin $343.47, naming, at last,
an odd figure.

Grimsley said he had held a conversation with Partin in
July, 1963, when Partin had related that "inasmuch as he
wouldn't be in circulation too much he had only one request
and that was for the benefit and care of his children that he
would like to have some money sent to them."

Grimsley was asked if he knew that Partin was indebted to
the U.S. government for close to $5,000 in income taxes, and
that his debt had been forgiven. Grimsley said that he never
had known the amount, but that he had been aware that
Partin had been in some tax difficulties. (It is worth noting,
as an aside, that ex-convict Partin, in exchange for some

highly questionable favors to a government engaged in some borderline-illegal activities, was "forgiven" $5,000 in taxes.)

Neal clung tenaciously to the incredible story that the payments to Partin were for expenses and developed this theme with his examination of Grimsley. This placed Grimsley in an awkward position when the angry Schiffer resumed questioning the witness.

Schiffer's examination brought out the fact that Grimsley had received no itemized bills and exchanged no vouchers with Partin.

Q. Well, tell me, wasn't the arrangement made you were going to send his wife $300 a month for support?

A. The $150 twice a month.

Q. One hundred fifty dollars, twice each month. And so it was not based upon what his expenses would be as he told you he was spending money and in expenses, but rather for the support of the children.

A. But we . . .

Q. Is that right?

A. More or less; that is correct, yes.

Q. Did you know the amounts of money—and these amounts you have testified to and as reflected by these checks —were, in fact, the alimony or support payments to his family?

A. It could have been. It's the same amount.

Q. Pardon, me?

A. It could have been. It's the same amount, $300 per month.

So there it was. These weren't payments for expenses at all, but actual payments for being a witness, admitted to be such by the very man who made the payments, Grimsley.

The government of the United States had broken the law, committed the crime of paying a witness to testify.

On the strength of Grimsley's admission, we demanded all of the records: all of Grimsley's accounts, any vouchers, and memoranda, etc., concerning the government's monetary transactions with Partin.

The government's minions, headed by Neal, fought bitterly against such disclosure, but Judge Wilson, faced with Grimsley's testimony, ordered that the evidence be presented. And among those papers was a memorandum, dated July 3, 1963, from Walter Sheridan to S. A. Andretta, administrative assistant attorney general.

It read:

Subject: *Confidential Fund Item*

In connection with the forthcoming trials in Nashville, Tennessee, it is requested that a check in the amount of $300.00 be drawn against the confidential fund beginning July 8th, made payable to A. Frank Grimsley, Jr., Attorney in the Criminal Division. . . . He will cash the check and give the money to a confidential source.

It is also requested that a check be drawn each month through November, 1963, made payable to Mr. Grimsley and mailed as above.

If there were any lingering doubts about whether the Justice Department, in violation of federal law, had paid a witness to testify, it seemed to us that they should have been dispelled when Harvey Silets queried Grimsley about the purpose of the "confidential fund."

Grimsley said that he didn't think the fund was used exclusively—or "altogether," as he put it—to pay informers, implying that it might also be used for some other purpose as well.

Then the following exchange took place:

Q. Now, isn't it a fact, sir, that at the time this memorandum was issued that the intention was to make a payment to Mr. Partin and that that was a flat payment of $300 a month?

A. It appears that way—Yes, sir.

With this admission, we had come full cycle. Partin had

been exposed as a paid witness, a spy hired to eavesdrop on the defendants as they made plans for the trial with their lawyers, and an *agent provocateur* who tried to entrap us.

Evidence had also been introduced so that Partin's record as to his character left something to be desired, casting at least some shadow on his credibility as a witness. But all of this came much too late, and the jury heard little of it. In fact, Judge Wilson himself estimated that the jury heard only about 40 percent of the testimony.

Then, too, the Grimsley testimony had seemed to establish the fact that Partin was a paid witness, and that, as such, his testimony had no credibility whatsoever. The testimony, we thought, should have been thrown out and the jury instructed to disregard it. But such was not the case in Judge Wilson's court.

In addition, while the proceedings were continuing, the prosecution kept insisting that it had done no wiretapping, no eavesdropping, no cloak-and-dagger snooping.

The one enormous flaw in these protestations of gemlike innocence was that earlier in the proceedings Partin had admitted that the government had taped his original conversations with me, when he called me from Baton Rouge. And certainly the judge knew about the taping, for he had received the evidence as a sealed document, along with the sealed tapes, early in the trial.

Therefore, when, on February 20, Grimsley admitted on the stand that Partin's telephone calls to me had been taped, Jim Haggerty again reminded the court that in his opinion a fair trial was "absolutely impossible," because of the government's "chicanery," and reminded the judge that the defense had made repeated motions demanding the recordings of Partin's conversation with me, and that the government had denied their existence.

In answer to Haggerty, Judge Wilson said he hadn't realized that the content of the taped conversations between Partin and me had not been made known to the defense.

The prosecution certainly should have made that clear to the defense, the judge tut-tutted. But no great harm had been done, he concluded, because he would see to it that the defense would have access to the recordings "at the appropriate time."

The appropriate time was toward the end of the trial, long after Partin had testified and left the stand for good.

Only when just about all the evidence was in, and the trial, in most respects, completed, did Judge Wilson let the defense have access to the taped recordings of Partin's wiretapped conversations with me. Yet these recordings contained information the defense should have had at the time it was cross-examining Partin. The defense had been deprived of it, we could only conclude, by an unethical ploy of the government, protected and upheld by Judge Wilson.

More important, it seems to me, is the fact that the government put a perjurer on the stand as a star witness and deliberately kept the tapes from the hands of the defense so that the perjury might be perpetrated; for the tapes revealed that it was not I, Jimmy Hoffa, who invited Partin to Nashville.

The tapes made it crystal clear that Edward Grady Partin had pleaded with me to spare him the time to talk to me.

It will be recalled that Edward Grady Partin was permitted to appear as the government's star witness after Judge Wilson had decided to believe Partin when he said that I had invited him to Nashville, and to disbelieve me when I had protested that he invited himself.

The following is from the recordings:

Partin (on October 8): Ah, what I was thinking, Jimmy, after I get this thing straightened out, and everything, if you have an opportunity or something, I would like to get with you and talk with you and talk this thing out.

Hoffa: Well, I'll be here all week [in Washington].

Partin (on October 18): I hate to interrupt you, Jim, but I need to talk to you on—when can I see you—you'd said you'd be there on the 22nd in Nashville—what's the best day to come?

    Hoffa: I'll be in Nashville on Sunday the 21st.

    Partin: Will Sunday or Monday be all right?

    Hoffa: Right.

Who lied? Partin or Hoffa?

In court I swore under oath that all that Partin had to say about me was an absolute lie: his statement that I invited him to Nashville, his claim that I asked him to stay there, his testimony about the Tippens affair, his statements about my meeting with Ewing King and my comments about him, his report of my comments about Gratin Fields, his claim that I made reference to Larry Campbell, his report of my comments on Paschal. I repeat myself now: it was an absolute lie.

Subsequent testimony even in that prejudiced court of law proved me right. Partin proved himself a liar on the witness stand.

Partin came to Nashville (at his own request, as the tapes proved) to plead with me not to put his Baton Rouge local under trusteeship of the International. I had previously spoken to Partin about shaping up and cleaning up his operation under threat of trusteeship. I was not inclined to judge him because he had so many indictments against him —after all, I had had a few myself, and I know from experience that being indicted doesn't necessarily mean that you're guilty. But things were happening so thick and fast at the Nashville trial when Partin arrived that I had no time to sit down with him and have a serious talk about the intolerable conditions down in Baton Rouge or about the personal problems that he said were plaguing him. I begged for time, and that, of course, was just what he was hoping for—he and Sheridan and Grimsley and Neal and their boss, the Attorney General.

I paid little attention to the fact that Partin was always around, seeming to be in on almost every meeting I had with members of the defense council. After an attempt was made to break into the room where we kept the defense records —the door had been jimmied—Partin served as a volunteer guard at the door. Since this door was one of those that lead to my suite, in time Partin became a sort of official "greeter" and a permanent fixture there.

No one paid much attention to him, one way or the other. Indeed, the trial was nearing its end before I had a chance to catch my breath. And it was only then that Bufalino and I sat down with Partin to go over his problems.

I don't know now what they really were. He rambled on from one subject to another. He seemed incoherent, nervous, unable to concentrate on what he was trying to say. He was upset, he said, because his opponents in Baton Rouge were making too much out of his business dealings with Castro.

I told him that if he was smuggling arms to Cuba, not only would I remove him from the local union, I would expel him from the Teamsters. At this he rambled off into a story about how anything like that on his part was insignificant. I repeated my threat.

When we began to consider the finances in the Baton Rouge local, we found that Partin was squandering money with needless trips around the country. The upshot was that I read the riot act to him and told him that unless he sat down and ran the local the way it was supposed to be run and cleared up the many charges against himself, I would have to act against him—meaning that I would force his removal and invoke the International's trusteeship.

In due course I related all of this on the stand, in an attempt to convince the court that Partin was a spy, that he had been planted in our midst by the government, and that on the surface, from the very beginning, he was perjuring himself.

It seemed impossible to persuade Judge Wilson that the

prosecution could be guilty of any wrongdoing whatsoever, and to me, a layman (though one who had been exposed to an inordinate amount of law and legal practice as a central figure), it seemed that I entered that courtroom as a guilty man in the eyes of the judge, and that I was only grudgingly being accorded a chance to prove my innocence—the reverse, of course, of the tenet of Anglo-Saxon law that considers a man innocent until his accuser proves his guilt. If I failed to prove my innocence, it was because we were simply unprepared to tackle that assignment, having geared ourselves not to prove my innocence but to disprove the government's charges.

Of course, as I have pointed out repeatedly, we had little assistance from the court. And another example of the court's failure to help occurred when Jacques Schiffer presented Judge Wilson with Bernard Spindel's second batch of FBI radio interceptions, all transcribed and sealed in an envelope. Judge Wilson declined to open it. "The court," he said, "is just not familiar with the practice of a stranger to a lawsuit filing a sealed document in which no attorney and no party alleges to have any knowledge whatsoever."

Of course, the judge had a valid point of order here—except for two things. First, Judge Wilson was not so finicky about accepting the tapes of Partin's taped phone conversations with me. And second, although the FCC regulations and Justice Department rules assert that no intercepted or tapped evidence can be made public until a judge rules that it is valid evidence, the FCC rules do not make it a crime to *intercept* such communications (such as the FBI's radio). It is a crime only to *divulge* them. Therefore, no one could state that the tapes contained relevant material, because no one but Spindel had heard them.

But in any case, the judge must have known this, for at the time the first intercepts made by Spindel were turned over to the court, Neal threatened action if he found a "violation of 605 of the Federal Communications Act." And in that first batch of intercepts Judge Wilson must have heard the FBI agent at the control post commenting to an agent in one of the cars engaged in the surveillance on the fact that probably "that fellow is listening to all you said," at which the man in the car reminded the eavesdropper that it was a "violation of the Federal statutes over which we have jurisdiction."

Indeed, when Spindel was called to the stand, it seemed to some of us that Judge Wilson was trying to force him to break the law by opening and introducing as evidence the sealed transcripts. Judge Wilson wanted to know why Spindel had made the intercepts, and Spindel replied that he had sealed and filed them as an aid to the court. Judge Wilson suggested he hadn't asked for any aid. He pressed the point. Hadn't Spindel expected them to be opened and disclosed?

"It was not for me to decide," said Spindel. It was, he said, a decision for the court to make.

"I'm giving you no directions, sir," Judge Wilson said. "You are the one that stated what your duty is. Proceed in accordance with your desire."

Spindel desired to hand the sealed transcript right back to the judge.

Silets asked if the court wasn't going to open the packet.

"This is your witness—Proceed, sir," Judge Wilson said.

Harry Berke then reminded the court that it had a duty to see if the constitutional rights of the defendant had been violated.

"What authority does this court have that any attorney would not have?" Judge Wilson asked.

Berke therefore pointed out that the judge had opened the first batch of intercepts.

Judge Wilson explained his reason for opening the first set this way. "I had no idea that any counsel was attempting to proceed by devious means. The court opened the docu-

ment thinking all the time that this was a document that
everyone knew about.

"The court now understands that there was some attempt
to put something over on the court in regard to delivering
a sealed document in that manner."

Judge Wilson refused to open the second batch of Spindel
intercepts. They remained sealed, concealing whatever it was
that Spindel was able to record.

The point I would make here, again as a layman, is that
when the government breaks the law, a defendant has recourse only to the courts. But when the courts seem bound
to the prosecution, the defendant is helpless against any violations of the law on the part of the government.

When testimony was taken about the surveillance, the
government produced another subterfuge, one as inadequately disguised as the business about paying Partin only
expenses. The contention was that the FBI had never deliberately observed me or any of the other defendants or any
of the defense counsel; it had, instead, been "observing" a
number of other persons who just happened to be near us
most of the time. If I or any other person connected with
the defense got caught up in the observation that was directed at people just beside us or just behind us or just in
front of us, well, that was too bad. In any case it was
unintentional.

Everett J. Ingram, the FBI's supervising agent in Knox-
ville, headed the Chattanooga operations with twenty-five
agents and twelve radio-equipped cars, he testified. These
agents, called in from offices throughout the middle South,
were in Chattanooga to keep an eye on four Teamster officials who were in no way connected with the trial—John
Cleveland, William A. Test, George E. Hicks, and Chuckie
O'Brien—and on Spindel.

Examination brought out the fact that the FBI had taken

723 pictures from the vantage point overlooking the Federal Courthouse. Strictly by "accident" I appeared in these photos fourteen times, and others in the defense appeared in various photos numerous times—Allen Dorfman, for example, appeared fifteen times.

The purpose of this major photography project was to see if any persons repeatedly turned up around the courthouse for some "ulterior motive."

There were people there who had ulterior motives, all right, but I'm sure they were well known to the FBI.

Finally, it became necessary for Judge Wilson to interrupt his post-trial hearing on the surveillance issues to hear the jury's verdict on the jury-tampering charge.

The jury dismissed identical charges against Dorfman and Tweel, but they convicted me along with Ewing King, Larry Campbell, and Thomas Ewing Parks.

After the verdict was in, we resumed the hearings on how the FBI had maintained surveillance and the prosecution had engaged in wiretapping and other eavesdropping techniques. And then, on March 12, 1964, Judge Wilson, the hearings completed to his satisfaction, sentenced me to eight years in the federal penitentiary and fined me $10,000. King, Campbell, and Parks were each fined $5,000 and sentenced to three years in prison.

Jacques Schiffer, counsel for Parks, was fined $1,000 and sentenced to sixty days in jail by Judge Wilson for "willful and criminal contempt" of court, which the judge regarded as "an attempt to degrade and debase the court." Schiffer asked for a hearing before another judge; Judge Wilson turned a stern eye on me and said:

> You stand here convicted of seeking to corrupt the administration of justice itself. You stand here convicted of having tampered, really, with the very soul of this nation. You stand here convicted of having struck at the very foundation upon

which everything else in this nation depends, the basis of
civilization itself, and that is the administration of justice
because without fair, proper and lawful administration of
justice, nothing else would be possible in this country, the
administration of labor unions, the administration of business, the carrying on of occupations, the carrying on of recreation, the administration of health services—everything that
we call civilization depends ultimately upon the proper administration of justice itself.

Surely no one can disagree with Judge Wilson's view of
the role of the administration of justice in our American
society. But it took many months for me to sort out the
events of the trial in my mind and to place them in proper
perspective. Finally, however, I think I have come to realize
the truth about Judge Wilson.

At the time of the trial, as I have said, I was outraged at
his seemingly partisan behavior. I have already told what I
thought of such actions and of the threat I consider such
activity to imply. But after much thought I came to the conclusion that Judge Wilson *is* a dedicated man, a militant de-
fender of the legal order and the judiciary. I now believe
that if a defendant, including myself, were to appear before
him on almost any other charge, there would be careful,
thoughtful administration of justice.

I was brought before him on a charge of despoiling the
very system to which he had dedicated his life, and he was so
upset at the thought that anyone would dare to tamper with
justice that he unwittingly accepted everything the prosecution presented in its efforts to establish my guilt.

I now think that his deep sense of outrage blinded him
to the unethical and unlawful methods employed by the government prosecutors—methods that denied me my right to
a fair hearing and caused me to be convicted of something
I hadn't done. Before his very eyes the government itself was

defiling the system of justice, but he could not see that what the government prosecutors were actually doing was far worse than what I had been accused of doing.

And this is the essence of "the Hoffa Case."

This was more than a trial of Jimmy Hoffa. It was a trial of the system of justice in the United States, and I charge that the U.S. Department of Justice, in great measure, and Judge Wilson, in less measure, share in the blame for placing that system in jeopardy.

Even if I had committed the crime of attempting to rig the jury—and I did not do so, and I believe that prosecution failed to prove that I did—I would pose less of a threat to our society and our civilization than a Department of Justice that ignores the law in its zeal to prosecute a defendant and receives the cooperation, even unwittingly, of the judge charged with administering justice.

The record bristles with admitted distortions in testimony by the government witnesses. It is redolent with sworn statements about threats to witnesses and intimidations—threats of indictment and loss of jobs. No one can read the record without being convinced that the government was guilty of deceit, deliberate evasiveness, and planned unfairness.

In prosecuting me, the government deliberately violated basic guarantees of the American system of justice, and thus it vitiated the lofty declarations made by Judge Wilson when he sentenced me.

A nation is in frightening danger when justice can be *used* by those in authority—when the Attorney General says someone is a bad man and belongs in jail, and those in power use "justice" to put him in jail, whether or not he's guilty.

After the trial was over and the post-trial hearings were ended, our defense investigators really went to work to try to learn just how far the government had gone in its violations.

Just before I was sentenced, we filed a series of affidavits that allege that the government, during the course of the trial, pampered the jurors with liquor, food, gifts, and entertainment. Sworn statements from bellhops, elevator operators, room-service waiters, and others in the hotel where the jurors were sequestered tell of liquor and party-type food being delivered to the jurors and describes scenes of jurors standing around the corridors of the hotel clinking glasses and having a high old time.

One interesting affidavit was that of Mrs. Dorothy Vaughn, of 420 Oak Street, Chattanooga. She deposed that during the trial a federal marshal in charge of the jurors rented a room from a neighbor, Mrs. Margaret Daves, and that on the night of February 21 Mrs. Vaughn visited Mrs. Daves and saw a number of gifts, wrapped, arrayed on the kitchen table.

Mrs. Vaughn alleges that she asked who the gifts were for, and that the marshal said, "For my jurors."

Mrs. Vaughn said she counted sixteen gifts on the table. Counting the four alternates, there were sixteen jurors.

Mrs. Vaughn further deposed that another federal marshal came to the house. He was to deliver the gifts. This second man, whose name, she said, was Erwin or Ervins, said of me: "That little imped son-of-a-bitch, that cocky bastard! We're going to do everything in our power to convict him!

"We're going to convict him one way or another. We know he's guilty and we're going to convict him."

Mrs. Vaughn relates that when this second marshal called me a son of a bitch, he struck the table with his fist so violently that he knocked a glass over.

The phrase that lingers in my mind is: "We're doing everything in our power to convict him."

Some of the people sharing that determination controlled awesome power.

"We're going to convict him one way or another," said the marshal-turned-deliveryman.

One way or another, they did.

And if those in power are allowed blandly to deprive me of my right to a fair hearing, who says they can't do the same thing to anyone?

Appendix: The Cast

ALBIN, J. D.: a critic of Edward Grady Partin's union activities who corroborated A. G. Klein's testimony before the grand jury. Albin was severely and painfully beaten by the same sextet that assaulted Klein. Albin still opposes Partin's Baton Rouge local administration, but as of this writing, his charges are being assiduously ignored by the Justice Department and the Attorney General's office.

BERKE, MARVIN: Chattanooga lawyer, one of the defense counselors. Marvin Berke figured in the FBI's shadowing of our forces.

BRANSTETTER, CECIL: Nashville lawyer representing Larry Campbell. Branstetter reported to the court that analysis of the first one hundred names submitted for jury-selection showed they would not be impartial toward me if only because of their backgrounds, many of which indicated antipathy to the labor movement.

BROWN, HAROLD: Chattanooga lawyer for Ewing King.

BUFALINO, WILLIAM E.: Detroit lawyer, a counsel for the Teamsters Union.

CAMPBELL, LARRY: Business Agent of a Teamster local in Detroit. Campbell was indicted on five counts of jury-tampering.

DANIELS, WILLIAM (HAWK): Special Investigator for District Attorney Pitcher's office. Daniels investigated Partin, then became his lawyer, then served as contact man between Partin and the Justice Department's A. Frank Grimsley.

DURKIN, JAMES: Special Assistant Attorney General. Durkin met in his own office with Shobe and Bishop St. Psalm.

ELLIS, HARRY: Detroit numbers operator. Ellis refused to participate in a frame-up to implicate Parks.

FIELDS, CARL: son of the juror Gratin Fields. Carl first testified that through Walker he had met Parks and that Parks had told him he would give his father $10,000 if he would throw the Hoffa jury. Under cross-examination Carl Fields totally repudiated this testimony, saying he had told "a pack of lies."

FIELDS, GRATIN: the one Negro juror on the Nashville panel. Gratin Fields was alleged to have been sought-out for a "fix" of the jury.

GRADY, EDWARD: Tweel's attorney (not to be confused with Edward Grady Partin). Grady claimed that Tweel did not even know me.

GRIMSLEY, A. FRANK: member of the Justice Department staff. Grimsley met with Partin "at least two times, possibly three," in Pitcher's office. Under oath, Grimsley admitted that Partin was acting as a spy for him when he first contacted me, and that he, Grimsley, paid Partin through devious methods.

HAGGERTY, JAMES E.: former president of the Michigan State Bar and a Director of the Detroit Bar Association. Haggerty testified that the planting of Partin in my quarters as an undercover agent was an "improper intrusion on the defendant's right."

HOOKER, JOHN: Nashville attorney working with the prosecution. Hooker tried to get Bernard Spindel to open the sealed report he had turned over to Judge Wilson—a request that, if complied with, would have caused Spindel to break the law and have jeopardized the admission into court of his vital evidence proving the surveillance of me and my counselors by the FBI.

KING, EWING: former President of Teamsters Local 327, Nashville. King was indicted with me on five charges of jury-tampering.

KLEIN, A. G., JR.: killed when a sand truck "fell on him" in Louisiana not long after he had testified against Partin before an East Baton Rouge grand jury that indicted Partin for forging a withdrawal card in the union, thereby removing a severe critic. Prior to his death Klein was severely beaten by six men he identified as members of Partin's union.

LEATH, MATTIE: Carl Field's sister and Gratin Field's daughter. Mattie Leath is alleged to have been approached by Walker at Parks's instigation and to have refused to have anything to do with the bribe.

LEBLANC, JUDGE FRED L.: of East Baton Rouge, Louisiana. Judge LeBlanc ordered Partin's bail reduced from $50,000 to $5,000 and further ordered his release so that he might assume his duties as a spy in my home and living quarters during my trial in Nashville.

McKEON, THOMAS: an employee of the Michigan office of the Justice Department. McKeon acted as go-between, sending Frederick Shobe from Detroit to Louisville and Nashville with instructions for operating and orders to call Walter Sheridan at Nashville 242–2106 each day and to report to him.

MEDLIN, LAWRENCE (RED): the neighbor who was supposed to have told Tippens it would be worth $10,000 to throw my case. Medlin never appeared in Chattanooga. He was tried in Nashville. Though Medlin was found guilty of trying to bribe his friend, the government produced not one iota of evidence or testimony linking Medlin to me or the Teamsters. Indeed, Medlin swore he never heard of me. His statement remains unchallenged.

NEAL, JAMES F.: U.S. Attorney in charge of the prosecution. Neal's influence over witnesses who completely reversed their testimony under cross-examination played an important part in the conspiracy to frame me.

O'BRIEN, CHARLES (CHUCK): Business Agent of the Teamsters in Detroit, a friend. O'Brien is closely associated with me. His identity was the subject of considerable FBI radio conversation.

OSBORN, Z. T., JR.: Nashville lawyer of the firm of Leftwich & Osborn, my local counsel in Nashville.

PARIS, LEO D.: an airman stationed at Lackland Air Force Base, Texas. Paris brought suit against Partin as a result of a hit-run accident in Cuba, Alabama, on Christmas Day, 1961, in which a fellow airman was killed. Partin was subsequently indicted for first-degree manslaughter and leaving the scene of an accident.

PARKS, THOMAS EWING: Campbell's uncle, Nashville resident employed in a funeral home. Parks was indicted on five counts of jury-tampering.

PARTIN, EDWARD GRADY: Business Agent of the Teamsters Union in Baton Rouge, Louisiana. Partin posed as my friend and acted as a major domo or sergeant-at-arms at the door of my suite in the hotel in Nashville, but he testified against me, revealing he had been planted in my room and had gained my confidence as a spy in the employ of the Attorney General's office. In testifying against me Partin perjured himself, and so admitted in court. Partin is under indictment on 26 counts pertaining to union activities alone and has been indicted, but not tried, on a number of other more serious charges.

PASCHAL, BETTY: member of the Nashville jury. Betty Paschal was alleged to be one of those selected for an attempt at influencing the jury.

PASCHAL, JAMES MORRIS: Betty's husband, a Tennessee State trooper seeking a promotion. Paschal said he talked to a go-between and was told he would be promoted if he influenced his wife to decide in my favor. Under cross-examination Paschal completely repudiated his testimony and reversed his story.

PITCHER, SARGENT: District Attorney of East Baton Rouge, Louisiana. Pitcher investigated Partin, had him on a charge of aggravated kidnapping. Pitcher released Partin when he learned the latter was going to work as stool pigeon for Attorney General Robert F. Kennedy.

PITTS, OSCAR (MUTT): employee of a trucking firm. Pitts was the go-between who contacted Paschal and was alleged by the government to be representing Ewing King, then President of the Teamsters Nashville local. Pitts later changed his testimony to swear that *he* approached King on behalf of Paschal, that King made no mention of the trial, and that when he, Pitts, broached the subject, King demanded that he desist and further ordered him not to mention the trial or Hoffa to Paschal or Paschal's wife.

ST. PSALM, BISHOP: voodoo practitioner and publisher of a small magazine in Nashville. St. Psalm was promised advertising by Special Assistant Attorney General James Durkin if he would work voodoo on Parks, the funeral parlor employee.

SCHIFFER, JACQUES: attorney representing Parks. Schiffer reported to the court that questionnaires filled out by one hundred jurors called for jury selection were withheld from defense counsel.

SHEETS, WILLIAM: FBI agent. Sheets was active in the surveillance in Chattanooga and was one of those alleged to have influenced Paschal to tell the story he later repudiated.

SHENKER, MORRIS: St. Louis lawyer, one of my attorneys.

SHERIDAN, WALTER: hand-picked by Kennedy to head his special investigation of labor rackets and to be a field commander of the special "Get Hoffa" forces. Sheridan had worked with Kennedy on the McClellan committee, successor to the McCarthy committee, where Kennedy started his career. Sheridan went to work for the National Broadcasting Company after completing his chore for Kennedy. He acknowledged that Partin had been used as an "informer" (his term).

SHOBE, FREDERICK MICHAEL: parolee from Michigan State prison. Shobe, who had been convicted for burglary, forgery, and armed robbery, testified that he was framed with a parole violation for associating with known criminals (at a job on the docks) but was given a chance to avoid returning to prison if he'd help Sheridan to "get Hoffa." Shobe testified he ranged the country for two years on his task as an *agent provocateur* (his term), and that he was told to use "any means, legal or illegal, fair or foul," to get Hoffa.

SILETS, HARVEY M.: Chicago attorney for Dorfman.

SIMPSON, SIDNEY: Partin's co-worker. Partin helped kidnap Simpson's two children from a motel where they were staying with their mother.

SPINDEL, BERNARD B.: Rome, New York, electronics expert. Spindel, one of the foremost authorities on wiretapping and bugging, tracked down and recorded the FBI's two-way radio hook-up installed to keep a twenty-four-hour surveillance over me and my attorneys during the Chattanooga trial.

Tippens, James C.: Nashville insurance broker. Tippens was the first juror to be seated at the Nashville trial. On the day after he was seated, Tippens reported that a friend told him it would be worth $10,000 to him to vote for Jimmy Hoffa.

Tweel, Nicholas J.: alias Anthony Quinn. Tweel, a total stranger to Partin, was alleged by Partin to have accosted him in the lobby of the Andrew Jackson Hotel in Nashville and confided to him that he was working on a method to "get the jury"—my jury. Tweel was one of the five others indicted with me on charges of jury tampering.

Walker, James T.: a Nashville police department patrolman.